The Full Burn

By the same author

Stud: Adventures in Breeding

The Full Burn

On the Set, at the Bar, Behind the
Wheel, and Over the Edge with
Hollywood Stuntmen

Kevin Conley

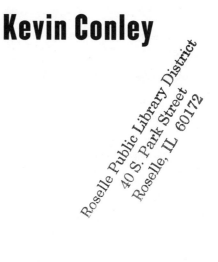
BLOOMSBURY

Published by Bloomsbury USA, New York
Distributed to the trade by Macmillan

All papers used by Bloomsbury USA are natural, recyclable products made from
wood grown in well-managed forests. The manufacturing processes conform to
the environmental regulations of the country of origin.

LIBRARY OF CONGRESS CATALOGING-IN-PUBLICATION DATA HAS BEEN APPLIED FOR.

ISBN-10 1-59691-023-2
ISBN-13 978-1-59691-023-2

First U.S. Edition 2008

1 3 5 7 9 10 8 6 4 2

Typeset by Westchester Book Group
Printed in the United States of America by Quebecor World Fairfield

To Amy, for lighting the fire

Contents

Prologue

This is not a how-to book. You can't do this stuff at home. You may want to. Stuntmen make it look like so much fun. But before you try anything rash, ask yourself: Am I a World Champion Something or Other? Am I nationally ranked? In tae kwon do? Rhythmic gymnastics? Street luge? Am I an ex–Green Beret?

You get around these guys (as I have for the past few years) and you start to think it's rubbing off. The problem seems to be universal. One stuntman told me that once he'd gotten to the point in his career where he was hiring other stuntmen and stuntwomen, arranging fight scenes, and directing car chases, his wife started thinking, "Hey, maybe I could take a stab at this. The money's good. Maybe he could throw me a bone." The stuntman pointed to the coffee table, which was short, in the living room, which was carpeted, and he said, "Fine. Just jump off that." She got up on the table.

"And land flat on your back," he said.

She looked down from her perch.

"Give me something else," she said.

There are deeds that your body will not let you do. Stuntmen do them anyway. They aren't foolish about it. They're incredibly ingenious at devising ways to make it look as if they've pulled off something far more painful and dangerous than what they actually did. Nothing in the contract says that they must defy death, no matter what the shooting script says. For all the riskiest maneuvers in the stunt arsenal—full burns and high falls, cannon rolls and cable-offs, pipe ramps and running Ws, boat transfers and descenders and drift-reverse 180s—there are, in most cases, provisions to ensure a stuntman's survival. Cars are crash-proofed, bodies are padded, cameras are angled just so, and this allows the stuntman to survive the stunt. Death is an unlikely outcome, a remote possibility due only to miscalculation or mechanical error.

But from time to time, a stuntman will face a stunt that is exactly what it looks like: sliding between the legs of a team of horses in full stride and straight on between the stagecoach wheels, say, or racing off the highest bridge in California in a Corvette convertible and then climbing out the backseat, while airborne, and BASE jumping to earth. Death is a distinct presence, haunting every step of preparation.

This book is about both situations, and about the rare sort of person with the skill and guts to deal with either one. Even among stuntmen such people are rare. There are about three to six thousand people who work a few days a year in stunts. Most of them perform what the call sheets refer to as N.D. or nondescript stunts: they tussle around the background of bar fights, drive in the opposite direction during chase scenes, move away from the restaurant table just when the stunt double crashes through the skylight and lands on the wedding cake. The business is brutal, and these N.D. guys almost never get the chance at the one signature job that would put them in the big leagues.

But a lucky few do get the call: "How's your Tuesday? Would you like to jump in a gator pit for us?" Or "We need somebody your size to go through a Hummer windshield. Can you do it in a bald wig?" The list of top professionals who prove reliable in this situation—who can pull off the gag, take after take, without dying or endangering the crew, or breaking the cameras—is as short as the roster of NBA players, for many of the same reasons: the jobs are scarce and the skills difficult, and the ones who make it tend to have an unusual personality, something beyond athleticism that allows them to perform consistently under pressure in the public eye.

For a writer, it wasn't easy to get to this elite group. Stuntmen, like special-ops agents, must commit acts of courage without sacrificing their professional invisibility; they don't always like it when their cover is blown. But after I made it onto a few sets, the men and women who wrecked the cars and shot each other started to share their expertise—and their misadventures: how one, known for his unworldly calm before a stunt, fell asleep on the set just before he was to be set on fire; how another, after messing up a high fall on a sword-and-sandal movie, ended up bare-chested and unconscious in the emergency room in a centurion skirt and Caesar wig with pin curls; how a third, after breaking his wrist falling for the fourth time to the concrete through the windshield of a truck, did eight more takes because he didn't want to lose the job to some young gun.

All our lives we have been watching these athletes drop out of the sky or race through the alley and down the stairs, straight into oncoming traffic, showing up at the crisis points in our favorite entertainments. As it turns out, their personal lives are every bit as pyrotechnic as what they do for a living. They ride expensive bikes and ruin the fastest cars (both tax-deductible activities) and they encourage their kids to do things you or I would never dare. They attempt the impossible, get hurt, and dust themselves off for another take as if nothing happened. And in between they tell stories that, coming from most people, might sound like exaggerations. For a stuntman, it's all in a day's work.

CHAPTER 1

The Art of the Crash

Ever since the days of the Keystone Kops, Hollywood stuntmen have called the dangerous stuff they do "gags." A punch is a gag. A car jumping across an open drawbridge is a gag. An aerial dogfight requiring elaborate flight plans and FAA oversight is a gag. And so is a fiery explosion that blasts your hero off a pier and into the Gulf of Mexico.

In late August, I stood on a thousand-foot-long pier just outside St. Petersburg, Florida, with the crew of *The Punisher*—yet another movie version of a Marvel Comics property. We were watching Mike Owen, a stunt double, get ready for a fire gag. He knelt on the edge of a floating dock just off the pier, wearing three layers of thin, fire-protective long underwear known as Nomex under his costume. The Nomex layers had been soaking in a cooler at forty-two degrees. Once Owen put them on, it didn't matter that it was noon and so hot that nearly everybody on the pier was dripping with sweat; Owen wanted to hurry up and do the gag, just so that he could stop shivering. In addition, his face and his hair had been slathered in a gel that protects you from burns—but only as long as it's wet. After a crew member finished putting it on, Owen had about five minutes in which to complete the gag safely.

The explosion would be the climax of an extended chase scene, which was being shot in Fort De Soto Park. The scene would take about a minute of screen time, but it required a week of shooting and included a fair selection of thrills. In addition to the fire gag, there was a series of car jumps, an SUV rollover, and a tricky car crash that Gary Hymes, the second-unit director, who had choreographed the entire stunt sequence, was saving for the last day on location. For that final stunt, Hymes somehow had to make a motorboat that was hitched to a trailer suddenly come loose from a car pulling it down the road, bounce high in the air, then slam down on a Ford pickup racing behind it—without killing anybody.

The chase down the beach comes early in the movie, and it's meant to establish the motivation of Frank Castle, a.k.a. the Punisher. He is the darkest character in the moral universe of Marvel Comics; this sequence, in which his wife and child are killed before his eyes and he himself is shot, blown up, and left for dead, helps establish why. The Punisher first appeared in 1974, as a mercenary hired to kill Spider-Man, and in 1986, after several bloodthirsty cameos, he got his own series. The philosophy of the gun-toting vigilante superhero is simple: "I kill only those who deserve killing."

The Punisher, relying on righteous anger and government weapons training, has no superpowers, and this gives the movie's stunt sequences a human scale that's missing from most Marvel franchises. As Owen rehearsed the fire gag, he and the film's director, Jonathan Hensleigh, discussed the scene's narrative elements: at the start, Castle, barely alive after being shot in the chest, sees a tongue of flame approaching—it's supposed to be gasoline that the executioners have poured on the dock and then lit. (The fuel is a mixture of unleaded gasoline and diesel, which photographs better and has a slower burn rate.) Hensleigh wanted Owen to recoil as the fire closed in, a movement that would, coincidentally, bring Owen out of his collapsed position to a nearly upright stance, allowing him to be both more visible to the cameras and better situated for the ensuing gag.

The crew had positioned two propane-filled canisters so that they were aimed directly at Owen. The fireball they were set to deliver was rigged to flare at the same instant that a ratchet cable, which was hooked to a snatch harness hidden under Owen's costume, jerked him off his knees and tossed him thirty feet away, into the Gulf. The equipment was hidden in plain sight—the ratchet line was threaded through a standard hoist, the sort you'd hang your prizewinning tuna from; if any wires did show up in the shot, they would be digitally erased in post-production. Owen had been rehearsing all week, hooking himself to the equipment, varying the height and velocity of his trajectory, and trying different rag-doll motions in the air. He and Hymes had gone over the video playbacks until they found the most convincing manner in which to be blown sky high. As Owen walked to his mark on the edge of the dock and knelt down, he said, "Finally, it's happening." Six cameras—two on each of two barges in the water, and two more stowed in explosion-resistant iron canisters on the dock—were focused directly on him. The extra cameras were there partly to ensure that the gag wouldn't have to be redone if one camera slipped out of focus. The array of angles also increased the chances of getting a shot that would make the audience gasp.

Hensleigh's assistant yelled, "Let's go hot on stunts," and somebody else called out, "Remember to hold your breath, Mike," and then the effects man hit the gas feed from six propane tanks that had been hidden out of camera range. The tongue of fire raced across the dock and ignited a fireball that hit Owen full in the face just as the ratchet jerked him off his knees, up into the sky, and out into the water.

A few seconds later, the director said, "Cut!" and two safety divers swam over to the spot where Owen had landed. He surfaced and shot a thumbs-up. Everyone on the pier clapped and hooted, but nobody moved until the divers had brought him back to the dock and they could see him walking on his own power. Hensleigh sat before the video monitor to see how the shot had turned out. The coverage was excellent: the cameras had picked up both the blast of flame and Owen's flight. As he wiped gel off his face, Owen watched the monitors for a moment, then walked away, looking slightly dazed, like a man getting a standing eight count. A producer rushed over and said, "How are you? Seriously, what did you feel?"

"I felt warm," he said, shrugging off the attention. "I feel fine. I love it."

Complex fire gags and chase sequences aren't sketched hastily on location or improvised on Hollywood soundstages. They're planned and storyboarded weeks in advance. In August, while *The Punisher* was still shooting, I dropped by the preproduction offices of *Cellular,* in Santa Monica, to watch the director, David Ellis, and his second-unit director, Freddie Hice, plan a chase scene. Ellis and Hice had worked together before, most recently on *The Matrix Reloaded*: Ellis, the second-unit director on that film, choreographed the high-speed chase scene in which Carrie-Anne Moss drives a motorcycle recklessly into oncoming expressway traffic. The scene gained renown for its computer-generated effects, but Ellis shot most of the sequence using real stunt drivers. The most memorable segments—the cameras racing in dizzyingly close, in traffic, either leading or shadowing the drivers—bear Ellis's stamp.

Shooting was scheduled to begin in less than four weeks, but Ellis sounded relaxed. "Go to your script, page twenty-four," he said to a team of five consultants, as he pulled Matchbox cars from a zippered bag. Ellis, a big surfer-blond guy who started his career performing stunts (*Smokey and the Bandit*), nimbly arranged about a dozen tiny cars (Jeep, minivan, police car, Mercedes SUV, Hot Wheels muscle car) inside Magic Marker lines on a posterboard on his desk. The consultants glanced at the script, then watched two lanes of traffic take shape under his fingers. In the scene, which was to be shot near Dodger Stadium in September, the young hero of *Cellular* is speeding across Los Angeles, desperate to track down his old high school teacher, who has been kidnapped and is being held in an attic (and is secretly communicating with him by cell phone). "So what he's going to see ahead of him is this Oriental driving-school car and some chick in a Mercedes who's talking on a phone and not paying attention," Ellis said. "And he's stuck here." He moved a little Jeep into an empty lane. "He can't go around this way: there's oncoming traffic. So he's going to make this move to the curb lane and yell to the chick, 'Get off the freakin' phone! Pay attention to the road.' Even though he's on his phone. And, as he's yelling 'Pay attention,' and he looks back, we'll have a trash truck, with its flashers on, picking up a Dumpster."

Ellis and his colleagues immediately digressed to discuss the timing and hydraulics of various automatic lift arms on garbage trucks—the up-and-over type, the in-and-up, the curl—and the effect that each might have on the staging of the final sequence, where, as luck would have it, the arm rises just enough for the hero, in a Ford Bronco, to squeak by. But Freddie Hice, who, as the second-unit director, oversees the stunt doubles and drivers, brought them back to business: he wanted to know what kind of move and countermove they should plan for the moment when the hero recklessly veers into oncoming traffic.

At this point, a lesser team might throw in some "power slides"—the flashy controlled skids that are the stock-in-trade of the stuntman or stuntwoman—but Ellis knows the difference between spectacle and bombast. Some TV directors back in the heyday of stunt driving (*The Dukes of Hazzard*, *The A-Team*) weren't so abstemious, and viewers grew bored with the unvarying diet of 180s, 360s, rollovers, and bridge jumps. He and Hice decided that all they really needed was a *zhoom-zhoom*—that is, an exploratory swerve into oncoming traffic followed by a hasty retreat.

In the course of the meeting, Ellis employed similar technical terms, such as *fweeshhhh* (the feeling the viewer gets as the camera quickly closes in on the garbage truck), *RRRR!* (the sound of tires locked in a skid), and *vwumvwum-vwum* (the rapid appearance and disappearance of opposing traffic in the foreground of a side-angle tracking shot of the Jeep). Apparently, the basic language of car stunts hasn't changed since you were six years old. However, the applications have grown more sophisticated. Every *zhoom* and *RRRR!* was followed by a lengthy discussion of camera angle and equipment. "We can still go in here handheld and get a clean POV," Ellis would say. Or, "We'll get a crane, a super-techno."

When it came to plotting the actual stunt—exactly how the Bronco driving just under the garbage rig would be filmed—Ellis spoke in a tone of restraint, saying, "I don't think we're going to do any big 'Olé!'" They discussed, then quickly discarded, the idea of filming the sequence backward—with the Bronco starting in contact with the garbage rig and driving rapidly away from the crash—then reversing the footage in the editing room. They also rejected CGI, or computer generation—it's safer but far more expensive. (And although no one admits it, to a career stuntman CGI feels like cheating.)

Ellis and Hice wanted to avoid a "cliché shot" in which the vehicle emerged from a seemingly inevitable wreck miraculously unscathed. So they decided to have the Bronco clear the lift arm but not the garbage can it was lifting: the top of the windshield would smash into the little wheels at the bottom of the trash can. To sell it to the audience, they planned an over-the-shoulder shot of a stunt double smashing the hero's car into the trash can (shot on location), followed by a separate closeup of the hero as the windshield shatters (shot in the studio, with safety glass).

Performing the on-location stunt would be dangerous. As far as Ellis and Hice could tell from sitting around a desk strewn with toy cars, the stunt driver would have to duck right before impact—steering up to the crash and then lying down on the seat at the last possible instant, driving blind as the windshield shattered around him. "The guy's got to go down," Ellis said, confirming his decision. "Whoever's driving the car there, you're down." Both Ellis and Hice had performed this duck-down maneuver themselves, and they knew they'd have no trouble hiring someone to perform the trick for them. The crash would be worth about fifteen hundred dollars for every take to the man who performed it, in addition to the standard Screen Actors Guild day rate for stuntmen, which is $678. "After that shot, we'll need a line of dialogue," Ellis said. "An exclamation, about what just happened to him."

"How about 'Shit'?" Hice said.

A few days later, I was back on the St. Petersburg set of *The Punisher*, where everyone was moving with a sense of urgency. Tropical thunderstorms had forced the crew to stop filming almost every day at five o'clock. And this afternoon was their last chance to nail the boat gag: at the end of the day, the crew had to clear out of Fort De Soto Park in order to make room for the Labor Day weekend crowds.

The boat gag, the one treacherous effect left to shoot, was the heart of the violent sequence in which the Punisher's family is gunned down by villains. It had been carefully designed by Gary Hymes, the second-unit director. The original script had left the sequence vague: "They jump in the pickup and give chase." Hymes had invented everything else. He had moved the chase from the pavement to the beach. He had added big jumps on the hard sand, a rollover, and enough mayhem to keep the audience from wondering why four hit men with submachine guns were having such a tough time taking out an unarmed mother and her ten-year-old son.

In the chase scene, Castle's wife and son are driving a Chevy Blazer that is pulling a twelve-foot motorboat on a trailer hitch. (The Castles enjoy scuba diving.) The four hit men pursue them in a Ford pickup truck. For most of the chase, the boat acts as an accidental shield, bouncing up and ruining the gunmen's aim or swerving into their path and preventing them from pulling alongside to shoot the Punisher's wife. Today's boat gag would mark the end of that sequence. When the Blazer ran over a large bump on the beach trail, the trailer hitch would break free, hurling the boat up into the air. The Ford pickup, practically tailgating, would smash right into it. The collision would provide the mother and son with a brief moment of false hope.

Hymes, a slim man of forty-nine with a square jaw, high cheekbones, and an Old West profile (in a long shot he could pass for

Robert Redford), was wearing shorts, a knee brace, and an Israeli Special Forces baseball hat. He is a former stuntman who came to the job from championship motocross racing. Stuntmen rarely come out of the circus or rodeo anymore; these days, you're more likely to find ex–X Gamers and converts from renegade sports like snowboarding and cliff diving. Still, Hymes's motorcycle background remains the stunt driver's gold standard; both disciplines require frequent power slides and a precise calculation of risk at high speed. Even though he's now at the top of his profession— Hymes designed the famous bus jump in *Speed*—he thinks his father would have preferred it if he were more like his two cousins, the accountant and the lawyer. He calls himself the black sheep of the family.

In fact, Hymes is merely embracing tradition: his grandfather was one of the original stuntmen at the Mack Sennett studios. Ask stunt people how they got into the business and they'll usually say, "I fell into it." The truth is that a hefty percentage are born into it. There have been at least twelve Eppers in the stunt business, all of them descended from a Swiss cavalryman who was delivering horses to MGM just when a director needed somebody to jump one over a moving car. There are stunt couples, stunt brothers and sisters, stunt grandmas and grandpas—even stunt babies. When I asked Hymes about his first big break as a stunt coordinator and he mentioned *The Untouchables*, I told him how much I liked the scene with the baby in the carriage rolling down the train-station stairs.

"That's my oldest boy, Collin!" Hymes said proudly. "He was eighteen months old at the time, and he loved it. As long as we were bouncing down the stairs, he was laughing and just thought it was great."

Hymes, who held the handles of the baby carriage throughout the filming, was trying to hit upon the same combination for today's boat gag: the illusion of danger with a guarantee of safety. Throughout the morning, as the director prepped for filming, Hymes kept coming over to the dogleg on the beach, where the landscaping crew was adding greenery along the sandy trail. While they worked, Hymes plotted camera angles. He went over the timing and the possible outcomes. Hymes envisioned that, just when the Blazer and the trailer hitch hit the bumps, a crew member would press a detonator and a charge of primer cord would detach the trailer from the SUV. Thinking aloud to an assistant, Hymes said, "Then the boat and trailer should—maybe it'll dig in its nose. Maybe it'll cartwheel. Who knows?" He paced back and forth over the patch of prepared ground. "All I know is it'll be a wreck."

It's impossible to eliminate chance from a stunt—Hymes and his crew were planning an accident, after all—but Hymes kept going over every detail of the scenario. He called in Donna Evans, the stunt double for the mother, and Sean Graham, the hit-man stunt double who would drive the Ford pickup, and went over the scene again. Hymes wondered whether he should replace the truck's glass windshield with one made of Lexan, a high-impact clear plastic used in race cars, in order to protect Graham. He decided to have the outboard motor carefully tied down so that it couldn't fly off. Then he had the mechanics take out the motor's insides, to make it lighter and less dangerous in case it actually did. Graham stood by, appreciatively watching the preparation. "This one's going to be a fart-knocker," he said.

Graham, who is one of the three hundred or so stunt people who work steadily and earn several hundred thousand dollars a year, is a former cliff diver and extreme snowboarder who has turned himself into one of the industry's top wheelmen. (He did Mark Wahlberg's driving in *The Italian Job*.) Graham's specialty, the high fall, is an all-or-nothing gag: you don't break a leg or crack a rib if you miss; you either hit the air bag and live or you don't. So high-fall guys are meticulous about preparation. Graham is a gag man's gag man, who keeps the stunt doubles laughing while they're waiting out the downtime under the shade trees. But when I asked him to confirm certain stories I'd heard—of stuntmen racing their rental cars, power-sliding into the hotel parking lot, and then rappeling out of their hotel-room balconies—Graham said that he took a Stanislavsky approach. "The more time we spend honing our craft, the better it's going to look in the movie," he said. "It's our job, as professionals, to try to eke out a little extra time with the equipment to physically prepare."

The way Graham looks at it, you're more likely to die from mistakes than from daring. In the 1923 cliffhanger *Plunder*, the first-time stuntman Johnny Stevenson jumped off a New York bus toward an elevated track at Seventy-second Street and Third Avenue; according to *Stunt*, a book by John Baxter, the bus driver drove faster than was planned, and Stevenson missed the girder; he fell to his death in front of his wife and daughter, who were playing extras on the bus. In the 1977 biker flick *Hi-Riders*, Vic Rivers successfully drove his car off a bridge and did a rollover in a three-foot streambed; he climbed out of his car but grew dizzy and fell in the muddy water and drowned. A year later, on the set of *Steel*, A. J. Bakunas successfully landed a record high fall; then the seams on his air bag broke, and he was killed. Stuntmen defy death so regularly that their own tragic deaths under relatively normal circumstances—like those of Dick Bullock and Jack Coffer, who died in car accidents on the way home from work, or Gene Coogan, who fell asleep in bed with a cigarette—can seem almost ironic, like one last gag.

At 5 P.M., the stunt was ready to film, and Hymes began scrutinizing the final camera setups. Two cameras were hidden by palm trees that the landscaping crew had installed just beyond the bumps; another was situated on a forty-yard dolly that ran parallel to the path of the cars; one was placed on the front seat of the Ford truck that Graham would drive; and one was on the ground, tucked behind another artful set of plantings. Hymes, satisfied with the arrangement, signed off on it. Graham looked at me and said, "The number of cameras they have on this tells me they don't want to do it more than once." After a few minutes, I saw him putting some things into his pocket, and I asked him about them.

"Whenever I have a big stunt to do, I keep these with me," he said. "Although this isn't that big a jump, allegedly." He showed me a laminated picture of him and his wife, Tabby, who is a stunt double for Julia Roberts, with their sixteen-month-old son; a tiny angel that Tabby gave him for these occasions; and a medal that his grandfather used to keep in his car. "He was the original bad-ass," Graham said. "No fear."

The sky was darkening with late-afternoon thunderclouds, so Hymes called a quick safety meeting. It boiled down to this: "Nobody, for any reason, should be in this area." As Hymes spoke, Graham performed martial-arts stretches on top of the biggest sand bump. During the rigging and the other preparations, the Blazer and the Ford pickup had been resting just feet away from where the gag would take place. Now Graham, with his team of hit men harnessed in, backed the pickup around the bend in the dogleg, just out of sight. Then Evans backed the Chevy Blazer up to her starting point, a few yards ahead of Graham; she sat next to a man who was four feet six, cursed like a dockworker, and specialized in doubling for child actors. Hymes sat by the monitors and spoke into his walkie-talkie. All the walkie-talkies up and down the beach were tuned to the same channel, so Hymes's voice, and Evans's and Graham's answers, echoed behind the dunes, up on the hill, out in the parking lot, and down by the cameras.

"Donna? Set?"

"Set."

"Donna's set. Sean?"

"We're set back here."

"Going hot on the set. *Action!*"

Evans's Blazer came bouncing around the corner at thirty-five miles an hour—the speed they'd settled on—with Graham just inches off her trailer, gauging his speed by hers. Thirty-five looked pretty fast on the rugged terrain. When the Blazer hit the bump, the trailer hitch detached right on cue and the boat went airborne.

This is where Graham's skill came into play. He needed to stay close enough to slam into the boat, but he had to keep a slight separation, too—so that he could see what the boat wound up doing in the air, and then steer into it. All of this happened within milliseconds: as the Blazer and the boat took to the air, Graham, right behind them, punched the accelerator and took off from the bump even faster than Evans had. Both the Ford and the boat were in the air—the truck ascending, the boat descending.

The boat, it turned out, didn't do any of the things the crew thought it would. It didn't cartwheel. It didn't dig its nose into the ground. It rose almost lazily upward in a movement that Graham might recall from his cliff-diving days: the layout. And in that classic face-up, flat-out position the boat came slamming down on the truck, hitting the hood and the windshield at the same instant. The camera rigged to the seat beside Graham captured the windshield breaking on impact.

At this point, the only thing Graham could control was the steering wheel. What happened next was truly odd. It looked almost as if the truck were tackling the boat—still moving forward, the Ford hurtled into the boat's metal keel and knocked it sideways, causing the entire boat to tumble off the passenger side and hit a palm tree on the edge of the sandy path. Evans sped off as planned and, despite all the chaos in the air, when Graham hit the ground he braked and came to a stop right on his mark. Hymes called, "Cut!"

After the fire gag, the crew had cheered and applauded. This time, the celebration was quieter: it was the difference between one spectacular thing going right and many little ones not going horribly wrong. The crew rushed over and huddled by the monitors, watching the scene again and again as Hymes compared each camera's account. A few—one side angle and a head-on shot—had it all wrong: they minimized the danger and underplayed the collision of the two airborne vehicles. The cars looked slow, the crash seemed humdrum. Evans appeared almost distraught as she watched them: although it wasn't coming across onscreen, she knew that the Blazer had taken off and landed hard. Finally, one low angle confirmed her version—the Blazer roared up into the air, Evel Knievel style, and shook hard as it hit the sand—and she practically shouted, "That's what happened!"

But the low angle missed a detail that the dolly shot had recorded: after the boat slammed into the windshield, it slid back over the cab of the truck and almost smacked into the bald head of one of the hit men as he ducked. From this angle, you could see exactly where the fall of the boat and the rise of the pickup truck intersected. And in those one or two frames where the boat stopped, froze in midair, and changed direction you could also spot how small the clearance was between the bottom of the boat and the skull of the stunt double—a matter of inches. The first time the crew saw this rendering on the monitors, you could hear them sucking in their breath, wincing at the close call. Hymes, however, reacted with relief.

"That's the one," he said. At his request, the script supervisor recorded which camera had captured the shot. That was a print.

CHAPTER 2

Nine on the Balls Meter

On an empty stretch of swampy bottomland outside Baton Rouge, five cars race down a two-lane highway: four cop cars and a bright orange Dodge with racing numbers painted on the doors. As the chase hits the straightaway, the cop cars surround their target—a 1969 Charger, Georgia license plates, what sounds like a 440 under the hood, and, to make the thing just a little more conspicuous, a Confederate flag painted on the roof.

The cop cars work together, spacing themselves around the Dodge so that they leave no room for escape and no question as to their intentions. On cue, one of the cops taps the fleeing vehicle, using the bumper to deliver a slight but precisely placed impact just in front of the left-rear wheel, a bit of fender-bender jujitsu that seems designed to send a car spinning to a sudden stop. The technique was originally developed for Delta Force and Navy SEAL units, to bring a chase to an abrupt end. In law enforcement circles, it's known as a "precision immobilization technique," or PIT maneuver, for short. At speeds over thirty-five miles an hour, it has been legally classified as a deadly use of force.

But the driver of the Charger, which is otherwise known as the General Lee, shows some talent at shaking the law: reacting with an instinctive countersteer, he quickly—even miraculously—recovers control. Before the cops can regroup and try again, the muscle car returns the maneuver, applying the same tap at fifty-five miles per hour to the lead cop car to his left, setting up a kind of high-speed

Houdini act. The lead cop car spins right as if it hit a patch of
ice, careening across the two-lane highway and turning completely
around. In the process, his rear bumper thumps into the other lead
cop car, sending *that* car careening back across the highway in the
opposite direction. As the two cars pinwheel across the lanes, the
good old boy in the General Lee—actually a onetime rally racer
from New Zealand—taps the brakes just enough to let them spin
by, then steers safely between them, hits the gas, and disappears.
The lead cops spin off the shoulder of the road and go thudding into
the thick brush as the follow cars squeal to a stop behind them.

Up the road, somebody in a camera car yells "Cut" and two
paramedics from the Baton Rouge Fire Department rush across
the highway to check on the stunt drivers. Darrin Prescott, the
stunt coordinator for this film, *The Dukes of Hazzard*, is usually
all business and back to work after a stunt, but after watching that
spectacle—which combined the qualities of massive wreck and
miracle escape in exactly the proportions he'd dreamed of—he
spoke over the radio to the two drivers in the cracked-up cop cars:
"That was just about flawless."

Dan Bradley, the second-unit director who also choreographed the
action on the last two *Bourne* movies, had cast the driver of the
General Lee with care, choosing the former rally driver Rhys Millen
over a host of stuntmen with more experience in feature films.
Millen usually worked around L.A. shooting car commercials and
racing in the Formula D drifting series, a fashionable motorsport of
Japanese origin that turned the power slides you see in rally racing
and stunt driving into a form of side-by-side competition, in which
drivers are judged, as they are in figure skating, for their combination of speed, line, aggression, and style. He is, according to
Bradley, a "fantastic, awesome, awesome driver." But the newcomer
wouldn't do crashes. "So we had to offer that out to people,"
Bradley said. " 'Listen, you'll double Bo Duke for the car crashes.' I
literally had guys saying, 'No, we get the seat the entire time.' I was
like, 'Yeah, you're a really good driver. But what I want is what this

guy does, and he doesn't do crashes. I want to step it up a notch.' And guys turned it down." There seems to have been some difficulty in believing that anyone was good enough behind the wheel to make it worth getting a stunt double for the stunt double.

So on the day Millen was scheduled to rehearse a particularly challenging maneuver, Bradley had Prescott bring all the guys out to watch. Millen was supposed to race the General Lee into a three-lane roundabout in New Orleans—the Lee Circle, by coincidence, just a block away from the Confederate Museum—and drift the Charger through the entire circle. That is, he had to pitch the car sideways into a skid and maintain that position, controlling the skid at a steady and fairly high speed through the entire roundabout. Bradley had cars parked all along the outer curb and traffic circling through the inner lane, the one closest to the monumental bronze sculpture of General Lee at the center of the circle. So Millen would have to fit his car, skidding continuously at a diagonal, in the lane and a half of space between the parked cars and the traffic. When he set off from the starting line, it looked almost as if the car had been set up to steer sideways. Despite the smoke and the squealing tires, he could keep at it seemingly forever, maneuvering through traffic, passing the other drivers, looking as steady leading with his passenger-side door handle as any of the rest of them might have leading with the nose. One of the older stuntmen, Tommy Huff, an ex-boxer and onetime Robert Conrad double, watched from the roof of a nearby apartment building as Millen drifted the entire Lee Circle over and over and over, without stopping once. "Mother*fucker*!" Huff said—a standard Huffism, used this time to register astonishment and admiration. He got on the phone to the guys who'd turned the gig down, and let them know that sharing an assignment with this kind of a wheelman was no dishonor.

In the Formula D world, Millen has been given the *nom de drift* of Mad Skillz Millen. It's a perfectly apt description of his abilities, but as a marketing strategy it's way off: as amazing as he is in a vehicle, you just can't picture this slightly pudgy New Zealander with the wicked dimples and Hollywood smile as a creature of the streets. His crew in the Trophy Truck series, an off-road racing circuit whose season includes the Baja 1000, has come up with a nickname that suits him better: they call him Metro, short for metrosexual. ("He's all dressed in his argyle sweater and shit," one said, in explanation. "I said, 'Dude, we're in Laughlin.'")

The first morning I saw him stunt driving, he was working on a chase scene: Bo and Luke Duke are racing through the streets of Atlanta to avoid the same cops who wind up chasing them in the big crash scene later in the film. The segment they were shooting came early in the pursuit, before the cops figured out how slippery these Duke boys could be. In the setup before the shot, a cop car had parked in the middle of the street, setting up a roadblock for the General Lee. Millen was supposed to come in fast, slide his rear-wheel-drive Dodge to a stop right next to the cop car, then do a burnout neatly around the front of the police vehicle, escaping on the far side of the roadblock with a screech of tires and a wiggle of the car's rear end.

They decided to split the sequence in two, filming the slide and the burnout separately. The first time Millen did the slide, he came in at about forty miles an hour and slid his car ninety degrees so it screeched to a stop with slightly less than four inches of clearance between him and the cop car. "You couldn't get a hamburger in there," Bradley said. Nevertheless he asked Millen to do it again. The next take Millen just barely kissed the cop car with his side panels; neither car was dented by the impact, and after Millen drove away to get ready for the next take, a scenic artist knelt beside the cruiser and brushed off two small daubs of orange with a swipe of a handkerchief. On the third try, Millen came even closer than the first time; the fourth, he backed off to about five inches away; and on the fifth and final try, it was perfect again, about as close as you could get without touching. He came out of the car and held up his hands: they were shaking. "That gets your attention," he said. "I'm sweating like a bugger."

Even though Millen didn't do crashes, Bradley was still getting more out of him than he would have from even a talented stunt driver. His drifting skills helped in the Lee Circle scene, but Millen had also spent years as a rally racer (the pro circuit motto is "Real roads, real cars, real fast"), so in scenes where the General Lee had to rush through the woods on a moonshine run gone bad, Millen was able to negotiate the dirt roads at race speeds. "Bradley's used to shooting at twenty-one frames a second to make thirty, thirty-five miles an hour look fast and exciting," Millen said, referring to the common practice of filming at a deliberately reduced frame speed, then speeding it up to make safe driving look out of control (and slightly surreal). "And we were coming by the camera at eighty, ninety miles an hour down these gravel roads, sideways, sliding, and he came up to me and he said, 'This is amazing. I've never been so excited to watch one car come down a road solo. I'm having to shoot twenty-four frames a second, real speed, because the action is exciting at real speed.' "

Millen comes from a family of motorheads. For thirteen years, his father, Rod Millen, a rally champion who now runs a research and development company that builds concept cars and classified military vehicles (among other things), held the world's record for fastest ascent of Pikes Peak; Millen himself won the Formula D drifting championship the year that *Dukes* came out. Car talk with him can be disorienting, like discovering that the driver's ed class you signed up for has been changed to a course in computational neuroscience. Here he is, for example, describing drifting the Lee Circle: "To put a car into a slide, you're overinducing the traction that a car has produced. You're abusing the power that you have, flicking the car into a slide, initiating it with turn-in from the steering wheel and then giving it full throttle, and essentially backing out once the car breaks traction, to control that dynamic, sometimes steering the car more with the throttle than you would with your hands. So given a sustained circle or an angle you could just about drift all day."

To investigate the family trait, I went out to California to meet Millen at MillenWorks, his father's company. An earlier incarnation,

Rod Millen Motorsport, was formed in the early eighties to support Rod's rally racing efforts (he won six American rally championships in a variety of divisions, from 1979 to 1995). But in the past few years, Rod cut back on his competitive schedule (sort of: in 2007 he won the 7,100-mile TransSyberia Rally in a Porsche Cayenne), and the group of engineers and fabricators has shifted its focus to a variety of engineering challenges. The company developed the airless tire and created the mechanical innovations for the Jeep Hurricane, a 2005 concept car that can spin in place and "crab steer," driving sideways directly into an open parking space. Some of the projects—unmanned vehicle programs for the military, for example—were classified, so the two men met me at the reception desk, right by a full-scale model of a helo-transportable tactical vehicle, and steered me through the building's public areas to Rod's office.

Rod is soft-spoken and easygoing—his MillenWorks nametag identifies him as "employee"—and his manner seems more suited to curious tinkering than championship racing. The family resemblance is striking—Rod has a wry and weathered version of Rhys's dimples and smile—and they clearly share a talent for driving any vehicle you put them into faster than other earthlings. But as much as they appreciate each other, their relationship at this point seems mostly collegial, with a little of the polite distance of separated twins. Rod left New Zealand to follow the international race circuit when Rhys was still in primary school; they didn't see each other much for most of Rhys's childhood. Rhys raced in New Zealand, and even shot a car commercial there at the age of nine, but he didn't get his license until he was eighteen, when he came to the States for college. He preferred surfing and racing mountain bikes, and his father supported this, sending him new frames whenever he "tacoed" a bike on the trails. In fact, Rhys was studying fabrication, in the hope of starting his own company to manufacture mountain bike components, and his dad saw that he was pretty good with a lathe and put him to work.

So Rod had his son building his race cars for the Asia Pacific Rally Championship before he ever saw him behind the wheel.

When he finally took him out, in 1990, he was "blown away" by his feel for the car, which both of them attributed to all the time he'd spent sliding around dirt paths on his mountain bike.

"There's a sense of balance that Rhys had that helps his skills today," Rod said. "And as you get confident pulling off all those maneuvers or stunts on a bicycle or a surfboard, you end up having the same confidence doing it on four wheels as well."

Rhys agreed. "In a car, especially off-road, you get in a loose situation, and you're not so much steering the car as you're manipulating the weight of the car to steer itself."

"And it gets to the point, either off-road or with a rally car," Rod said, "where you look at the terrain and you don't ever say, 'I've got to do this.' You just say, 'That's where I'm going.' I don't know how many people have said to me, 'How do you do that?' I say, 'Well, I don't know.' Because you don't physically stop to do it. You don't think how—you just instinctively do it."

Very little of this ease behind the wheel appears to have been taught, since Rod left New Zealand permanently when Rhys was six. It seemed that Rhys makes the case for the existence of a driving gene, I said. "Unless there was something in the air that he picked up?"

"There might have been," Rod said. "At the age of three, four, or five, when I'd drop him off to kindergarten in the mornings, right?"

"Yeah," Rhys said. "It wasn't exactly the straightest route."

"With a bit of luck, the roads would be wet and even slippery still. And he would always thoroughly enjoy that. 'Come on, Dad,' he'd say. 'Slide it some more!'"

On the same trip to California, I got a chance to sit in a passenger seat beside Millen as he drove a Trophy Truck, the Formula 1 of the desert, during a practice session on a fifteen-mile off-road run out in the Mojave, near Barstow. The terrain was rough: ruts and hills, holes and rollers, rocks and gravel, blind turns and sudden drops. This sort of uneven layout demands a sophisticated suspension

system: ideally, the wheels bounce all over, traveling down and snapping back so that the right kind of driver—someone with a mogul
skier's sense of balance and anticipation—can keep the cab of the
truck floating almost serenely over the big whoops and gullies and
washboard straightaways. Watching Millen drive past the improvised work zone where the crew had set up its car haulers and toter
homes, you could see the Trophy Truck's bump-travel suspension
snapping the wheels every which way while the cab above swayed to
a gentler rhythm; the truck seemed to be split at the midsection, like
a Latin dancer. As I was picking out a helmet to wear on the next
run, one of the suspension specialists warned me, "It's the most un-
controllable controlled ride you'll ever have."

Under normal circumstances, you experience the willing suspension of disbelief only after you buy a ticket or turn on the TV.
You don't have to put on a five-point harness and a crash helmet
equipped with a communication system that allows you to speak
with the driver over the roar of the 700 horsepower engine as it ac-
celerates, over and over, from almost nothing to a hundred-plus
miles an hour. But even though this was easily the scariest driving
in my entire life, even though we were racing up and over the edge
of rock formations that Millen could not see the other side of, I
wasn't worried. It was as if the words "Closed course, professional driver" were flashing across my eyeballs.

There were a few moments during the fifteen minutes it took
Millen to complete a circuit of the course when we could talk a little over the helmet-to-helmet intercom—I made some remark
about his evident rally experience as we slewed up and over a hill,
catching a little air and somehow landing on a gravel run right in
the middle of a buttonhook slide. At other times I could barely
breathe, as the ill-defined "road" vanished, and we hit an uneven
stretch of pits and swales of indeterminate depth. Each one, to my
eye, looked deep enough to swallow the truck, but to Millen they
weren't worth so much as a tap on the brakes. He kept right on
going, sprinting over the mesa with a few shakes of the steering
wheel, and we bounced along, with an economical minimum of

rebound. He seemed to be solving a puzzle at full speed, sorting through the landscape as if he could simultaneously see it from above and still feel it through the wheels. Then out of nowhere, he stopped short: what looked like just another dip turned out to be a sharp drop that he drove down slowly then raced up the other side of, a moment of sudden caution that cast a retrospective terror over the entire run. It felt like the lost Trophy Truck scene from *Strange Interlude*. "Wow, nice brakes," I said over the intercom, while behind the mask I was ripping off a dark soliloquy about a desert rollover and death on the mesa. Millen launched into a professorial explanation of the stress factors and fatigue points of the metals involved, which proved his grasp of the engineering, and seemed to reduce the driving to a theoretical exercise. The next day I discovered a few black and blue marks on my arms and thighs. I vaguely remember slamming my arm against the roll cage during one bounce and I might have been pressing a fist into my thigh for a while to suppress a natural urge to brake. I don't know.

A little while after my drive-along, another stuntman and Formula D driver, Tanner Foust, who'd just worked with Rhys on *The Fast and the Furious: Tokyo Drift*, showed up to watch Millen's test runs and take a tour in the passenger seat. His risk assessment is more practiced than mine: apart from his drifting duties, Foust also test-drives advanced vehicles and trains government drivers how to handle their duties under adverse conditions, work that sends him to Michigan's northern peninsula a few months each year. By the time Foust rode the circuit, Millen had been through it a few more times, so the run was even faster. When it was over, Foust took off his helmet, blinked a few times, and shook his head.

I asked him about his view of the ride. He'd fiddled with his seat belt throughout, he said, and he kept looking over at Millen wondering how he could see where he was going. "It seems like whenever you get to a sketchy area you have to make a decision—either brake hard, and then hope you can lift off the brake enough when you get to it, or go full throttle. One or the other. And I'd say nine and a half times out of ten, it was full throttle." He felt like he was putting his life in Millen's hands. "I haven't trusted somebody from the right seat that much, ever."

Millen, unfazed, immediately began dissecting his performance with the mechanics. "I think the shocks are too soft. It's using up too much of the travel," he said. He'd felt it in a section of the course that he called "the fast stuff"—that mesa top of pits and swales. "And then up through here"—he gestured in front of us toward a flat but rugged section at the end of the run, a straight-away where each wheel seemed to follow its own separate path through the rubble. "Up through here I was getting bounced around a lot more than I was before," he said.

"We were right here," one crew member said, in gentle disagreement. "And it looked perfect."

"Yeah," another agreed. "The cab was riding up here and it looked steady."

Foust interrupted. "It looked scary as shit from my seat."

One of the biggest risks in stunt work has nothing to do with physical danger: the movie you're in could really suck. Every performer runs this risk—check out Sir Laurence Olivier and Dame Maggie Smith in *Clash of the Titans*. But stuntmen, given the nature of the films that call for their particular skills, are much more likely to wind up in, say, *Bloodsport III* or *Brain Smasher: A Love Story* than in *Othello*. They don't take any less pride in their accomplishments, but it does promote a certain ironical view of success when your best work appears in *Seed of Chucky*. I was walking around Venice, California, with a key stunt performer from *The Punisher* a few months after it opened, and we ran into one of his stuntwoman counterparts from the movie; the last time I saw the two together they were hugging after surviving the big car gag on a beach in Tampa, Florida. The guy asked, "Did you go to the premiere of that thing?"

The woman shook her head. She was not the type to go on record if she didn't have anything nice to say, but you could tell that she would also not be seeing it on DVD, cable, or pay per view.

The stuntman laughed. "Me, neither. And I'm sure not going to waste seven dollars on it." I said nothing. I'd seen it the day it opened, with two *New Yorker* editors, one of whom praised the accuracy of the gunplay, which had, he noted, clearly employed the proper three-round burst typical of an M16.

I sort of enjoyed *The Punisher,* not just because it was the first movie where I knew nearly all the stuntmen; it was dark and bloody and featured John Travolta in a daringly listless performance and Rebecca Romijn in a housedress. But *The Dukes of Hazzard* truly did suck by the time it wound up onscreen. Dan Bradley said he doesn't even bother putting it on his résumé. From a stunt perspective, the failure seemed inexplicable. Bradley considered the footage he'd supplied the director, Jay Chandrasekhar, some of the snazziest vehicle work he'd ever done, and the producers had agreed. The director just didn't know how to work the stuff into the final product, so the best parts never made it to the screen.

But the professionals on the shoot that day knew how smooth the work was, by Millen and the others. Tim Rigby, who was behind the wheel of the lead cop car in that first big crash, was exhilarated by it, even though he wound up with the branches of roadside trees in his face. "It was as precise as dominoes, because once the chain reaction started we had to be in critical speeds, at critical distances, with critical spacing," Rigby said. "But you're not going to look at that and go, 'Hah, I wonder how they do that.' I don't know how it's going to look on the screen, but it's very possible people are going to look at it and think, '*That* wasn't meant to happen.' It looks that much like a wreck."

Despite the high-profile nature of such gags, a good portion of the art of the stunt lies in its invisibility. For most in the trade, anonymity is part of the professional code, and Tim Rigby, a slim, six-foot-two Brit with bluff, second-generation military diction, likes it that way. At thirty-eight, he's been in the business for sixteen years, and his feats have inspired awe even among the professionally fearless. Still he'd rather not be known at all, let alone as the signature figure of the three-year-old stunt group Brand X. There's only one catch: all his best work is captured on film.

Rigby is modest to a fault—a purist in the old-school style, he seems equally drawn to the daring and the invisibility of the job. But he is also rigorously straightforward and reliable, so if you ask him he will forthrightly describe his accomplishments, even while downplaying them. He has, for instance, BASE jumped from the Petronas Towers, in Kuala Lumpur, the world's tallest building at the time; from Angel Falls, in Venezuela, the world's highest waterfall; and from man-made landmarks in downtown Los Angeles that he will not specify because the jumps were, strictly speaking, illegal and because the BASE jumping community would like to continue making them. He often wears a wing suit for the jumps, which allows him to fly at speeds of greater than a hundred miles an hour. He played me a DVD that showed him jumping and then flying down the face of Kjerag—a spectacularly craggy 3,380-foot cliff in the Lyse Fjord in Norway—in and out of a thick layer of fog. When I recoiled in spite of myself, he said, "Oh, I could kind of see. It wasn't that bad."

Rigby has BASE jumped in movies twice, for *xXx* and *Along Came Polly*; both times the producers wanted to meet him before they'd sign off on the stunt. In the rigid Hollywood caste system, producers do not ask to meet stuntmen, but these producers were nervous and needed to be reassured. BASE jumping is famously dangerous—since you can never be absolutely certain which direction you'll be facing when your chute opens, you run a great risk of flying into the object you just jumped off, and death rates are high. Precise statistics are not available, because the sport is still largely clandestine, but Rigby could quantify the grave risks in personal terms: he'd had four friends die in the past four years, one of them immediately after Rigby had finished a jump and was standing in the valley below, watching and folding his chute. He seems to carry the seriousness of the event with him—the gravity of it, in every sense of the word. "I think the producers are a little

shocked when they meet me," he said. "They kind of think I'm going to turn up with a bunch of piercings and tattoos."

Rigby described the line that every stuntman must walk: You
need to command respect for being a good technician and for "having some balls." But, he said, "there's a line that you cross over
where you become a lunatic and then all that respect just goes right
out the window. It's almost unfair in a way. You could score a nine
on the balls meter and that gives you all this respect, but all of a sudden you go to a ten and now you're just an idiot." Rigby gets respect on both counts. As he tells it, any recklessness he had in him
disappeared one day when he was still in the Navy, working in the
Explosive Ordnance Disposal unit. It was his first big job. He dove
to the seafloor, traveling down on the same line as a 625-pound
German ground mine from the Second World War that a fisherman
had trawled up in his nets. The mine was live but unarmed—like a
loaded gun with the safety on—and Rigby threaded a wire around
the whole thing so it could be raised again and towed out to sea. In
training exercises, the mines he'd wired had been resting on mud, so
he'd tunnel his hands underneath the mine and wrap the wire
around it. But this time the mine was on the rocky seabed; tunneling
and poking was impossible. Because he was a rookie and knew he'd
get yanked out if he came up to ask questions, he *simply rolled the
mine over the wire.* "I really wanted to do this job," he said, with
the mixture of calm and excitement that you'd expect from a capable executive who'd just landed a plum account. "It was a dream
job. You could go your whole career and not get a mine like that."

Once they were out to sea, he dove again, packed the mine with
plastic explosives, set the timer, and returned to the ship, where the
whole crew watched and waited. And then it blew. Rigby was
shocked by the enormity of the explosion. "It wasn't cool," he said.
"You got a huge dose of wisdom in that second of seeing that.
Thinking, you know, 'This is not a game.' It changed me from a
gung-ho kid into, you know, 'Okay, let's get serious about this.'"

Fifteen years later, the Hollywood producer Arnie Schmidt,

impressed by Rigby's seriousness, agreed to let him perform one of the most audacious stunts ever put on film—a BASE jumping sequence in *xXx*. For that stunt, Rigby, wearing a Vin Diesel face mask, drove a red Corvette off the Auburn-Foresthill Bridge, the tallest bridge in California, 730 feet over the north fork of the American River, in the Sierra foothills. Then he climbed over the backseat, out of the car, and started his BASE jump from there. The stunt earned him two Taurus awards for best specialty stunt and best overall stunt by a man. Rigby described it with his typical blend of modesty and fatalism. "Once you've thrown your pilot chute, you're done. It's out of your hands. From that point on you just enjoy the view or panic," he said.

Rigby's path to the job was typical only in its eclecticism. After he left the British Navy at twenty-three, he began wandering around the globe, dedicating himself to what you might call a pre-stuntman course of studies: He taught windsurfing in Cap d'Agde, in the South of France; dove for pearls in northwestern Australia; rock-climbed on Mount Arapiles, a technical climbing challenge that is Australia's equivalent of Joshua Tree National Park. In 1992, he came to the United States and began his long professional apprenticeship, moonlighting on live stunt exhibitions like the *Miami Vice* show at Universal Studios, scraping boats as a commercial diver to make money, and riding everywhere he went—in L.A., mind you—on a bicycle. He remembered one conversation he had with a top stuntman early on: The guy laid it out, how many people try to do it and fail, how few made any real money at it. He had a reaction he remembered having once before, during his training for Special Forces: "Good, I'm glad it's not easy," he thought. "The harder the better, because I know I'll stick it out."

Unless your entire family is stuntmen, having a stuntman in the family is unusual, but Rigby says his family always supported him, well before his career looked like the sound financial decision it does today (a top stuntman like Rigby earns something in the mid six figures). The career was by no means inevitable, though.

His mother and sister could barely swim, he says, and while his father was a redoubtable figure—he led a Ghurka regiment in
Malaysia—he never spoke about the experience or pushed his son
in any direction at all. Still, the father's quiet influence is hard to
miss: two of his kukris, the sickle-bladed Ghurka combat knives,
hang over Rigby's fireplace, practically the only decoration in
what you couldn't in good faith call his living room. The room
that does, in fact, reflect his life is his office, with its two comput-
ers (one equipped with a flight simulator and Cessna-style controls
so he can practice flying) and his "glory wall," the pictures, many
of them taken on set, of his many stunts: Rigby rappeling; hanging
from a chain below the landing pod of a helicopter; doubling the
twins in *The Matrix Reloaded* with a friend from Brand X; Rigby
and forty-four others in a memorial skydive for Harry O'Connor,
a close friend who died paragliding during the filming of *xXx*;
Rigby, in the British Navy at age nineteen, readying for a dive.

Practically all of the figures in the pictures with Rigby are stuntmen, and most of them belong to Brand X. They're a miscella-
neous crew, of varying height and heft and character. But there's
something unmistakable about them, beyond the simple fact that
they're all clearly in shape. It's like looking at tintypes of fron-
tiersmen or Arctic explorers: you see boldness in every body type.
"It never ceases to amaze me," Rigby said. "Whenever I turn up
for work on a movie or a TV show, whatever, and it's your first
day, you don't know anyone, you're just looking for where you report to, and some production assistant will catch sight of you and
go, 'Oh yeah, stunt guy, your trailer's over there.' Maybe because
of the giant bag"—filled with rigging and assorted gear for a wide
range of conceivable stunts—"that's probably the giveaway. But I
always think, 'Is it that obvious? Couldn't I be a cameraman?' "

Rigby's most audacious stunt so far, his BASE jump in *xXx*, was
caught on film by eighteen cameras. It was not the sort of gag you
planned on doing twice. The special-effects crew had gutted the
Corvette, removing its motor and drive train, installing the lightweight shell on a motorized track leading over the bridge railing.

For weeks beforehand Rigby and the special-effects team tested the speed and acceleration and trajectory of the rig, riding one shell after another, junkers stripped to the same weight as the Corvette, into a dirt bank in Simi Valley. Meanwhile, Rigby said, the effects guys prepped the hero car for safety. "I'd go in," he said, "and they'd tell me, 'Well, we thought your foot might get stuck here so we plugged that hole—in case you get your foot trapped behind the seat as you speed off.' Little things like that."

Rigby had done a hundred and fifty BASE jumps in his life, and he did forty-five more of them to train for the *xXx* jump. "I got myself upside down, and in all different body positions," he said. "So that I would be more comfortable if I jumped off the car and was all out of shape and upside down." On the day of the jump, the effects crew sent off a test Corvette first. It plunged off the bridge as planned, but something went wrong, and the car twisted in midair, fell flat, and backflipped. Rigby was inclined to discount the bad run—they had added two hundred pounds to the back of the car to stand in for his weight, but he knew that once he and the car flew off the bridge, he'd quickly disengage and weigh next to nothing. Still, to avoid a repeat of that eventuality—which could conceivably pin Rigby underneath the car, where he'd be unable to open his chute—they added more weight to the engine compartment. "I would have rather it front-flipped," he said. "At least then it would send me over the end—catapult me forward. Which wouldn't have been great either, but it would have been better than a backflip."

The primary unknown—among many, since nothing of this sort had ever been attempted—was what Rigby called the burble: the disturbed air behind a moving object that could interfere with the opening of the pilot chute, the small round chute that the BASE jumper throws out to tug open the main canopy. Rigby, who had clearly thought a lot about burble, explained it thus: "Like in the back of a pickup truck, you sometimes see a piece of trash just going round and round and you think, 'Wow, how come that doesn't just get sucked out?' " He'd seen pilot chutes bouncing around like that, caught in the tiny burble created by a BASE jumper's back, and knew that the huge burble behind a plummeting Corvette would be considerably stronger.

He did one BASE jump from the bridge in costume to prepare—the film crew would have a chance to practice focusing on him while he sailed under canopy, and he could try once more to prepare for the worst-case scenario. He did a gainer, a reverse flip, not to show off, but to be upside down again, then pulled the chute, snapped himself upright, and landed smoothly. And then he went back up to the bridge and—contrary to his normal BASE jumping routine, in which, he said, he jumps as quickly as possible, as soon as the wind is right—he sat down to wait. Film sets are notoriously slow moving. All he could do was stash his good-luck charms—his mum's jewelry—and get nervous. He had about a half a day to sit around and stew.

"Then right before I went, when I could hear cameras rolling," Rigby told me, "once I was on the car and it's imminent, I was probably as calm as I'd been all day. And then once it starts, you just deal with each half second at a time. What's going to happen three seconds from now doesn't really matter at that point. It's just: Let me deal with this half second, and then this half second."

He rode the lightweight Corvette up and over the handrails of the bridge, and the car sailed into space. The weight held and the car floated and he stood up and jumped free. On the ground, his aerial coordinator, Harry O'Connor, worried about his safety. It looked to him as if Rigby was waiting too long to pull his chute, and he was partly right: Rigby, hoping to sell the stunt, wanted to make sure that the camera could see him floating away from the Corvette. But one element of the delay had nothing to do with showmanship: Rigby waited to be absolutely certain that he was free of the turbulence to be sure the pilot chute would work.

"And then when I threw out the pilot chute—this happens to me on every BASE jump—I think, 'This is the one it's not going to open. And there's nothing else I can do about it.' The delay that I have programmed into my brain—the amount of time it takes from when I throw that pilot chute to when I feel that parachute open—it's seconds. But in my mind, whenever that happens on a normal BASE jump, every single time I say, 'Oh, this is longer than normal. This is not right. This is not right.' Then, *Whack!* It opens. But on 'Triple X' it really was longer than normal. So I thought that anyway, then I had to combine that with the fact that it actually was longer than normal.

"And then it opened. I have never been so relieved in my life."

CHAPTER 3

Is There a Problem, Officer?

The day I met Jeff Galpin, he was the busiest stuntman in the state of Louisiana, maybe in the entire United States. Not that you could tell just then from looking at him. We were standing in a warehouse in the French Quarter, near Tchoupitoulas and St. Joseph streets, trying to get a good look at the chase scene unfolding outside. The warehouse was serving as the makeshift commissary for the *Dukes of Hazzard* shoot, and it was cool in there, and all the cameras—it was a big shoot, so there was one on a nearby rooftop, a few more down at the corner, another bolted to a chase vehicle— faced our direction, but if you peeked at the scene from a certain angle you could watch the drivers nearly crash into each other without ruining the shot. Galpin talked about how much he was working—the 2002 tax incentives that had brought so many Hollywood productions to Louisiana also made it attractive to hire a certain percentage of locals. He talked quietly, between takes, mostly unspooling a long story about being shot at, during his days as a police officer, by a drug dealer he'd been following undercover. I remember him being friendly and angry and distracted and sad. I later learned that the week we met, his wife had taken their two kids and left him for good.

Galpin stands out from other stuntmen. First of all, he doesn't share the sunniness that you see in so many of the pros flown in from Los Angeles. Those guys all know one another and work together well when the cameras start rolling. And when the director calls "Cut," they're just as good at horsing around and bullshitting in the shade. To an outsider, the setup can look suspiciously like a hiring haul—a system designed to keep all the jobs and money within a small group of buddies—but the practice makes sense professionally: in dangerous and precisely timed gags, stuntmen are more likely to perform confidently with somebody they trust. The practice also makes sense socially, since nobody wants to hang out with a grump every day for three months. Notorious jerks, even highly skilled ones, don't get hired for long shoots in the middle of nowhere.

But different standards apply for local hires like Galpin, who works nearly all the time despite his pit-bull disposition (in the year after we met, he appeared in at least ten films). The Louisiana hiring incentive helps, but it doesn't entirely explain how Galpin became the state's top stuntman. First, he's what stuntmen call useful—rugged, versatile, and uncomplaining. He combines skills you don't often find in one package: he's a licensed animal wrangler, a certified EMT, an ex-cop, a weapons expert, and a crane operator. So on low-budget films and big features looking to save money (the main reason films wind up in Louisiana), he looks like a great hire; a producer who puts him on the payroll can effectively fill two jobs with one paycheck. And since he has actually worked around town in all of his various capacities, he's connected. He knows the roundabout ways the city functions and who to call when it doesn't, from the governor's film commission to his boys on the NOPD. Hire Galpin and you get a film-industry Huey Long who can do high falls and bar fights and gator wrestling—and a savvy local ombudsman in the bargain.

When he trades stories with the guys, his contributions tend to be cop stories. For much of his career, he'd work a full day at stunts, then get right into his police uniform for the graveyard shift. The jobs blended well: Being a cop, for instance, gave him both the means and the motive to practice chase scenes. He'd drop into the NOPD motor pool, grab a car, take it out on the interstate, and hit the emergency brake over and over, downshifting, sliding the car sideways, teaching himself control at high speeds. Then he'd bring the cruiser back to the motor pool and tell the mechanics to fix it. This on-the-job training paid off both on the set and on the streets. He started to notice that whenever he got into a real chase, he'd look in his rearview mirror and see the other cops wiping out behind him. "I always got the bad guy," he said. "Stunts actually helped me in my police career." Sometimes he made that claim the other way, saying that stunt work looked easy after all he had to face on his patrols. "After my cop training, this wasn't hard. Think about it. What do cops do? Basically we shoot, drive, and fight. I just had to learn to shoot away from people."

He said this with a laugh that was sharp, dark, and hard to laugh along with. Galpin seems to sense this quality, because he doesn't laugh a lot. Usually, when he gets to his punch lines, he just shuts up and watches you with his eyes gone flat. And it's mostly this look that lets you know, even five years after he quit the force, that the man looking at you is a cop.

Actually, first he was a narc, starting in college, when he led a double life pretending he was a high school student in order to infiltrate dope rings. He was a natural—young and good-looking and easy to get along with, with an unflinching quality that came off as cool and remote. But then one night, as he unlocked his door—he lived in a camp house on stilts out on the Tangipahoa River—Galpin was attacked by a suspect he'd been tracking, a hash-selling son of a Saudi general. The kid stuck a pistol under Galpin's chin and squeezed the trigger. When the gun didn't go off, Galpin knocked him down and ran, pretty sure that his assailant couldn't keep up with him in the swamps at night. After that experience, he decided to get out of narcotics and into uniform, thinking it'd be safer, and he joined the street-crimes team of the New Orleans Police Department.

Galpin is not physically imposing. His résumé says he's five-ten, a hundred and eighty, and in his head shots he's dimpled and boyish, almost pretty. He's polite on the set, with a "ma'am" and "sir" for superior and subordinate alike. But you'd have to be almost oblivious to misinterpret his everyday mood, which is at once well-mannered and unmistakably threatening. "I don't know what to tell you," he said. "I was an aggressive cop. I loved to chase people down. I loved the car chases. I loved for you to run from me, because when I caught you, I would beat your ass. It's called 'contempt of cop.' It's contempt of cop when a guy runs from you and you take it personally—like, 'How dare you run from me? I'm the police!'"

Stuntmen often get acting credits playing thugs, longshoremen, orderlies, soldiers. Galpin usually winds up as a cop. Directors appreciate his realism. But he is also a good actor, with a narc's ability to shape-shift into all manner of lowlifes, and when he tells stories, he interrupts himself in other voices and accents, carrying on entire conversations with the characters that a cop can meet: crack whores, preachers getting blow jobs, vagrants, drunks, and all-purpose assholes. "You don't need to harass a guy to get him," he starts out. "But if you want him, you got him. There's so many laws. We used to call them the fuck-fuck laws. You know what I mean? You wanna play fuck-fuck? Let's play fuck-fuck."

I was laughing (an honest cop!) and he warmed to his theme. "I remember one car: This woman was a bitch. She was an absolute bitch. It was a speeding ticket, running the red light, which she really did. And she called me an asshole: *'You're a dickhead. You ought to be catching crackheads.'* So I told her, 'I'll be right back.' I wrote her another ticket. *'You're a fuckin' asshole'* . . .'I'll be right back' . . . Wrote her a third one. *'You're just a fuckin' loser. You need a real life'* . . .'I'll be right back.' I wrote that bitch fifty-two tickets. I broke out the air-pressure gauge. Checked out the tire tread. Made sure the windshield wiper squirted fluid. I mean, literally, I was in the book going, 'Uhhhh, that applies! Write that ticket!' Two and a half hours writing tickets on this one car. 'Cause she pissed me off. That's the little fuck-fuck rules, you know? Wanna be a bitch? Let's be a bitch. I'm the bigger bitch, I promise."

The next time I saw Galpin, it was August, eight months later, and he was coordinating stunts on the set of a low-budget film called *Little Chenier*. Actually, I ran into his gator first: an eleven-footer in a crate on the flatbed of his Chevy Avalanche. Trace Cheramie, the Cajun stuntman slated to wrestle the gator under Galpin's direction, showed me the hide through the crate's breathing holes. He'd never wrestled a gator before, he said, and got the job largely because he didn't mind getting the Mohawk needed to double the lead. But he had a good feeling about doing it, "as long as that mouth is taped, bro." Cheramie's ancestors were all fishermen— highly uneducated, he said, except in the habits of local aquatic life—and wrestling a gator was a big item on any Cajun to-do list. "I'm pretty eager about it," he said. "As a true coon-ass"—a derogatory term for Cajuns that Cajuns use affectionately among their own—"I can earn my stripes."

Cheramie was one of the first to arrive on the set, and he stood by the truck, stretching, calmly answering questions about the gator's size. ("I don't know how big it is, but they picked it up with a cherry picker and when they put it down, the truck went *whhhump!*") A German assistant director named Tanya came over and quizzed Cheramie about the particulars of the stunt. "We have to rig the gator, tether him down to some trees," Cheramie told her, quickly sketching the technical prep work that the gag required. He spoke to her in the low tones you'd use to calm a spooked horse, and neatly avoided the issue of his inexperience by pointing out that the biggest question mark involved whether the scene would be filmed on land or in water, and if in the water, where—matters that Galpin and the director still had to decide.

"Well, let's hope we get some clues at some point," Tanya said, turning to leave. "Otherwise, we'll have to change it to a duck."

Once she was gone, Cheramie considered the dangers of his job that day. With oversize prey—say, a hundred-and-eighty-pound man from Lafourche Parish—a gator's favored tactic is the death roll: it'll clamp down, dive, and begin spinning wildly to disorient the prey as it rips off bite-size chunks. Whether or not the gator actually did go into a death roll during the stunt, "he's going to go down," Cheramie said, "and take me along. My biggest concern is the depth of the water if he does get to spin, and if the cables do come loose and I get wrapped in them." This would be the worst-case scenario, since it would add the possibility of mutilation and strangulation to the risk of drowning.

When Galpin arrived, things started to move quickly. His cousin Jared and another stuntman, Cord Newman, had come with him to work as safeties. They drove the Chevy over to a shady spot near the shore, slid the gator crate out of the flatbed and onto a mover's blanket spread out on a tiny patch of grass be-tween the shell road and the sand. They opened the crate and lifted the gator, lethargic from his stay in the hot close space, onto the grass. One production assistant, a big guy well over two hundred pounds, was instructed to sit on the tail.

Galpin wore swim shoes, a blue T-shirt, and a wet suit rolled down to his waist. Jared, a taller, younger version of Galpin with a brighter, less troubled smile, spent a lot of time straddling the snout, helping restrain the gator while Galpin ran aircraft cable around its waist. He was meticulous, because the safety of the gag would hinge on its proper placement: he threaded the ⅜-inch steel cables through a sleeve-and-thimble kit, tightened the cables, then crimped the sleeve shut. Throughout all this, the gator lay motion-less, and during one of these spells I put my hand down and felt the ridges and the scales along its back: It was just like touching gator skin on boots or a belt or a watch strap, except this one was attached to something hot, solid, and huge. I could feel it breath-ing. Every once in a while, it would let out a long, shuddering sigh, and everybody standing around to watch would scatter, then laugh and slowly inch closer again. "Long as he don't bust me in the nuts," Jared said. To the gator, he added, "I love you."

"This a he or a she?" a cameraman asked.

Galpin looked up. "You know how you can tell?"

"Stick your finger up his rectum," Jared said. "If you feel something, it's his prostate. Make him feel good."

They were filming on a shady bend in a river about twenty minutes from Lake Charles, in Calcasieu Parish, Louisiana. Cypress trees grew in the water and along the shore, and the ground was riddled with knot-like stumps poking up from their roots—hazards that pretty much eliminated the possibility of wrestling the gator on land. It was buggy; a production assistant came over to squirt Hot Shot roach and ant killer anyplace the director, Bethany Ashton, set up to watch the action. Except when a banana fish jumped out and skipped across the river, the water was still. When the assistant director called out, "Quiet for tone," so the sound crew could record the bayou background noise, everyone stopped what they were doing, and you could hear the rattle of crickets rise and fall like the sizzle of fish in a frying pan.

In the movie, two good ol' boys, the ex-con T-Boy and his retarded younger brother, run a bait shop and get in trouble with the law. But in that day's scene, the two come upon a family in danger out in the bayou, pinned in a cut in the bayou by a gator that T-Boy recognizes. After a little speech ("Hey dere, ol' girl. 'Member me? You miss me fuh the pass ten year?"), T-Boy flings away his gun and wrestles the creature fair and square.

For much of the early afternoon, they filmed parts of the scene without the gator in the frame: the family in tears; T-Boy and his crew arriving in his shrimp boat; T-Boy bare-chested, jumping bravely into the water; reaction shots from the people in both boats. To Galpin's mind they were wasting the day, and he blamed Ashton—a Lake Charles native who'd moved to Los Angeles—for nervously putting off the gator scene because she'd never done a big gag. "I told them I'd do it because it was a local show," he told me. "I didn't know it'd be a cluster fuck like this."

Finally, they'd run through everything they could film without the gator, and the director called everybody to the waterside for a safety meeting. Safety meetings are required by the film's underwriters, and mostly they're an exercise in the obvious. The director or stunt coordinator is still obligated to get through it all, like a flight attendant explaining how to use a seat belt. But before a truly dangerous stunt, these meetings lose their pro forma quality. At such moments, whoever is detailing the precise sequence of dangers about to unfold ends up—intentionally or not—building the tension and stoking the excitement, like a ringleader at the circus. This time, the ringleader was Galpin.

He stood up in front of the cast and crew, the stand-ins, the makeup girls, the teamsters, the medics. "Basically," he said, "at one point T-Boy's character is going in the water. Trace is gonna be the stunt double, he's gonna grab the alligator. This gator will roll. It's gonna throw him around. Medics: If we're not running sound when Trace is doing his thing, I'd like the ambulance running and ready to go.

"This gator is tied in by the hip. He's got two cables around his waist. They're crimped in. He's gonna have two separate lines, one running to the other cypress tree—not cypress tree, whatever the hell it is. Anyway, he's tied off. He will not be able to bite. His mouth is taped with clear tape, but he is still as dangerous as he could ever be. The tail can literally break your legs. His teeth are exposed on the sides. He will rip you. So as long as we got the gator out everyone stay back unless you're one of the stunt guys. Anybody have any questions?" He'd gone through the whole speech like a policeman, underplaying it all, but still sounding commanding. "Al'ight. Let's do it."

For long stretches of the afternoon, you could see Cheramie standing by himself with his eyes closed, slowly moving his arms and raising his legs, practicing the choreography in his mind's eye. Under his new Mohawk, he made this practice sequence look peaceful and poetic, like some tai chi exercise he performed every morning: Wrestle the Gator.

When it came time to put the gator in the water, it took six guys to carry the creature, his eyes now uncovered, and lower him in. Some thirty feet away, another crew grappled the aircraft cable cinched to the gator's hips, pulling it tight on Galpin's command. Jared and Cord Newman remained in the water, ready to tug the cables to rile the gator into movement whenever the director called "Action."

For most of the first takes, Galpin, now fully wet-suited, bobbed in the water near the gator's head, just out of the frame, fishing for sludge and greenery to put on the gator, a bit of camouflage so nobody could tell that the snout was taped shut. The director sat on a crate about ten yards away on the shore, watching takes on a clamshell, a portable clam-shaped device that allowed her to see playback immediately. "So, Jeff?" she said.

"Yes, ma'am?"

"Where can we put the camera to see the gator head on?"

In most shots, she said, the gator stayed too low in the water or disappeared too quickly. So to make the gator behave more like an actor, Galpin suggested putting a new cable around it, which he could use like a bridle to control the movement.

That sounded good, Ashton said. And now it fell to Galpin to put this bridle over the gator's head. It took some doing. By this point the gator had stopped objecting to the cable around his hips. But when Galpin tried to slip more steel over his head, the gator churned around, and there was silence on the set. Everyone watched Galpin snapping out of the water and then back underneath. The first time he surfaced, Galpin yelled "Bitch!" and the next time, Cord Newman asked, "You got him?"

"Yeah, I got him," Galpin said. The waters calmed. He was suddenly in control, and looked at Newman. "You think I'm a pussy?"

Galpin got the harness on and bobbed on the water just out of the shot while Clifton Collins Jr., the actor playing T-Boy, finished filming all the speeches and preparatory lunging toward the gator. Finally, the time came for Cheramie to get in the water and do the gag. He wore the same outfit as Collins: bare-chested, with cowboy boots and jeans. Cheramie added a mouthpiece—his face would be turned from the camera—and he'd sanded down the bone handle on the knife that the character wore so it wouldn't cut him up in all the commotion. Galpin asked the guys in the ambulance, from West Calcasieu Cameron Hospital, to get as close to the water as possible and leave their doors open. One of the producers, Gavin Boyd, had worried all night about this stunt. Now, his voice a little strained, he shouted, "You're a rock star, Trace!"

Galpin and Cheramie stood side by side in the water, going over the best way to grab hold of the gator. They'd taken off the noose so it couldn't ensnare Cheramie. The only thing left to hang on to now was the gator's front legs. Cheramie had played football in college, but this was wrestling. As at a wrestling meet, there was a calm before the match began, when you could look at the combatants and gauge their chances. The gator was eleven feet long and weighed about five hundred pounds—one of the biggest at Bayou Pierre Alligator Park, in Natchitoches. He was restrained at the waist, so he couldn't drag Cheramie too far down or pull him out to deeper water. But he could roll all he wanted and could still pummel the stuntman with his snout or slap him with a whipsaw chop of the tail—two natural moves designed to stun prey and channel it within range of his jaws. Cheramie was stocky, about five foot ten and a hundred and eighty pounds, and his power seemed evenly distributed between his chest, arms, and legs. He was forty, a ground-pounder with an easygoing vibe. You place your own bets.

Galpin and the safeties steadied the gator. Cheramie tucked his right arm up and under the gator's right front leg, then threw his other arm over and around its neck in the combination half-nelson and choke hold he'd practiced onshore. Through all this preparation, the gator seemed to be biding his time. When the crew let go and moved away, Cheramie held the gator on his own. The cameras were rolling. The cue to begin would come from him. Galpin had assured him: Any sudden move on his part, and the gator would unleash.

Cheramie bent as close as he could, pressing the bare skin of his chest and belly against the gator's side. He tightened his grip.

Suddenly—and with a quickness that was terrifying in such a large creature—the gator rolled to his left, and Cheramie's legs flew up and around as he held on. The two of them sank beneath the brown swamp water and reappeared almost immediately five feet away. Cheramie's legs whirled through the air again. That was his flourish. Galpin had wanted him to tuck himself against the gator so he'd stay close, like a jockey riding a horse, but Cheramie preferred to play it like a rag doll. After the second roll, Cheramie darted clear of the gator and emerged from the water to a round of applause.

But the director watched the playback and wasn't satisfied with the gator's performance. On that last take, it had uncooperatively rolled out of the frame, and this time they wanted to shoot it as a closeup. Cheramie got back in position, and again tugged hard, but on this take the gator swung his head quickly and caught Cheramie in the stomach, a chop to the body that knocked the wind out of him. He fell back and swam away as quickly as he could. When he'd gotten far enough, he shook his head and let out a big zydeco yell: "Whooo!"

On the third take, they got it right: Cheramie's legs swung wildly through the air, and the gator rolled violently in place—and on top of the water, mostly, so that the camera caught it all. "There's something in there," the director said when they were done, as if she couldn't wait to get to the editing room to piece it all together. Then she decided to lay off the directorial talk for a while and she just stared in admiration. It was her first big stunt, too. "You guys were fantastic."

Galpin never intended to be either a stuntman or a cop. He'd gone to college hoping to be a vet. As a teenager, he'd gotten serious about raising wildlife and become a licensed rehabilitator in the state of Louisiana; he'd take in wild animals that had been hit by cars and nurse them back to health. Through the veterinary program at LSU, he got an internship at the Audubon Zoo, in New Orleans, and he was working in the swamp exhibit there when somebody from the movie *Undercover Blues* came in looking for the right kind of person to throw over a railing into a pit of alligators. Without thinking too much, the zoo's herpetologist told them, "Jeff is the one you want." He didn't know it but he'd been launched on a new career path. After two days of watching Galpin handle gators on the set, the producers hired him for the rest of the film. And when that one was finished, he got called for *Interview with the Vampire*. Then *Hard Target* wanted to find out if he was scared of rattlesnakes. Hell no, he wasn't. He started telling productions not to bother bringing in handlers from Los Angeles, to let him take care of the animals instead. And once he got those jobs, he persuaded producers to put him on stunts, too.

When the film business dried up in the early nineties, Galpin began his stint as a narc. In 1993, he added construction to his skill set, holding down a job as a crane operator from 7 A.M. to 3:30 P.M., followed, at that point, by the six-to-two shift on the street-crimes unit. Whenever film work did come to town, he simply juggled another ball: he could handle the crazy schedule partly because a crane operator might make only one lift a day (so the other seven and a half hours he could sit in his cab and sleep), and partly because he dosed himself with ephedra and forty-ounce coffees.

He was dropping in for a coffee the last time he saw his ex-partner, Jimmy, at the Circle K, in 1995. He'd moved from the street-crimes unit to driving a patrol car, and was working a morning shift. They ran into each other at the end of Jimmy's shift and the beginning of his. When they got back in their squad cars, a call came on the radio: armed robbery, purple four-door, black male. There were only four routes out of that part of town, and Galpin quickly blocked off one, and was waiting there when Jimmy came over the radio asking for another description. Galpin gave it to him. Five minutes later, another call came on the radio: an officer had been shot.

"I remember asking that dispatcher, 'Is it an officer or is it one of those rent-a-cops?'" Galpin told me. "And the dispatcher says,

'The lady says she's blind and old but she saw a policeman fighting with somebody and shots fired.' So I hauled ass. I actually passed one policeman in the air at a hundred and twenty miles an hour. I hit a bump and I passed him and looked down at him. And when I got there I didn't even recognize Jimmy. I didn't know who he was. He had a weird color. I ripped his shirt off, started doing CPR, and watched the blood shoot out of his chest. And I couldn't figure out why I'm watching blood, why is it coming out of his chest? It just didn't register. All I remember is: This is a policeman, he's down, he's one of us. And I looked at one of the paramedics and I said, 'Who the fuck is this?' And he says, 'It's Jimmy.' "

Galpin jumped in the ambulance with the paramedics and worked on Jimmy all the way to the hospital, but when they arrived the presiding doctor said Jimmy had been dead on the scene. That's how Galpin told it, without mentioning explicitly that his ex-partner had died in his arms, or under his hands, minutes after they'd said goodbye. He later heard that Jimmy'd been fighting with his wife, which might explain why the guy had worked all day without his vest and then took an extra shift despite how tired he was—two ways of saying he didn't want to go home.

After the shooting, the New Orleans Police Department put Galpin on administrative duties for two weeks. And, as he put it, "they made us go to the loony bin." All of Jimmy's close friends on the force spent eight hours a day talking with a psychiatrist. "It gave me a new respect for one female cop I really did not have any respect for," he said. "Because we had a roundtable deal where they went around asking, 'What's the first thing you thought of when Jimmy was shot?' They asked me, 'What was the first thing you wanted to do when you left the scene where Jimmy was dead?' The first thing I did, I stopped every black male everywhere. There wasn't a black male in the entire Jefferson Parish that didn't get stopped, no matter what kind of car he was in. And taken out at gunpoint. Literally. So I said, 'What I basically wanted to do was, I was going to shoot him, whoever it was. I was gonna find him, kill him, and then worry about the consequences later.' This female detective, they asked her, 'What was the first thing you thought of?' And she said, 'The first thing I was listening for on the radio was someone to shoot him and me helping him cover it up.' And I went, '*There.*'"

Galpin was unapologetic about all this. "Anytime you shoot someone, they give you time off, as much as you want, to let you clear your head. Me, anytime I was involved in a shooting, I just went hunting." He let out his laugh. "Kill some more." He'd actually never said that he'd killed anybody, but I wasn't about to follow up with him on the matter then. "At some point, you develop a sense of not caring: Man, life doesn't mean shit. I could play in your guts tomorrow and it wouldn't bother me none. I'm still like that to this day."

I later did ask, and Galpin told me that he had been involved in firefights on the force, with results he preferred to leave unspecified. He did say that those events had a lot to do with his decision to abandon the line of work entirely. He had a family, so he stayed on the force for the benefits, but as soon as the stunt work looked steady and secure enough, he turned in his badge to be a full-time stuntman. Since he was holding down three jobs, it took him a little longer to break in than it might have somebody else, but because he was such a workaholic, he did it. By 2002, when the tax incentives kicked in, he was working nonstop on indies, big-budget features, commercials, and television.

He has gone back to police work once: A few days after I left the *Little Chenier* set, Hurricane Katrina hit the Gulf Coast, and Galpin made sure his family was safe in Baton Rouge, then returned to the city. He'd heard about policemen quitting or leaving town or just refusing to show up, and he wanted to help. They were deputizing practically anybody from the nearby jurisdictions. But he didn't want to just go out and get shot at. He stuck to the safer zones, helping launch boats or just watching for looters. He sent me some pictures he took out on the streets, and it's easy to see that he works in film. He tells a story in just a few snapshots, and his point of view comes across: a woman floating facedown, above the caption "St. Charles Street"; a man standing by a shopping cart, his hands at his midsection as if taking a piss ("He had a gun"); a skinny white couple, the man shirtless and waist-deep in the water, pushing his woman on a launch piled high with six-packs ("Gotta have the beer").

The downtime after the hurricane doesn't seem to have affected Galpin. In the past three years, he's been averaging twelve films a year. When I last spoke with him, he'd been doing a lot of coordinating. In one, *Pride*, in which Terrence Howard plays a swim coach in inner-city Philadelphia, the director also pegged Galpin to play—what else?—a cop who has a run-in with Howard. Galpin told the actor that it was a good omen. "Last time I beat up a black actor as a cop on a show was *Ray*," he said, laughing. "And Jamie Foxx got an Oscar for that. So hopefully it works for Terrence Howard, too." He sounded excited about the film, didn't play it down in any way. One of Galpin's most attractive qualities is his frankness: he has no illusions about the sort of behavior he's capable of, and in all our conversations, he never second-guessed or prettied up his stories from the streets. But for all his gruffness, you couldn't miss his contentment, his amusement that he wasn't doing things much differently than before. Just that this time, all the rough stuff was happening safely, on time, under budget, and in the frame.

CHAPTER 4

Gravity and Blondes

The first stuntmen weren't stuntmen first. They started out as something else and got ambitious or bored or desperate. They were extras. They were circus clowns and acrobats, prizefighters and barnstormers, steeplejacks and flagpole-sitters, out-of-work roustabouts from the California oil fields, rodeo riders from the Wild West show circuit. One account credits the first stunt to an unnamed L.A. hypnotist who, in 1908, accepted five dollars to dive into the surf in a blond wig on *The Count of Monte Cristo*. Another gives the honor to a drunken Indian named Eagle Eye, who, during the shooting of D. W. Griffith's *Intolerance*, in 1916, accepted a three-dollar bump in his daily fee to fall from a Babylonian tower onto a hay cart.

These men and the ones who came after probably called what they did gags because they did so many in comedies, especially in Mack Sennett's Keystone Kops series. Sennett's props could be elaborate—his studio was filled with wind machines, moving sidewalks, and a fleet of trick Keystone Kop wagons that could spin out seemingly forever (liquid soap on the road facilitated this effect). But the ex-vaudevillians generally did their own gags, with very little trickery. If a scene called for a line of twenty hapless cops to hang off the end of a wagon and be dragged through the streets as the driver weaved around telephone poles, all they did was spread a little sand on the ground and go. These slapstick specialists prided themselves on their ability to pull off, as

Sennett wrote in his autobiography, "any foolish stunt my psychopaths in the writing room could think up." And they kept at it when the cameras stopped: one of their favorite offscreen gags involved wiring the studio's urinal so that it would shock anyone who used it.

It wasn't just Sennett comedies that relied on the bravery of gag men. Chapter plays and cliffhangers like *The Hazards of Helen* and *The Perils of Pauline* owed much of their popularity to spectacular and often improvised stunts. To a degree that was often foolhardy, the action in these serials was real; taking little or no precaution, stuntmen would somersault from plane to plane, jump out of an upper-story window into the trees below, drive a motorcycle off a cliff based on a few scratch-sheet calculations about when to pull the parachute's ripcord. On a Clarence Brown film in the twenties, Gene Perkins agreed to swim the rapids over the six-hundred-foot Nevada Fall. "When I get here," he told the director, pointing to a spot only two feet from the top of the falls, "throw me a rope and try not to miss me. The water looks cold." Plane gags, which profited from the ready availability of barnstormers and former military flyboys, proved the most dangerous of all, and studios learned to take advantage of the publicity bonanza that followed the spectacular aerial deaths. In 1920, Lieutenant Ormer Locklear crashed coming out of a spiral in a night shoot lit by flares; there were no identifying remains, except for a special-delivery letter to his mother that he always carried in his coat pocket. Three weeks later, Fox delivered *The Skywayman* to the theaters, complete with footage of the fatal spin.

When the movie business was in its infancy, action stars and gag men competed freely for popular attention. Stuntmen like Fred (Speed) Osborne and Suicide Buddy Mason trumpeted their feats in the press, and stars like Tom Mix and Richard Talmadge and Douglas Fairbanks played up claims that they actually performed all the acts of derring-do that showed up onscreen. This led to the occasional conflict of professional interests. In one such incident, Yakima Canutt, a saddle-bronc champ who would later become arguably the most influential stuntman in the history of film, was spending his first off-season doing "picture work" in Hollywood when he overheard Mix bragging to visitors on the set. The onetime Oklahoma City bartender regaled them with tales of the horse thieves and outlaws he fought singlehanded, the horses shot from underneath him in the middle of heated gunfights. When the group left, Canutt said, "Tom, you're a bit reckless with the truth, aren't you?"

"As long as a lie don't hurt anyone, there's no harm done," Mix said, once he'd calmed down. "They ate it up, didn't they?"

Canutt left Mix's show a few days later; the star wanted Yak to grow a beard and play an outlaw, and Canutt, who was tall, handsome, and twenty-four, thought the look would interfere with his nightlife. But he stayed in Hollywood, where there was plenty of work for a man of his abilities. Like all rodeo riders, Enos Canutt (Yakima was a rodeo nickname that nodded to his roots in Washington state) knew how to hit the ground. His acting, in silent features such as *Ridin' Mad* and *Hell Hounds of the Plains*, ranged from jumping off a cliff on horseback to jumping off a cliff onto a horse's back. But he excelled at fistfighting scenes—especially brawls that involved the smashing of saloon windows. Over the next few years, he grew into a silent-movie action hero in low-budget Westerns, the blood-and-thunder quickies that the studios started to churn out weekly.

Unfortunately, his voice couldn't make the jump to talkies—he said he sounded "like a hillbilly in a well"—but he adapted, playing bad guys and doubling stars like John Wayne and Clark Gable. Later, Canutt moved behind the camera to oversee the action in such movies as *Spartacus*, *El Cid*, and *Ben-Hur*. It was here that he'd have his greatest influence: over the ensuing decades, his technical improvements and canny modifications of familiar gags helped turn stunt work from a primitive trial-and-error proposition into a sophisticated, even relatively safe branch of movie magic. He is thought to be the first person to have positioned the camera over the shoulder of the guy getting coldcocked during a screen brawl;

the camera, which has no depth perception, records the punch be-ing thrown and the head snapping back without detecting that the punch never actually connected. He began shadowing the explo-sives teams and the rigging crew and giving the directors tips for staging stunts more effectively. Eventually, the producers simply handed him scripts and told him to write in the action scenes. (He designed and filmed the *Ben-Hur* chariot race.) Thanks largely to his efforts, the second-unit director became the chief figure on the set in charge of stunts and spectacle, and in 1966 he received the only Oscar ever given in recognition of a stuntman's work—an hon-orary award "for developing safety devices to protect stunt men everywhere" and "for creating the profession of stunt man as it ex-ists today."

Canutt cut the template for a lengthy and successful stunt ca-reer, but for all his work behind the camera he is still best remem-bered for a gag that's widely regarded as the most amazing stunt sequence on film. He did it three times: first in *Zorro's Fighting Legion*; then, a few months later, on *Stagecoach*; and finally, three years after that, on the Roy Rogers film *Idaho*. Each version offers small variations, but the basic outline is this: Canutt, on horse-back, chases a stagecoach that's trying to outrace him. When he catches up, he leaps from his saddle over the leader of the six-horse team, landing on the wooden hitch that connects the team to the wagon. At this point, Canutt either gets in a fistfight or gets shot off his perch; either way, he soon falls underneath the hitch and slides right between the two rows of galloping horses, then passes both axles of the stagecoach. In *Idaho* and *Zorro's Fighting Le-gion*, he finished the sequence by catching hold of a bar at the back of the coach, clambering back on, and making his way over the roof to jump the driver. In *Stagecoach* he simply let the wheels pass over him and lay still on the dirt, while his fellow Apaches continued to chase after John Wayne and Claire Trevor, leaving him for dead on the Monument Valley dirt.

Though it's old-fashioned, the gag is impressive, filmed without trickery and presented without any of the quick cuts that might have allowed Canutt to divide the action into safer segments. Whether or not it's the greatest stunt ever is irrelevant. What's important is that it's the gag that *stuntmen* bring up when they're talking about the best stunts of all time. If they ever build a Stuntman's Hall of Fame, Canutt's stagecoach gag will be the first film clip you see as you walk in the door. For stuntmen, it's the best and most intimidating example of the career-defining stunt, that signature blend of talent and bravado that each stuntman prays he will someday get a chance to bring to bear before the cameras.

Only one other stuntman has pulled off the gag on film: Terry Leonard, a onetime decathlete and strong safety in the Canadian Football League. He did it most memorably in *Raiders of the Lost Ark*, doubling Harrison Ford, slipping underneath a cargo truck. "I jumped from the horse to the truck, then went out the window and down underneath the truck and up the back," Leonard told me. "And everybody remembers that stunt so vividly. It's become a classic. But three months before, I did the same thing under a stagecoach in Monument Valley." Like Canutt, Leonard pulled it off with horses first, in 1980, on *The Legend of the Lone Ranger*, a dismal picture that didn't make back its shooting budget. "Now the point I'm going to make is that doing it with six head of horses and a stagecoach is the wildest thing I've ever done as a stuntman. The thing under the truck—the only danger of that was maybe getting run over by the truck if my buddy Glenn Randall wasn't driving it correctly. But the people remember the *Raiders of the Lost Ark* so much because it was poignant. It came at a point in the script when Harrison looked at Karen Allen and they see the truck leaving, and she says, 'What are you going to do now?' And he says, 'I don't know. I'm making this up as I go.' And he takes off after that truck on this gray Arab stallion. That's the difference between those two stunts, one being the wildest thing I've ever done and the other one being not quite so wild, but memorable because of the way it's placed and interjected into the film. Everybody remembers the *Raiders* stunt. Nobody remembers *Legend of the Lone Ranger*."

Like Canutt, Leonard has now moved behind the camera as a second-unit director—the only one I've ever seen praised by name in a movie review, for his work on *The Fast and the Furious: Tokyo Drift*, in *Variety*. At this stage in his career, Leonard has become the unofficial ambassador of stunts, the one the news crews call when they want a few words from a stunt legend with the scars to prove it. He does not disappoint. At six-one, two hundred and ten or so, with a square jaw and a saddle-sore hitch in his stride from his three hip replacements, he looks the part. He's rakishly handsome with a full head of white hair, a ranch-hand squint, and a craggy face that could stop a haymaker or two. Even better, he talks the way a stuntman is supposed to talk. "I've never been scared of anything," he said, as we sat together in a production office across from Paramount Studios. "But my two biggest enemies have been gravity and blondes."

Leonard doesn't dwell on his injuries, but it is impossible to talk about the turning points in his life without mentioning them. In 1964, at the Olympic trials for the decathlon, he twisted an ankle he'd broken playing football at the University of Arizona; that injury knocked him out of the trials and kept him out of the L.A. Rams rookie camp. Two years later, a bulging disk brought his career in the Canadian Football League to an end. As he was thinking of things he could do next, he remembered a few days he'd spent working on a movie set in college, watching Chuck Roberson, a Texas cowboy turned stuntman, doubling John Wayne. "I saw what jumping off buildings was all about and I said, 'Man, I can probably do that.' But it didn't enter my mind until I bagged up in Canada playing football." He called Roberson, who told him to come down to L.A. and give it a try. Roberson taught him the Western business out in his backyard, all the things that only stuntmen can do with a horse: saddle falls, and back rolls, and running Ws. (The running W is a type of horse fall in which a trip wire sends the horse tumbling forward when it reaches the end of the wire. It has been illegal since 1940, but up through the late seventies, when the American Humane Association managed to close the loophole, it was still a common practice to shoot scripts that required a certain brand of spectacular fall in places like Mexico or Spain, where more genteel notions of animal rights did not apply. Leonard owns a ranch in Agua Dulce that he has named the Running W, "because that's how I paid for it. Going end over end.")

Leonard grew up in West Allis, Wisconsin, stacking hay bales, jumping fifty feet into a rock quarry pool, driving a ton-and-a-half International truck with a load of grain on it at the age of eleven. He thought it was a hell of a background to be a stuntman. "I'd been an athlete. I'd farmed. I'd been around livestock. I had a work ethic that was second to none." At Roberson's, instead of hauling in a truckload of sand to soften the ground for horse falls, he liked to go out with a pick and shovel and dig the spots so the horses wouldn't get hurt. "It was nothing I take credit for," he said. "It was just the way I grew up, the way my parents raised me."

I tracked him down one evening when he was roping at the ranch of his friend and fellow stuntman Walter Scott. The two both started out back when, as Scott put it, "the backbone of this industry was cowboys." That night, while they waited by the gates for their turn, letting their horses do a little footwork, they talked about why cowboys made such good stuntmen. It had less to do with their famous ability to hit the ground, and more with country intangibles. "They're raised different than city boys," Leonard said. "They have more try, more heart."

"They take things in stride more," Scott added.

Scott was breaking in a pair of colts he'd just bought in New Mexico, so he wanted to stretch their session. Leonard had just finished a shoot, so he felt a little rusty and he, too, was happy to keep going under lights. "There are thirty-five hundred stuntmen in Hollywood, six thousand nationwide," he said. "And maybe twenty-five guys that can do this." Then he and his roping partner took off after another calf.

They settled into the rodeo pace—long sideline stretches of insult and reminiscence interrupted by bursts of action. This is also the natural rhythm of the stuntman, and nobody's better at this part of it than Leonard. His colleagues respect him for his stunt work, but the universal reverence he is accorded derives as much from his off-camera persona—his rollicking accounts of personal misadventure and late-night cowboy charisma. Still, he's not entirely happy about stuntmen stepping into the spotlight, although he admitted, "I'm probably as much to blame for that as anybody." He has an old-school preference for anonymity, and even though he freely divulged the how-tos on his biggest stunts, he still thinks that part of a stuntman's job is maintaining a sense of mystery. "It's becoming a visual effects business now, and the magic is lost. I meet people and not only have they seen the stunts, they've seen the DVD on how the stunt was done." One DVD extra revealed a key preparatory measure for his *Raiders of the Lost Ark* gag: before they filmed him sliding under the truck, they'd dug a trench that would both guide the driver and help channel Leonard between the wheels with a few more inches of clearance. People have even come up to him and said they knew now how he did it. Leonard curled his lip scornfully as he sat in the saddle. "Yeah," he said, "that's what made it *easy*."

In some ways, he'd rather talk rodeo. He has a team-roping arena at the Running W and his own roping steers. "Oh, man, you come over to rope at my house and it's the best ground you ever seen in your life. I work that like a Beverly Hills lawn. It's wet and there's no dust in it. It's been tractored and I use a drag going through there, and it just looks gorgeous. There's nothing prettier." He smiled. "One of the most beautiful things in the world is well-worked farmland. I love to work out at the arena and do it the way that I want to do it, and then I look at it, and I say, 'Man, cool.' If you've got to have those horses, you don't want them running on hard ground. I like a lot of air in the ground."

His obsession with the softness of the ground is understandable: he's hit it often enough. As a young man, he earned a reputation as a high-fall guy in the days before the air bag. He'd build his own catchers out of empty boxes, stacked in layers and roped together, then he'd plummet through the air about as far as anyone ever dared. Falling on boxes may seem like a primitive way to cushion a landing, but it was and still is standard procedure for falls under thirty feet or so. Stuntmen usually have to assemble the things themselves, on location, before every take, which should ensure that the catchers are soundly assembled. "I hit the street once in Pasadena," he said. "I was doing a high fall in a movie called *Black Samson*," a 1974 blaxploitation flick. "I got a little cavalier about my abilities and I didn't build my catcher right. My ego got in the way, and I went through it and hit the street" after about a sixty-foot fall. "It knocked me out. When I woke up I was in the worst pain in my life. I couldn't see and my legs were paralyzed. I guess the catcher was just good enough to keep me from getting killed."

A year later, shooting in Spain on *The Wind and the Lion*, he was slated to ride a horse through a third-story window—Sean Connery and his Berber henchman were abducting Candice Bergen. Leonard nailed the gag the first time, but the cameraman missed the shot, so he had to do it again. On the second take, the horse turned over in the air and landed on him. "You see me and the horse crashing through the window and starting down," Leonard said. "But what the audience doesn't see is that we're another ten or twelve feet in the air with this horse and down he comes. Knocked me out cold, and when I come to, I was flopping like a chicken on the ground. They sent me up to the American Hospital in Madrid. And they X-rayed me and said, 'You're fine.'" He went back and finished the film, somersaulting horses in huge battle scenes, breaking his nose when another horse landed on him and fracturing his collarbone when he slammed into a flag standard just before the movie wrapped. A year later, some doctors giving him an MRI asked, "When did you break your back?"

"I didn't break my back."

"Yes, you broke your back. You've got a cracked sixth thoracic vertebra."

"That was that goddam window I jumped out."

Apart from the concussions and broken back, he'd torn up his knee repeatedly, wrecking a train on *Rio Lobo*, and jumping off another one on *The Legend of the Lone Ranger*. He used to see a doctor in Arizona who'd always clear him to go back to work—production companies didn't want to be responsible if they knew you were injured. "I'd go see Doc Chester and he'd stick a big old needle in my knee and pull that junk out and I'd go back to work. Under normal circumstances, you'd let yourself heal. But when you're healing, you're not making money. Stunt business, just like rodeo cowboys, you get hurt, you're out of business." After Chester fixed him, he came right back to *The Legend of the Lone Ranger* to do the stagecoach gag. On that one, he held on just a split second too long and both coach wheels ran right over the knee he'd torn on *Rio Lobo*, tearing it again. As Leonard said, "Most people like to think they treat their bodies like a temple, whether they do or not. I treated mine like a South Tucson beer bar."

But for all his decades' worth of injuries, Leonard can still sound as if he'd just arrived, straight out of Canadian football and into a Hollywood version of the Summer of Love. He talks about flying over to Spain in 1968, wedged in an airplane between Raquel Welch and Burt Reynolds, eating chateaubriand and drinking champagne, on his way to double Jim Brown in *100 Rifles*. "He doesn't like it, but there weren't any black cowboys and I was the only guy big enough back then," Leonard said. "So now you work about an hour out of Almería, come home at dark, go to the bar. The Grand Hotel is just a crossroads for the continent. The bar was jam-packed every single night. You come in there dressed as an American cowboy working off a movie and I'm telling you what: you never went to bed. God."

I asked him if that didn't bother him, losing all that sleep and then facing a full day of fistfighting.

"Never," he said. "Man, thank God for youth, huh? Stupidity or youth."

From time to time, though, it was the specter of a stunt that kept him up. He had one high fall in Jamaica, for the 1970 Burt Reynolds movie *Skullduggery*, that had him looking at the ceiling all night, second-guessing himself. "They had us camped out in a pretty fancy place called the Mahoe Bay Club. And they didn't give us a per diem. You just signed for everything, because everything you needed was at the hotel.

"So I didn't have a per diem, and I'd go out and meet an airline stewardess and bring her back for dinner and I'd be signing. And all of a sudden I got more money signed on my ticket for the hotel than I'm going to make doing this high fall. And I get out there and look at it, and I turn to Buzz Henry, the guy that brought me down to do it, and I said, 'Buzz, man, this is a lot higher than what you told me.'" Leonard had to jump about eighty feet down a canyon to a ledge. He'd done the pre-drop—pushing a rock off the cliff to show him where he'd land. So he knew, rationally, that he'd get to the bottom safely. "But my mind is telling me that ain't right—my mind is telling me that I'm going to go where this rock doesn't." To make matters worse, he'd had an extra day to stew over it. "We were ready to do the deal, and the camera was pointing into the sun. They said, 'Now we can't do it today. We've got to do it tomorrow.' So I get the benefit of laying awake all night trying to conquer my mind.

"I got to get hit with this arrow, and sell the shot, and come off the cliff. As long as I don't over-amp and push too hard, I'm going to be cool. But I can't rationalize at this juncture when it's midnight and I'm thinking, 'Oh, what did I get into?' And I can't quit. I can't say, 'Guys, I'm not doing it.' They've got the whole company out there, trucks and everything. It's called the cockpit area of Jamaica, and we're out there three hours from the Mahoe Bay Club, and I'm thinking, 'Jesus, I'm going to have to pay this tab for all these gals I've been squiring around. Now I've got to go off this cliff, because I can't afford not to make the money.' Finally, at about four in the morning, I'm out there sitting on the beach, looking at the Caribbean, and I got my mind back, and it was so relieving. It was like having a broken arm and somebody gives you a shot of morphine or Demerol and all of a sudden this agony that you're going through, you relieve it, it anesthetizes you."

I asked him how it turned out.

"Hell, I hit the boxes and off I went. I took a vacation at the Playboy Club."

This figure, the twenty-four-hour Leonard, is the one who has inspired generations of stuntmen, but the truth is that even at twenty-seven, when he was staying up all night, Leonard was planning his move behind the camera. The slipped disk that forced him to abandon football and his athletic career had devastated him. And he knew that it could easily happen again and he'd wash out of the picture business. "I said, 'This could hurt you. And it could hurt you bad.' Getting hurt in football is one thing, but getting hit by a car, and having both your legs wrapped around your head, busted, and you need new hips, you need a new back—you can get seriously hurt doing this stuff. So how do you duck the bullet? You'd better learn what direction is all about. I'd go to dailies and see something on film that didn't look as good up there as it did to the eye. I wanted to know why. I wanted to see what was going on behind that camera. That camera, to me, was magic."

As a second-unit director, he's now in charge of running everything, scouting locations, devising the action, arranging the cameras, vetting the effects. The stunt coordinators do most of the hands-on work with the stuntmen, setting up the action. Freddie Hice, who called Leonard Ol' Hollywood, worked with him on the Colin Farrell Western *American Outlaws*, in 2000. "I was the stunt coordinator, and he was the second-unit director," Hice said. "So I'd set up the stunts. I go, 'Now, Terry, this is how we're going to do it.' And he'd go, 'Okay, but back when I was on *The Wind and the Lion*, we did it like this.' Then he'd stop a second and go, 'Nope—that knocked me out. So it probably wouldn't work very well. You guys do it the way you want.' And all of us fall on the ground laughing. We'd go, 'Terry, sit in your chair, would you?' Every one of his stories ended with, 'Oh, that didn't work out too well. I got knocked out.' Or 'I went to the hospital.'"

Leonard laughed when I told him about that characterization. "I didn't really plan on staying in this business," he said. "It was like, 'Let's go to Tijuana and get drunk.' But if it ended today, I wouldn't have regret one."

A lot of guys who were never "hard-core, bag-carrying, fly-all-over-the-world, do-the-big-number kind of stunt guys" parlayed their familiarity with gag work into management positions and second-unit directing. But almost none of them have the rare combination of stuntman savoir-faire and managerial say-so that have made Leonard a hero to newcomer and veteran alike. "It's like the guy that inherits a lot of money from a death in the family, goes out, and buys a yacht." he says. "And then he buys a white captain's hat, blue blazer, and the white pants, the white deck shoes, the whole thing. And his grandmother says, 'To yourself, you're a captain. To me, you're a captain. But to another captain, are you a captain?' "

CHAPTER 5

The Craziest Stuntman in the World

The first time Mike Kirton died on a film set, it was on the movie *Striker* and he was twenty-eight years old. He sustained two concussions in the space of a single sixteen-foot fall: one when a pipe knocked him out on the way down, and the other when his unconscious body landed on the concrete below. That's when his heart stopped. But Kirton didn't let this discourage him. He was a tough guy, and he'd live to die another day. A few years later, on the Italian TV miniseries *Extralarge*, he jumped a van over a bridge at sixty-five miles an hour and landed nose down on the pavement, crushing the truck and breaking his skull, collarbone, shoulder, ribs, and ankle, in a series of traumas so massive that he drowned in his own blood. That was the second time. "The funniest thing about it," he said the day I met him, "I was so fucked up with the concussions that it doesn't scare me, because I don't remember. I roll cars all the time now. I'm doing one tomorrow."

Kirton was sitting behind a shot of Goldschläger and a screwdriver, in flip-flops, green shorts, and a Hawaiian shirt, a bit of South Beach transported to the Angry Dog, a Dallas dive with a lengthy menu of draft beers and a couple "best hot dog" awards from the local paper. He's compact and more than a shade on the heavy side now, but even at forty-eight he's still full of a teenager's nervous movements. He jiggles, he drums, he flicks back his sandy hair with a snap of his neck, and when he talks, he likes to stand close to you or lean forward and block your exits. He talks fast, and his voice is loud and permanently hoarse, and when he gets to the scariest parts of his stories—the big crash, the fistfight in Rome, the narrowly averted fall from the cargo door of a helicopter—he often rasps out the word "fuck" in a half-whisper that's meant to represent yelling at the top of his lungs: *faaawwck!* It's a motto of sorts, of terror and delight; a redneck "Geronimo!"; a call, across the years, from the original Narcoossee, Florida, farm boy who still cannot believe his luck.

He was nineteen when a talent scout for an Italian movie crew discovered him performing at a racetrack, jumping cars into school buses (not over them, *into* them: up off the ramp, then— slam!—straight down into their passenger compartment). His father, a dairy farmer who thought the whole "Italian movie" proposition sounded a little shaky, advised him to get his cash up front, so Kirton and the producer made an arrangement. He showed up, did one car jump over a thirty-five-foot river—in a convertible and without a helmet—then, when it was discovered that the film had broken on the first take, shrugged and did another one. He walked out with more than seven thousand dollars in cash for a day's work. On the way home, he stopped in a Chevy dealership and bought a brand-new 1979 pickup with four-wheel drive. *Faaawwck.*

A few weeks later, the Italians showed up at his door with a first-class ticket to Rome, and the next day he was sitting on the top floor of a 747 in his cowboy hat. The Narcoossee farm boy, it turned out, had a gift for languages—during my stay with him I heard him sprinkle his stories with rough, confident bits of German, Italian, Spanish, and Bulgarian, and he claimed to speak four more—and he quickly found his niche as an export American badass anchoring stunt teams on European action films, doubling actors like Franco Nero, Rutger Hauer, and Bud Spencer. He worked most often with the director Enzo Castellari—in fact, he was working for Castellari both times he died. Castellari, at the height of his career, had specialized in crime films, spaghetti Westerns, and war epics (including one, *Inglorious Bastards*, that inspired Quentin Tarantino to write a movie of the same name). But by the time Kirton came along, Castellari had been reduced to directing *Rambo* knockoffs and TV miniseries, low-budget stuff even by Italian standards. Kirton, who was ready for anything, was a perfect fit.

I learned about Kirton because I often asked folks on set to name the craziest stuntman they'd ever worked with. The story of Kirton and his van jump stood out—not just because he'd died doing it, but also because he'd purportedly stolen the stunt vehicle the night before. When I asked him if that was true, he laughed. "We did *buy* the van," he said, "just from a questionable source. Let's say it came without a title and the guy didn't need a receipt. That was Italian filmmaking in the old days." He worked all night on it, adding a roll cage and stripping the extra weight and putting sandbags in the rear end to make the thing more flightworthy—in other words, trying to make sure it wouldn't do exactly what it wound up doing. "The gag was a pipe ramp," he said, a maneuver in which the stuntman drives off a tilted ramp that sends the car spiraling through the air. "And I probably hit it about twenty-five miles too fast. It was supposed to be forty, and I was doing sixty, sixty-five. So instead of rolling and doing a spiral, the van came down on the driver's corner first. It just went up and over, hit the driver's side, and augered in." His friend has a video of the whole thing that includes the aftermath with the medics trying to revive him. "I was so crushed inside the car, the guy can't shock me like this," he said, pushing an imaginary pair of electrode pads at me. "They had to scratch the pad and reach underneath my arms and rip my shirt and shock me like this." He came to hug me from behind. "They kept shocking me and shocking me. For like six months afterward, I had two huge burns here and here," he said, pointing to his chest and side.

According to Kirton, he and Castellari were at each other's throats all the time, back and forth, "Italian style." In the director's defense, Kirton did seem to require a jolt of anger to spur his best work; many of his stories kicked off with the recollection of a vague slight that somehow incited him to perform a stunt twenty, thirty, forty miles an hour faster than originally requested. He didn't even have to be working, really, and something could set him off, like the time he spotted Castellari's 1957 Mercedes convertible parked across two handicapped parking spots. He and some friends, an actor and a couple of stuntmen, were leaving a Hooters outside Miami when they noticed the transgression. "We're in the car, they go, 'Look at that motherfucker.' I go, 'That's Enzo's car! Put on your fuckin' belts, dads.' I back up this rent-a-car, in a parking lot, about sixty yards." He drove straight into the sports car with his rear end, demolition-derby style, and "beer-canned" it, hitting it so hard that the director's vintage Mercedes jumped the curb and slammed into a nearby concrete barrier, effectively crashing the car from both front and near. The director literally never knew what hit him—until Kirton told the story a few years later on an Italian talk show.

When Kirton got up to go to the bathroom in the Angry Dog, I was left alone at the table with Jane, a friend of his, an ex-stripper who'd joined us a couple of rounds earlier. Even with the bar noise (the Spurs were winning a playoff game on the TV), there was an awkward silence in his absence. Jane was slim in a haunted, night-owlish way, but she had no trace of showgirl exhibitionism. She'd stopped dancing a while ago—her peak years corresponded with Kirton's—and her shapeless summer top and khaki shorts fit her current profile: single mom studying for a real-estate license. I asked her how she knew Mike, and she said from L.A., back when she was a Clippers cheerleader. Also, she'd dated a stuntman—a guy from the cowboy era, a John Wayne double, her senior by at least twenty-five years.

"So what made you want to write about stuntmen?" she asked. I told her what I liked about them—all their pranks and derring-do, the intricate trade secrets, and the long bullshit sessions as everybody waited for the cameras to roll. But that line of argument was getting nowhere with her, so I cut it short: basically, I said, I like to write about passionate people who tell great stories. "Like Mike."

"He loves to talk about himself," she said. It was obvious that she'd stopped being impressed a long time ago, maybe not by men in general—an occupational hazard for a stripper—but certainly by stuntmen.

"Which is why they're so good to write about."

"Yeah," she said. She picked at her plate of chicken-fried steak with gravy and fries. "They are a little bit narcissistic."

I'd thought finding crazy stuntmen would be easy, but most guys I approached about it could offer me no help. They'd mention somebody funny, or they'd talk about a standout, unbelievably daring stunt they'd seen someone do, but that wasn't what I was asking for. Finally one stunt coordinator set me straight. "There's too much pressure, too much money riding on every shot," he told me. "I've got to have guys I can count on every day. You can't hire a crazy man. You can't even hire your buddies anymore and expect to hide them in a car. Those days are over. There's too much at stake." Plus, as the coordinator explained, the stuntman stereotype that rules in the popular imagination is a big liability at the bargaining table. "It makes it harder to get a good rate when the producers think you're just some daredevil idiot."

Kirton knows that he's a throwback to an earlier time. He talked disdainfully about new-school guys with their BlackBerries and extolled the virtues of "everything guys" like himself, who never cheated on a gag, who would always tough it out—a phrase that often occurred in his conversation. To him, toughing it out was an all-embracing concept. Part of it had to do with partying hard: how he'd downed a pitcher of Kamikazes in a bar in Haifa, outdrinking a marine and ex-USC football player in front of Terry Leonard and Lou Gossett Jr. Part of it had to do with a willingness to try anything: he fought a tiger and a grizzly on film, and he never let lack of experience get in the way of a job. To snag one underwater scene, he told the stunt coordinator Ronnie Rondell that he knew how to dive. He just hung back when it came time to suit up, watching how everybody checked their gauges and hoses.

The approach worked, he said, until he got down twenty feet and his nose started bleeding. "I didn't know to clear my ears. I didn't have the guts to tell Ronnie that for ten years."

But it was toughing it out that got him into the big leagues. After a few Florida jobs and Italian shoots, he moved to L.A. He was down to his last ninety dollars, when he landed a job doing utility stunts—mostly as a background body in fight scenes, mass immolations, and the like—on a hokey sword-and-sorcery flick called *The Beastmaster*. (The film, which premiered three months after *Conan the Barbarian* and performed poorly, went on to become a cult classic on early cable: Dennis Miller used to say that HBO didn't stand for Home Box Office, it stood for "Hey, *Beastmaster*'s on!") The credits on *Beastmaster* list a whopping thirty-four stuntmen (and at least fifteen others who, like Kirton, got acting roles as heavies) and the set was filled with legends in the business—Ronnie Rondell, Buddy Van Horn, Jeannie and Gary Epper, Frank Orsatti, Chuck Picerni Jr. Kirton desperately wanted to show them he belonged. So he volunteered to do a gag that nobody else wanted: a forty-foot fall down the stairs of a Mayan temple wearing only a leather thong.

The set for the Mayan temple was built on a foothill in Pyramid Lake, just north of the Magic Mountain amusement park; an eighty-foot wooden structure covered completely with a hard shell of cast resin-and-fiberglass molds, a stand-in for the limestone blocks of the Mayan originals. The structure was lightweight but sturdy and realistic-looking on camera, and the telltale hollow sounds of the actors moving around on it—or falling down it—could be eliminated in postproduction. On the morning of the stair fall, Kirton checked the schedule and saw that the gag still had no one's name attached to it, so he walked up to the stunt coordinator and volunteered. Kirton insists that the gag had been turned down by all the veteran stunt guys—not just the ones on the set, but "everyone in town." But it's much more likely that the stunt coordinator had sounded out a few of them, and they'd all politely passed, so the casting of the gag was purposely left open on the production schedule as an invitation. It was a common practice with a rough but uncomplicated piece of work: the older guys sat on their hands, knowing that some eager young gun would volunteer. And if the kid didn't work out, if he balked or held back or mangled himself, well, hey, it's a tough job and the kid did have his chance.

According to Kirton, the stuntmen all laughed at him when he asked to do the fall, and the coordinator said, "You're a kid. You'll kill yourself." Kirton walked straight to the hair and makeup wagon to have his head shaved (the character was bald) and came back, pointed at his shiny head—a drastic step in the days before Michael Jordan—and repeated his desire to take the hit: "This is how serious I am. I'll fuckin' do this." I heard a few versions of the story during my three-day stay with Kirton (and in the months before and after), and in my favorite the coordinator okays the gag, but first pulls him aside to point out the assembled legends. "Just remember," the coordinator said, "that's Buddy Van Horn, who doubles Clint Eastwood. That's Glenn Wilder and Ronnie Rondell, who started Stunts Unlimited. All these guys you see here? If you mess this up or chicken out, get a new career. Just walk off the mountain and keep going all the way back to the little country shithole you came from."

The character who falls is a "Jun priest"—and a henchman of the bad guy sorcerer. Apparently Jun priests walk around virtually naked, which means that to do the stair fall safely a stuntman really should wear a flesh-colored wetsuit stuffed with padding. But Kirton wanted to tough it out, to do the gag dressed only in a leather loincloth, a bold but rather foolhardy decision that allowed the camera to shoot much closer as he toppled headfirst, flinging himself end over end, then tucking his shoulder and taking the rest of the tumble helter-skelter down the stairs. He broke two fingers and smashed himself black and blue in many places, but he still popped back up and said, "You guys want to see that again?" That night, the producers called after seeing the dailies to say the fall was fantastic and if he could keep his head shaved he could stay on for the whole show.

Huge stair falls like Kirton's have gone out of fashion, probably because they were used in so many eighties TV shows and still carry a whiff of that era's socko-cheesiness. Most moviegoers can now spot the ways that stuntmen protect themselves, by slamming into walls or tossing themselves dramatically from side to side on their way down a staircase. The top pros are critical of such cheats. In their eyes, the only way to pull off a stair fall is simply to fall down the stairs, to will your body to absorb the punishment. Kirton gets high marks in this regard. When I asked Ronnie Rondell about him, he said, "He was good, I gotta tell you. He was a tough guy. He could take abuse."

That sort of assessment (from a Rondell!) is the stunt world equivalent of a Morningstar five-star rating, so it's a wonder that Kirton's résumé is as spotty as it seems. Part of this has to do with location. Kirton now lives a few miles from West Palm Beach, and, to some degree, the pattern of his career—an appearance in a major action showcase like *Bad Boys* or *Miami Vice* followed by a mix of B movies and straight-to-video releases—mirrors the health of the film industry in South Florida. But it also reflects his tendency to run hot for a while, then drop everything to follow a whim—like when he parlayed a stunt job in Buenos Aires into a long-running gig as a villain on an Argentine telenovela, wearing beads and bleach-blond hair extensions to play *El Rubio Malo*, the Evil Blond. Being crazy allowed him to live with his own brand of no-bullshit purity, as a hard-drinking, high-impact version of the Lonely Planet wanderer: he'd do a high-profile gag to preserve his rep, then travel, pick up a low-budget location job—in East Germany, say, before the fall of the Berlin Wall, or in Prague, years before it became Hollywood on the Vltava—then he'd travel some more. At times these journeys might involve a chick. And every so often he'd feel the need to reaffirm his personal Declaration of Independence by pissing off someone important, just because he could.

He got called into *Bad Boys* because the stunt coordinator couldn't find or didn't trust anybody else to do a big gag early in the film: the villains hijack a police van with the help of a crooked cop, and then, on their way to committing an audacious heist (stealing a huge stash of cocaine right out of police custody), they shoot the crooked cop and let him fall straight out of the van's back door and onto the pavement. Kirton was scheduled both to play the cop and to do the gag—stuntmen often get such bit parts, a piece of double duty that allows the cameras to shoot the stunt much closer and edit without the quick cuts that mask the presence of a stunt double. When Kirton showed up on the set, the director, Michael Bay, seemed to have already run out of patience. He immediately started screaming at him, "Can you do this stunt?"

"Mr. Bay, I can do this," Kirton assured him.

"You *sure*?"

"Mr. Bay. I. Can. Do. This."

And he did: he rolled out of a paddy wagon going more than thirty miles an hour, while the cameras, following at a safe distance, captured it all. After the take, Bay asked him to do it again, only this time he wanted Kirton to roll off the camera car, so he could shoot it from the bad guys' point of view—or, more precisely, from the point of view of their tires, by placing a camera nearly at pavement-level, a low angle that would amp up the violence and demonstrate, in great detail, what it feels like to bounce out of a van and roll down the street. While the crew did the prep work, Bay and Kirton wound up waiting side by side and the director started muttering something about "Florida fucking stuntmen."

"You know what, Mr. Bay?" Kirton said. "I've done, whatever, five billion movies, and I've got this badass reputation. But I'm from here originally, and I don't appreciate that."

"Just fall off the fucking truck and show me what you're made of," Bay said. And the two men stopped talking until the start of the action. But Kirton kept stewing and by the time Bay gave the order to roll film when the camera car hit twenty-five miles an hour, Kirton had worked himself up enough to contradict the director, shouting "Don't roll yet" to the cameramen. To show Bay *what he was made of,* he instructed the driver to go faster—thirty, thirty-five. At thirty-eight miles an hour it finally looked fast enough for him and he let everyone know he was ready to shoot. So Bay wouldn't miss his point, just before dropping off to roll on the street for the second time, Kirton yelled, "Hey, Bay! Fuck you!"

Kirton tore his pants apart and knocked himself unconscious as he rolled over the streets, and the gag looked great. But that didn't matter: the first sound that greeted him when he came to was Bay heaping abuse on the high-speed cameraman because the film broke. Kirton, with his nose still bleeding, put his temper aside and walked over and told them both not to worry, he'd be happy to do it again. It's the sort of decent gesture that happens in jobs everywhere—one working stiff saves another from an angry boss. At most jobs, though, the gesture wouldn't require falling off a moving vehicle onto a Miami street.

A few months after this run-in, Kirton was back in L.A., walking down the Third Street promenade in Santa Monica with a couple of stunt buddies, when they all decided to duck into a club called the Renaissance. As they got their drinks and scanned the crowd, Kirton spotted a tall guy—"Michael Fucking Bay!"—talking to a "chick with a weird look on her face." It was a look that Kirton recognized immediately from his time abroad. Kirton said, "That girl can't speak a word of English. Watch this." His friends, who knew the history between the two of them, urged him not to do anything stupid, like knock out one of the most powerful action directors in Hollywood. Instead, he walked over and said, "Michael Bay! You don't remember me? I worked on *Bad Boys!*" Then he turned to the blonde. "*Sprechen Sie Deutsch? Hat er sich vorgestellt? Der Produktionsleiter und Filmregisseur der* Bad Boys?"

The girl complimented him on his German and started to explain what she was doing in the States when Bay interrupted. "Dude, you know me?" he said. "Well, maybe you can help me out then. Can you talk to her?"

Kirton said "Sure," and turned to the girl, and they chatted in German about things she should do in L.A. When Bay, on the sidelines of this conversation, started nudging him, Kirton told her that Michael wanted her to go get a little boy so they could have a threesome. She recoiled at the proposition.

"Dude, what did you tell her?" Bay asked. "What does *Kinder* mean?"

"Oh," Kirton said, laughing amiably, "I told her you're just a big kid!"

This story, and the schadenfreude for the director, spread quickly through movie circles. Once, Kirton got a call from a friend on the set of *The Rock*: Sean Connery hated Bay and wanted to hear it firsthand. By the time Kirton recounted it to me, he even had a moral at the end. "Dude, I fucked him so bad because I hate that guy," he said. "But you know, so many people are *scared* that they'll get fired off a show. They're *scared* just to be really crazy. You know what I mean? But I always go from show to show. Because I don't care. You know what I mean? No one gets hurt. I never hurt anybody. But I don't fuckin' care."

It was more than wanderlust that kept Kirton coming back to low-budget films. He was hooked on the atmosphere, the slightly disreputable style of doing business, the way the money flowed both on and off the books. A few years ago, he'd written and directed a film whose inflated budget was actually a clever dodge that allowed the producer to acquire and write off a $1.6-million condo in Puerto Rico. And the movie still turned a profit. After all those years slugging it out with Castellari, Kirton knew how to work fast, cheap, and dirty. He knew action, and he could fill a script with his own smartass brand of tough talk and turn out B movies and straight-to-video releases that appealed to a certain audience. "My crowd? Ninety-seven percent of them shop at Wal-Mart." He claimed to be making more money now in low-budget films than he ever had, he said, by cutting deals, getting producers to pay him by slipping him cash in the pages of a script. He gave the impression that he took all this money home, unlike his friends back in Hollywood, who had to pay state and federal taxes, the agent, the manager, the ex. Here he was doing a few weeks on a little shit movie down in Texas, for instance, and on top of whatever he was getting paid he had a deal where he got to keep the bad guy's Freightliner truck. This he could pass along to his brother's construction company, in which he was a principal investor. Where it would make him even more money.

On the morning after our trip to the Angry Dog, we got up early and headed to the shoot. He was in charge of the stunt crew for *Walking Tall: The Payback*, one of those B-movie sequels that doesn't have the star from the original or even the character he played, just the rights to use the title and the premise: man returns to his hometown and single-handedly cleans out its criminal element. As we drove off together in an old red Dodge pickup (the hero car of the movie), out to the day's location, on a Waxahachie country road, he outlined the principal elements of his unorthodox financial life.

He was basically set, financially, because of the cash he got from his brother's construction company. The idea for the company came to him when his very young wife—a Bulgarian woman, the mother of his six-year-old son—revealed that she was sleeping with her boss. Here's how he handled the news: He took all his money and gave it to his brother to start a construction business. Then he signed all the residuals from his fifty-something movies and TV shows over to his son Toshi, in an irrevocable trust, so she couldn't get a dime. Since his wife was "in love" with her new guy, she signed over her interest in marital property to Kirton. At this point the new guy still hadn't told his wife, so Kirton saved him the trouble. The ensuing divorce changed the lovebirds' financial picture so much that they decided to go after whatever Kirton had, which by then, on paper, was almost nothing. He was perfectly set up to wait them out. For two years, while the divorce proceedings dragged on, he stayed home, taking care of his son, writing children's books and screenplays, and filing modest tax returns.

He went to all this trouble for the sake of his son, to whom he seemed sincerely devoted. Often, when I made follow-up calls in the middle of a working day, I caught the two of them off somewhere fishing or swimming or walking through an amusement park. "Say hi, Toshi," he'd tell the boy. "You know, he's not really a kid. He's a midget Indian I saved from a traveling circus." He seemed to have no trouble adjusting to his new role in life as a stay-at-home dad. If anything he seemed grateful. "As much effort as it is being a dad," he said, "it's not as hard as being me when I was single."

Still, I couldn't have been more surprised when Kirton explained how he'd won his custody battle. The thing that cinched it for the judge, he said, was his job with the CIA.

"What?"

"Yeah. I've been to Iraq and Afghanistan."

"You mean now? No way. For what?"

"Training videos. And I shoot prisoner interrogations."

Kirton did not require much prodding to keep his stories going, so I tried to sound casual. "Oh yeah?" I said. The red light on my tape recorder was on—I moved it across the seat to make sure I got everything, over the sound of the old Dodge hemi—and my reporter's notebook was open. Kirton didn't seem to mind.

"Yeah," he said. "I do work for the CIA, FBI, Department of Homeland Security, Interpol." I was amused and extremely skeptical of the story at first, but he ended up talking about his double life in such detail that I started to believe him. Mostly, he said, he and his military counterpart, who was also a single dad, wrote training videos together over the phone, starting in the morning after the kids had left for school, breaking around two when they came back home, then picking up again after eight, once both their kids had settled down for the night. Sometimes he flew to a military base somewhere in the world to help with filming. Apart from his ex-wife, no one in his family had known about this stuff. He used to tell people that he was off on location. To back up his claims in court, his military counterpart, an ex–Navy SEAL, appeared at the hearings to substantiate everything under oath.

I hadn't asked about his divorce, but he kept coming back to the topic. He told me how he took advantage of his spook connections. He had his ex's phone tapped. ("You can't use it in court, but you know what's going on!") And on one occasion, after his ex's live-in boyfriend had yelled at Toshi, he uncovered a software program that could turn his caller ID into any number he wanted: Kirton decided to call the boyfriend using the home phone number of the guy's mother. "Hey, man," Kirton told him when he picked up. "Your mom's got a nice house!"

There are plenty of parents who show few scruples when it comes to a custody battle, but Kirton attacked the project with unusual gusto. When Toshi looked out the playroom window and spotted one of his mom's new friends snooping around Kirton's house, snapping pictures, Kirton called the new boyfriend, this time to say, "You send somebody to scare my son like that again you'll wish you hadn't. You're in your house, right? Now go look at the front pocket of your jacket. The jean jacket. On the chair." The guy pulled out his cell phone and it had a smiley sticker on it—even though the house he owned had an elaborate security system. Kirton whispered, "That's how close I can get."

"How *did* you get it there?" I asked.

He kept right on talking as if I hadn't said a thing—his one moment of tact in three days of conversation. "Then it stopped. All I told them was 'Just leave me alone. Come visit your kid on visitation days. You have your merry life and I'll have mine.'"

When we pulled into base camp, the crew was already setting up for the big gag of the day—the rollover that leads to the death, in Act One, of the hero's dad. Tom Harper, a Texas native and veteran stuntman, was overseeing work on the police car that Kirton would drive in the scene, installing a steel spring arm that he'd just invented, the centerpiece of his "exclusive cannonless rollover" system. Like many stuntmen, Harper considered the traditional rollover setup dangerous: mechanics cut a hole in the car floor and installed a homemade cannon, basically a steel cylinder filled with explosives and loaded with a log or sawed-off telephone pole. The cannon was aimed precisely straight down, and to roll the car the stuntman pressed a button that set it off. The combination of forces from the cannon explosion and the impact of the log on the pavement below sent the car somersaulting down the street. The gag took its name, the cannon roll, from the equipment, which often proved riskier than the stunt itself; Ronnie Rondell remembered one time when the log shot out and ricocheted straight up into the air, bringing down a helicopter hovering overhead, and on a lot of movie rollovers you'll see what looks like a big hunk of firewood skittering away down the blacktop. Even worse was the noise: most stuntmen, who had to be strapped into a driver's seat just inches away from the cannon blast, didn't worry about the car wreck or the telephone pole moving faster than a speeding bullet. They worried about winding up deaf.

Harper's innovation, which was making its feature-film debut that day, eliminated such dangers. The five-foot steel spring arm was hidden from sight, attached to the cop car's undercarriage by a hinge on the passenger side. When Kirton pressed a button, the arm would slam into the ground with two thousand pounds of pressure per square inch and flip the car instantly, but the only noise he'd hear would be the quiet hiss from the release of pneumatic pressure (and soon thereafter the crunch of the car's roof and its sirens hitting the pavement). Harper could adjust the pressure according to the circumstances, adding more if the filmmakers wanted to see a barrel roll like something from the highlight films at the Daytona 500, or less if they wanted the stunt vehicle to flip only once or twice.

While Harper and a few mechanics sweated to get the car ready, hoping to avoid shooting in the worst of the Texas heat, Kirton jumped into a brown Ford LTD and headed out to survey the road where he'd roll the car. "I don't need that violent a turnover," he said as he took me down a two-lane stretch between cornfields and windbreaks and chigger farms. "That's part of the secret of a stunt: to be realistic, for the story. So I'm Charlie, driving," he demonstrated, pacing through the beats of the sequence out loud, mostly for his own sake. "There's a big semi coming this way, I get scared, start going fast . . . I slide around here, and the semi tucks in behind me, because the bad guys are orchestrating this . . . The semi's bumping me in the back." He interrupted himself to make a shockingly loud air-horn noise. "That guy's banging my fenders, I'm doing this, that." It would be hours before the production shut the road to traffic, but the road was naturally deserted, so Kirton did a couple little slides, catching gravel on the shoulder each time, doing a solo version of the scene's desperate give and take. "Now we're in the final stretch, fender banging. They're trying to kill Charlie. The big semi—" He startled me again with his air-horn imitation. "That guy's bangin' me, bangin' . . . You got about five million miles of that shit, right? Setting up that they're going to kill Charlie."

He cleared a bend in the road and headed into the final straight-away. "Now we get in here, where it's more open and we can shoot it from the field. See that yellow sign? That's about where the wreck's going to be, so in a perfect world, we'll be going, go-ing, and somewhere in here we'll do the setup. The truck will pull behind me and stuntwise I'll do something like—" He did a three-part cha-cha-cha with the steering wheel: left, right, left. "Boom, boom, then I'll throw the car this way, try to end up something like this." His final move was hard to the left, and he slid just a touch down the road, with the passenger side (my side, just then) facing forward.

Drivers always start a rollover after a sharp turn into a slide, since it helps ensure that the car rolls sideways. If the driver did hit the button and send the car up into the air when it was heading straight down the road, the gag would not be a rollover but a slamdown. To a stuntman's way of thinking, a rollover is a nice, survivable wreck. A slamdown, on the other hand, is an unaccept-able risk: instead of rolling down the road and dispersing the en-ergy gradually, a car going straight would jackknife end over end and come to an abrupt stop on its roof, transferring the combined propulsive forces of the car and the cannon directly to the driver's brain. A racing helmet is no help in such a situation, since the collision is internal: as the brain, which is suspended in fluid, continues moving at full speed, it shears away from its connective tissue and slams up against the inner surface of the skull, deforming on impact like a rubber ball hitting a brick wall. Stuntmen want no part of this. Like the rest of us, when they get behind the wheel of a car, they observe the line between what is safe and what is unacceptable. They just draw it in a different place: between the spectacularly violent and the potentially fatal.

Kirton, however, seemed genuinely unconcerned about his day's work. "I was worried the first hundred times, okay?" he said. "I'm up to about five hundred." In fact, he wanted to start the day's shooting with the turnover, following a rule of low-budget filmmaking. "We have two identical cars, the stunt car and the hero car," he explained. "So if we do the turnover first, we've got an ending. Then, if we shoot the start of the chase, we have a beginning. The idea in all battles is to shoot the ending and the beginning, and however much time you have left over? Well, that's the middle. If you're behind schedule, it's just a shorter car chase." But the director, Tripp Reed, had his own ideas about time management, and they turned out to be the opposite of Kirton's. So, soon after Kirton got back from scouting the route with me, he and the other stunt doubles were sent off with the camera crew to spend most of day racing down the road, banging away at each other in the hot Texas sun, shooting the middle of the chase.

Nobody back at the base camp seemed to miss him. As a boss, Kirton followed the confrontational Italian style, so once he was out of the way, everybody could relax and sit around the catering tent telling stories. The conversation grew even more festive around noon when a few other stunt performers showed up; some Hollywood types from another film shooting around Austin had heard about Tom Harper's new setup, and decided to drive the two and a half hours to Waxahachie to see how it worked. The visitors were all stunt elite: Corey Eubanks, a Taurus World Stunt

Awards winner and one of Tom Cruise's (officially uncredited) stunt doubles, was the most charismatic of the gang, chatty and relaxed in a black Hawaiian shirt decorated with yellow tiger lilies; Mike Owen, another Taurus winner (for his fire gag on *The Punisher*), played his easygoing sidekick, in a sleeveless muscle shirt and black sweats; and Jennifer Badger, who specialized in doubling the more curvaceous stars (Angelina Jolie, Drew Barrymore, Jennifer Lopez), wore a black tank top and talked less than her traveling companions but still attracted attention by rubbing cold water bottles on her bare arms to beat the heat.

People don't get into stunt work just so they can join these epic bullshit sessions, but I'm sure that quite a few stick around the business, signing on for safety work or background traffic, just to trade stories a few more times. At first, the discussions sound aimless, just random shoptalk to fill the vast stretches of downtime, but it doesn't take too long to make out the rules. First, don't talk about a successful stunt, although it's okay to brag about crashing a rental car or embarrassing another stuntman. Second, gossip can never be the point of the story—although it's fine to say, in passing, that so and so showed up drunk or wound up in a trailer with a woman not his wife. Third, and maybe most important, death is a forbidden topic, although you may acknowledge a tragic accident, especially if your story involves you and the victim in some previous ballsy and hilarious disaster you both survived. Because, really, that is the only kind of story that stuntmen tell in these situations. The good ones can go on for hours.

Eubanks opened the discussion by mentioning Tommy Huff, an older, well-loved, and profoundly foulmouthed stuntman who'd died at home a few months before, after a day's worth of wheel work on a Paris Hilton movie. They first met after Eubanks got in a crash on *The Dukes of Hazzard* TV show: he'd been driving a car blind, from a hiding spot in the backseat, doing all the steering based on directions he got via walkie-talkie, when another stuntman, also steering via radio, confused his left and camera left and slammed straight into him. The collision landed Eubanks on a gurney in the hallway of a Valencia hospital, which is where he was lying when they wheeled in another gurney and parked it right beside him. "And here's this man laying there: '*Oh, mother-fuck!*'" Eubanks is the son of Bob Eubanks, the onetime host of *The Newlywed Game*, and he's a born showman, able to keep everyone within earshot involved, interrupting himself to tease somebody, or breaking into spot-on imitations. "I'm like, 'You all right?' He's like, 'Aw, I broke my hip. Awwww.' 'How'd you break your hip?' 'I'm a stuntman. I was working on *Airwolf*.' I said, 'Really, what's your name?' He goes, 'Tommy Huff.' I go, 'I'm a stuntman, too. Corey Eubanks, *Dukes of Hazzard*.' And he goes, 'I guess we're not very good, huh, motherfucker?'"

After that, the stuntmen traded horrible injury stories, spitting them out fast, like brokers at the stock exchange. One stuntman they all knew came back to a dock on the set of *Pirates of the Caribbean* and dove into the water for a relaxing swim—without knowing that since the last time he was there the crew had installed a steel plate just below the surface for the actors to stand on. He cut his scalp badly—"peeled his head open," as Badger put it. Tom Harper brought up an ironic injury: after a day working with explosives on the set of *Pearl Harbor*, he was cleaning up in the locker room and cut his heel walking into the shower. Talk of *Pearl Harbor* led to a story about a mouthy stuntman who'd teased some Navy SEAL on the set and wound up getting duct-taped to a chair and submerged in a tank. Badger remembered a more ominous aquatic-movie moment, recalling a German scuba pro who'd gone underwater to prep a scene for the actors just before the director decided he wanted to shoot elsewhere, and since nobody on the boat remembered that the pro was underwater, they just took off, abandoning the German in the middle of the ocean, a real-life version of the scenario in the movie *Open Water*. This led to discussion of sharks and shark movies, Jessica Alba's ability to hold her breath underwater, and, in a gentle leap back onto land, movies with trained bears. One of the stuntmen had been advised by an animal trainer that if the bear in his scene ever got out of line all he had to do was rub two sticks together, because the bear knew that sound: it meant that he was about to get an electric shock. Eubanks mentioned a trained bear who loved SpaghettiOs: he'd go anywhere as long as his trainer was right ahead of him with a pot of the stuff. They were shooting a beer commercial, and luring the bear across a rocky stream, and the trainer tripped and the SpaghettiOs landed all over the cameraman's face! Everybody laughed as Eubanks imitated the bear slurping down the treat. "The guy lives in a rubber room right now, I'm sure."

"I don't have any bear stories," Tom Harper said. "But I have a funny tiger story. We were working on *Jungle Book* up in South Carolina, shooting nights. They had camels, bear, donkeys, horses, all this stuff. And the tiger—in the story he comes in and steals a little kid out of the camp. Well, they don't feed these tigers is the way they get them to do what they want. The trainer would show him the food and then run through the set with the tiger chasing him, and when the tiger got where he wanted him to go he'd give him the food, right? So, most of the nights we'd sit in the trailer and play cards and stuff. And at three or four in the morning they'd come get us, we'd do like two or three shots, then go home, play golf, and go to bed. So one night they came to get us at like four o'clock and we go to the set and there's all these portable fences up, right? And the camera crew's inside them."

Everyone around the catering table could see where this was heading and laughed.

"So they're bringing out the tiger. They had *twenty-one* trainers with this tiger."

"For one tiger?" Eubanks asked.

"One tiger. It was a two-year-old, three-hundred-pound female. And in the story, there's a lot of havoc going on in the camp, the tiger's already stolen the little kid—so she's running here and there." Harper, who was once turned down for a gig as Patrick Swayze's stunt double because he was better looking than the star, wasted no more time with the setup, jump-cutting to his own point of view as he did the stunt, remembering the trainer's advice about what to do if the tiger ever deviates from the script. " 'If he comes at you,' the trainer says, 'whatever you do, don't run, because you're not going to get away. Lay down and play dead.' Okay, that works."

"I thought that was for bears."

"So I jump across the little thing that you tie the horse on— what do you call it?"

"Hitching post."

"Hitchin' post. Yeah, I jump across the hitchin' post right after the tiger goes running by, right? I hit the ground on all fours, and I look up, and just as I do, when I hit the ground, she just went *shwoooot* like this and looks right at me. And she's about from here to that gas can," about fifteen feet away. "Now I'm on all fours and I'm going, 'Okay, let's see what she's gonna do.' She started coming at me. So I laid down." He said he exchanged glances of an "oh shit" variety with another stuntman as the tiger came closer. "I just laid down on the ground like this"—he curled up in a fetal position. "And I had on this little helmet that went down in the back like this. And the tiger came up and started"— Harper pushed roughly at a pile of Styrofoam plates leftover from lunch—"moving me around like this, waitin' on me to see if I'd try to get away. And I swear I laid on the ground seemed like hours. And nobody did anything!" Harper spoke in a deep Georgia twang, the sort of folksy voice you often hear on dirt-track racers and airline pilots. "It was awfully alone."

Again the table roared with laughter.

"I can feel the thing slobbering on me, pawing at me to see if I was still alive. And I'm like, 'Shoot this fucker!' "

"Omigod!"

"Finally, they all come running in. Of course, they put the tiger up at that point because it scared all the trainers. So about an hour later we were at the craft-service table, and I said to the trainer, 'Dude, you don't have a tranquilizer gun or anything?' He goes, 'Shit no, we're not going to shoot the tiger!' I said, 'What were you waiting for?' " 'Oh, we were waiting to see whether or not she was going to eat you, because if she was going to eat you there was nothing we could do.' "

The story brought out a combination of grunts and astonished monosyllables, and the silence that followed was filled with both shivers of recognition and a series of individual memory checks: it was a story any one of them could tell again at another assembly. After that, Sylvester Stallone's stunt double told a story about a stuntwoman on a horse getting chased by a lion. The Robocop double volunteered one about being shut in a cage with a tiger, in a bar in the Philippines, on an off day, just for fun. Then Tom Harper started another promising animal-gag story: he was doing a scene where pit bulls were supposed to maul him to death in a TV movie, but it went on too long, hinged on minutiae of execution, and somehow portrayed the day-to-day plight of stuntmen— their safety compromised by the incompetence of inferiors, their best efforts subject to the capriciousness of uncomprehending directors—in a light that was too close to the unglamorous truth. Mike Owen offered one more funny bit about a stuntman who, at first, didn't want to hang bare-ass off the side of the ship until he learned that the prep on the stunt would be handled by a girl in wardrobe that he'd had his eye on. But, really, Harper's shoptalk had killed the mood. Nobody seemed to mind when Kirton came back from shooting the fender-banging, bragging about his undiminished skills as a wheelman, bulldogging everybody to get the prep work done on the rollover.

By the time they finally got around to shooting the sequence it was five in the afternoon, and the new director and his crew were racing the sun. (In the finished product, the high-speed chase begins in noonday glare and ends, about a mile up the road, on the far side of twilight.) They'd set up shop in a hayfield that had been recently mowed, with a small tent providing shade for the main camera about forty yards from the spot on the road where Kirton intended to launch his rollover. Several remotely operated cameras, or "I-mos," had been hidden closer to the target area, inside protective canisters and camouflaged under a pile of straw. The designated safeties, Mark De Alessandro, who'd worked with Stallone since *Rocky III*, and Cord Newman, a young Florida stuntman whom Kirton was bringing along, would be stationed closest to the wreck, ready to race out from their hiding places in the shoulder-high corn across the road if anything went wrong: both wore shin guards and blue fire-retardant overalls and lugged fire extinguishers. De Alessandro had been in Kirton's position many times. "Whenever I'm going to do something like this," he told me, "I just kind of stay quiet with the Lord."

The farm road had been closed to traffic, and a couple of troopers sat at either end of what was now a movie set, checking in by walkie-talkie with the assistant director from time to time, letting him know how much traffic they were holding back. The stretch of road that would actually make it into the shot was bermed and raised about four feet above the level of the fields, and this paved platform—the perfect staging ground for a rollover—shimmered with heat waves, even at five o'clock.

For Kirton, the heat was the hardest part of the gag. Even though they were supposed to roll camera right after the safety meeting was over and everybody had been fully briefed about what was going to happen and where everybody should be, it still took more than twenty minutes for the camera car to get into position and for the driver of the Freightliner to find a working radio and for the director to sign off on the camera setups. Meanwhile the cop car was running, the police lights were whirling, the road was baking, and Kirton, strapped into the rig in a five-point harness, in his full-length fire-retardant overalls and a helmet, kept getting hotter and hotter. From time to time, a production assistant came by and spritzed him on the face with some mist. But that didn't help. He'd seen other stuntmen lose it at this point as their body temperature rose, amplifying the effects of a heart racing with adrenaline: they'd get light-headed or feverish and start making no sense. But it was out of his hands. There was nothing he could do except sit and bake and lose his mind waiting for the A.D. to call "Action."

I had found a good semi-inconspicuous spot to watch, in the field behind the camera tent. Eubanks, Owen, and Badger were just ahead of me, and right behind me one of the cops stood beside his black Chevy Silverado at a bend in the road. Finally, I could hear the A.D. yelling into a megaphone, "The car is hot, everybody. The car is hot!" By which he meant, at last the scene was starting. He yelled "Action," and the camera car started moving, leading the way, and then Kirton and the driver of the Freightliner stepped on the gas, accelerating to about forty. Just past the yellow sign on the roadside, Kirton shimmied left, right, left, and then went airborne. In miraculous silence, the car sprang up, and at the peak of its first roll it pogoed a bit on the spring arm, then slammed down on its roof and kept rolling, through one complete revolution and more, until it came to rest balanced on its passenger side, the police lights facing the cameras and still whirling. The A.D. called "Cut!" and De Alessandro and Newman ran out of the cornfield to check on Kirton. He unstrapped himself, and everybody nearby ran to the police car, to hold it steady so it wouldn't topple down while Kirton climbed out of the window. Everywhere underfoot you could see and feel the broken plastic from the police lights embedded in the hot asphalt.

Kirton was pleased. He wandered around near the wreck, accepting congratulations and praising the new system. "It done what it was supposed to do," he said. "It was awesome. What a nice piece of work, huh?" Harper and the Hollywood stuntmen came up to say how great it had looked. "What's up, bro?" Kirton said.

"Good job, man," Harper told him.

"Your arm is so smooth," Kirton said. "It was so quiet."

Harper agreed. "That's what's weird. It's quiet as hell, man."

Eubanks joined in: "It's like all of a sudden he's up in the air and . . ." Eubanks did a double take, as if he'd forgotten something. "Where's the boom?"

"Dude, that was state of the art," Kirton concluded. "Good job, buddy. You're the hero."

One thing that always startled me, no matter how many times I'd seen it happen, was how quickly stuntmen got back to work after a big gag. They'd review the footage for a few minutes, looking over the director's shoulder, oohing and offering their opinion about whether they needed a second take. (They decided that the rollover, which the director had covered from plenty of angles, looked fine.) But after a scant few minutes, they broke off and started prepping for whatever segment they needed to film next. In this case, the oncoming Freightliner still had to slam into the cop car, which then needed to careen off the road, onto the field, and burst into flame, and all of that had to be in the can before nightfall. So Kirton took a sledgehammer to the car windows (which makes the collision with the truck safer, and the cleanup easier, and also sets up for the dramatic final shot with flames pouring out of the windows). Harper began disassembling the spring arm; no need to have that ruined by the oncoming Freightliner. The other stunt guys helped hook the car to a cable, a tether that would ensure that, in the aftermath of the crash, the car would land exactly where they wanted it to—in the empty field, where it would be visible to the cameras and safer to set on fire.

The speed with which they all hurried back to work also served as a reminder of a basic truth: no matter how tough and handsome and talented they were, in the strict social hierarchy of a film set, they weren't stars. They didn't rate their own trailers. No personal assistant kept track of their lattes and Tic Tacs and dry cleaning and suppository creams. Sure, I'd come down to see one of them performing the film's headliner gag, and to me all these guys were high-level athletes and performers, but none of them ever got or expected star treatment. If a guy like Kirton wanted to become a myth, he had to do it on his own time, as a hobby. Ten minutes after he'd risked his life, there he was taking a sledgehammer to the car he'd crashed. And when the day's shoot was over, that was him driving the chase vehicles back off the set.

So it was well after dark by the time Kirton left base camp and drove back with me to Dallas. We went out drinking again, but it was a Monday night and all the crazy places he'd been to in Deep Ellum, the ones that had had pool parties in their parking lots on weekends, were practically deserted. At the last one, the bouncer, who was so heavy he seemed to be able to sit down on a bar stool without bending at the waist, accepted the attentions of a twenty-year-old who was dressed like a librarian but danced in such a manner as to reveal her back tat and thong. Her gay friends playing pool in back applauded. The bartender served us a drink she had concocted and named herself. Every once in a while, Kirton would say something like "Dude, I did such a fucking ass-kicking turnover it's not even funny. We're the heroes, man." Or he'd shake his head at the emptiness of the bar and the certainty that we would close this one, too, and he'd tell me, "I've got friends my age that are old! They're like, 'Shit, dude. You've got a twenty-five-year-old ex-wife?' Yeah, why not? Why not anything, you know?"

Even though we'd been talking about his ex from Bulgaria on and off throughout my visit, I'd never actually done the math (twenty-five-year-old ex minus six-year-old son) until just this moment. "Wait," I said. "That means you married her when she was nineteen and you were forty-two!"

"Yeah!"

"Dude!"

"Shit, why not?" he said. "It was all going to hurt in the end, right?"

CHAPTER 6

Wonder Women and Titty Twisters

At sixty-six, Jeannie Epper dresses like a grandmother, in champagne-colored sweats and comfy sneakers. Her neat house, with its garden knickknacks and family photos displayed on a golden easel, looks just the way a grandmother's house should. But nobody on earth looks and sounds more like a stuntwoman. Her voice scratches and rattles like skate wheels at the roller derby, and her face is worn and rumpled, as if she'd been through a few fights. Actually, "a few" is lowballing it. The more accurate number is "way too many," she says. "Before I actually became a Christian and turned my life around? Probably thirty bar fights. I don't think it's such a cool thing, but it was kind of expected of the Epper sisters. We were supposed to be rough and tumble and tough, and we were, in our hot pants."

You can find twelve Eppers with stunt credits in the Internet Movie Database, spread over four generations. ("We're like lemmings," she said.) From the start, she and her five sisters and brothers were groomed for the family business, although to them it felt more like just running wild. They grew up on a ranch in North Hollywood, back in the forties and fifties, riding bareback, chasing trains along the railroad tracks and jumping off their horses onto freight cars, just for fun. The property, nine acres on Longridge, between Vanowen and Sherman Way, today is crowded with upper-middle-class homes and pools and tiny parched lawn plots. There's nothing left of their stunt paradise, not a trace of the stables and riding trails where her father trained his movie horses. It vanished along with the world it belonged to, all those Westerns and swashbucklers filled with the he-men that her father used to double, stars like Gary Cooper and Errol Flynn, who came by the ranch to ride and drink with him and get away from it all.

Movie stars liked to hang around her father, she said, because he was a "man's man's man." John Epper, the stunt family's first stunt professional, was Swiss, an ex-cavalry officer who left his homeland because he indulged in certain habits, like drinking and riding and womanizing, to a degree that the local Swiss magistrates did not approve of. When he came to America in 1926, he didn't fit in on his first stops in Holyoke, Massachusetts, or Cleveland, Ohio, any better than he had back in Gossau, St. Gall. So he kept heading west till he got to California. There the former soldier wound up teaching proper form to young ladies at the Beverly Hills Riding Academy and, from time to time, wrangling Academy horses for the movie studios. Which explains why he was waiting around the MGM lot on the day that an English stunt rider repeatedly failed to get anywhere near the moving motorcar he was being paid to clear. Epper discreetly asked for a turn: on his first attempt, he sailed neatly over the rumble seat, and the producers signed him to the picture for twenty-five dollars a day.

Jeannie Epper refers to her father now, fondly and with no illusions, as a rounder. "He just liked to hang out and drink with the guys and have a good time and pop out kids," she said. But he was hardworking and strict about a few things. All the children learned to harness and drive a team of horses, from a one-horse gig to a four-in-hand. They learned how to ride in the proper English fashion, starting out bareback and graduating to the smallest of saddles, to be allowed a full-size Western rig only at the age of thirteen. By that age, her sister Steffi had already been a riding double for five years, on TV shows like *Fury* and *My Friend Flicka*; Jeannie had the same job on *The Dakotas*. "He didn't want us to be riding like cowboys," Epper said. "He wanted us to tuck it all in from the center, and we all ride that way: we ride collected.

It's really hard to dump us off a horse, because when you're that tucked in and collected, you're a part of the animal. You almost have to ride *that* good to ride bad. In order to look like you're falling off, you have to know where your center is at all times."

The kids weren't movie brats. They had chores—Jeannie plucked the chickens and hot-walked the horses after gallops. But after that, they made up their own challenges: They jumped off the top of the house or the stable. They strung a rope from a tree and slid down to the ground (and didn't mind hitting a few branches on the way down). They practiced bulldogging each other: Jeannie would wait in a tree for a sister to ride by, then she'd leap down and grab her and the two of them would tumble to the ground. From time to time, their father came by to supervise, so they could get the timing right. Epper isn't one to romanticize—her memories of childhood seem untinged by nostalgia (of the chickens, she said "I can still smell the smell"). But as a stuntwoman she has traveled all over the world, so she knows how unspoiled and prelapsarian her childhood sounds. Her dad taught them how to bleed out, skin, and butcher the cattle. The kids snuck food from the kitchen and rode down to the railroad tracks to feed the "hoboes," who knew them by name. "It was a different life," she said. "Simple, quiet, no TV. We had a phone, but it was in my parents' room with a lock on it."

Although Epper had been working as an extra, a stand-in, or riding double since the age of nine, it wasn't until 1957, when she was eighteen, that she landed what she considered her first big gag. Like so many stuntmen of that era, she got her start on a horse. She convinced a lady she knew at the Warner Brothers casting office to send her to *Maverick*—she'd be doubling Joanna Moore ("Ryan O'Neal's first wife") for a rear and a fall. "The guy I rode in with was Bing Russell, Kurt Russell's dad," Epper said. "And the people from the casting office came in to watch me perform. That was a lot of pressure on an eighteen-year-old girl. I had to come in riding really fast, pull up to a stop, rear him up, and get shot off. And I had to hit a mark." Epper mostly spoke about her own stunt work with professional detachment, but for this one she allowed herself the hint of a smile. "I did it the first time. There was no way on God's green earth I was going to make a mistake. I knew then that I had what it took to deal with stuff under pressure. And the lady from casting started giving me work all the time. It didn't even make a difference if I was their size—I doubled everyone on that lot for years and years. I doubled Connie Stevens, I doubled Diane McBain." She got married about then, to a roofer she'd met at a corner liquor store that he owned, and she named her daughter Eurlyne after the real name of an ingenue she doubled on *Bourbon Street Beat*, the former Miss USA Arlene Howell. Her daughter hates it, she says, and prefers to be called Earl.

Her experience at Warners gave her the confidence to go straight A—an old-school term for giving up the safer work reserved for members of the Screen Extras Guild (a separate union at the time) to switch to the Screen Actors Guild and be a full-time stuntwoman. It was a daunting step. Then, as now, it was hard for women to get by in the stunt business: there's a lot less work for them, men run the set, and the guys handing out the jobs aren't always sensitive, forward-thinking, women's-lib types. These days, the union contract requires three stuntwomen to turn down a gag involving a female character before a man can take the work, but when Epper began, men were the first and often only option for stunts, which explains the presence of so many hairy and broad-shouldered blondes in the action scenes of the black-and-white era. Stuntmen were used to looking at women but not to looking at them as competition, and they could easily disguise their selfish motivations as a form of gallantry: no one is more averse to seeing a lady get hurt than the guy who'd like to do the job, for pay, in her place. Epper knew what she was up against; she'd been around stuntmen nearly every minute of her life. And though she knew she was as fearless as any of them, she was also practical—she had to be, with three children at home by the age of twenty-five. She gave herself five years to make it, and her gamble paid off. Seven of her first ten movies were Westerns, but by the early seventies, between disaster films like *The Poseidon Adventure* and *The Towering Inferno* and Blaxploitation flicks like *Coffy* and *Foxy Brown* (as the white heavy), she had enough work for five Jeannie Eppers.

With horse operas on the way out in the seventies, a lot of old stuntmen who came up through the rodeo circuit disappeared, unable to adapt to the demands of a new era. Jeannie was young enough to learn the tricks the job now required, the car work, high falls, and karate-style brawls. For her, the high falls were the hardest. "I was not a high person," she said. "It tested everything in my being to have to go learn how to jump." But she made herself overcome the fear. Every free weekend, she'd go out to train at Bob Yerkes's place in Northridge. Yerkes ran Circus of the Stars and trained a lot of trapeze artists at his own home. His backyard, filled with high wires and air bags and Russian swings, was like a Juilliard School for circus performers. By that time, Jeannie's family had sold the ranch in North Hollywood ("Be worth trillions today. I wouldn't have to think about working"), but for her kids Yerkes's setup became the same sort of training-ground-cum-stunt-nursery that the ranch had been for an earlier generation of Eppers. Her daughter Eurlyne learned the flying trapeze and appeared for years in Yerkes's Circus, and by the time her son Richard was a teenager he'd learned the intricacies of rigging well enough to run the show whenever Yerkes was busy.

She needed to be comfortable in the air because in 1975 she landed the job as Lynda Carter's stunt double on *The New Adventures of Wonder Woman*. The role, which she held all four seasons the show aired, was a rare one—a big action vehicle with a female star—but the problems Epper faced were typical for stuntwomen. She had to do everything a man would do, only in a lot less clothing—especially after the first season when they modernized Wonder Woman's costume, eliminating the bloomer cut on her blue-spangled bottoms in favor of a sexier high-ride bikini that showed a lot of thigh. But for Epper, who had inherited the Swiss tendency to curvaceousness, it was the low-cut red top with the weird gold palm-frond design that gave her problems.

"I was running out," Epper said, explaining a typical costume glitch, "and I hit a minitramp to go over the hedge to bulldog whoever the bad lady was from Germany"—Fausta, the Nazi Wonder Woman, played by Lynda Day George—"and just as I hit the minitramp and I'm up in the air, *this* decides to go this way. And now I'm committed. And I know my top's off and I have to commit to the stunt or I'm going to kill myself." Donna Garrett, who was doubling George on the shoot, had to adjust at once. Garrett "was trying to put my costume back on, but we're still trying to fight and roll down this hill. To this day, when Donna and I see each other we just start laughing. She was trying to tuck my boobs in, and trying to fight, trying to get it all in one shot. And the crew's watching!"

By the third season, Epper eventually solved the boob problem with a tiny piece of nude-colored elastic, but the first few seasons the risk was real and recurrent. "Another time we had to do this thing where we were coming down, upside down, and we'd never tested the costume with me climbing down. And I couldn't touch the ground, because if I did an explosion would go off, and I had to pick up something with my arms outstretched, and that's when the costume comes off."

Epper's slapstick flashing anecdotes are somewhat at odds with her personal code. Her father, perhaps because he knew how a stuntman thinks, imposed strict standards of behavior on his daughters; he sent the teenaged Jeannie back to Switzerland for two and a half years to study in a convent, under the care of her aunt, the Mother Superior there. In the convent, improbably enough, Epper learned to sew and knit and cook—she can even darn socks, an un-usual skill among stunt professionals. But somehow it fits with her aura on the set, which is principally that of the mother hen, espe-cially around stuntwomen. For much of her career, she went about this mothering in an organized fashion—she was one of the found-ers of the Stuntwomen's Association of Motion Pictures. As presi-dent, in 1972, she sent a letter to Universal, complaining about the way the stuntwomen in her group, the most experienced in the busi-ness, kept getting passed over as stunt coordinators in favor of younger models. She didn't come right out and say it, but the way she saw it, the stunt guys were hiring their girlfriends, or, worse, women they hoped to sleep with, and that was hurting stuntwomen twice: the competent women weren't getting work they were qualified for, and the women who were getting the jobs didn't know what they were doing. She believes the frank letter got her banned from Universal for four years. "They silently got rid of me," she said. "Nobody knew it was really happening. I just suddenly wasn't working over there anymore."

Despite her time in the convent, Epper is not a prude. In 2004, the filmmaker Amanda Micheli made a two-fisted documentary, *Double Dare*, which followed Epper and the young Kiwi stuntwoman Zoe Bell on and off the set for nearly four years. In one scene, Bell joins Epper and Eurlyne in a limousine on the way to the Taurus World Stunt Awards, and as Bell bounces around in excitement and sips champagne, Epper catches sight of Bell's lip piercing. Epper's immediate reaction is "How do you do a blow job with that?" (Bell reassured her: "Omigod, I give great blow jobs with that!") But she keeps this side of her life separate. Her father's business tips covered more than just how to ride or tackle or throw a punch. "He was really strict with us girls about 'Don't sleep with those stunt guys.' He pounded that into us from early on. Because every one of those guys had been through five wives," she said. "Being a good stunt person, you have to have the whole package. You have to be built right. You have to have a good personality. You have to get along with people. You have to learn your morals."

She tries to tutor raw talents about "set etiquette"; she clearly wants to help young stuntwomen succeed. And nobody has any problem taking advice from Epper—her stature among stuntwomen is as exalted as Terry Leonard's is among stuntmen. She has a similar big-gag résumé—she did eighteen takes falling down a mountain in a mudslide for *Romancing the Stone*. She was the first stuntwoman to receive a lifetime achievement award at the Taurus World Stunt Awards. And, of course, she's an Epper, which multiplies her authority in stunt matters about a dozen-fold.

It helps, too, that she's never really been hurt, apart from getting whacked on the head with a picture frame once by Pam Grier, and getting some of her hair burned off when she got pinned under a burning crossbeam. Oh, and messing up her knee on the twenty-eighth take of a British commercial, when she caught her heel jumping from car to car, in the rain, on top of a moving train, just last year, at the age of sixty-five.

People listen to her for professional reasons, and she's fun, too, every bit as good a yarn spinner as Leonard. But a stuntman leaves you laughing, and the feeling is different when you walk away from Epper: you wish she were your grandmother. I'd like to say that all stuntwomen are that way—that unlike stunt*men*, they don't need to indulge in entertaining bits of bluster to distract a listener from the real pain of life—but Epper's frank and achingly undefended conversational style is her own achievement.

She has no problem telling you whatever's on her mind. The morning I visited, it happened to be her granddaughter's breasts. "Amber's going through this thing where all of a sudden she's got these boobs on her," she said. "And I have to go, *today,* to buy her bras. She just went kaboom. It's driving my son nuts, because he knows where all this is going. And she's in these tank tops, leaning over—she's full-breasted, you know, like Scarlett Johansson. That's the kind of breasts she's got. They're scary. They're beautiful. They're knockout breasts. This is what my fourteen-year-old grand-daughter's got: 34-C. We're very large-breasted in my family."

Her life has been hard—successful, even illustrious, but hard in ways that have nothing to do with career. In 1977, she was Wonder Woman, thirty-six years old, married with three kids and a brand-new house and car. Still, she felt something was missing in her life and she started looking in the Yellow Pages to fix it. She found a listing for the First Assembly of God in Northridge and she said to her youngest, Kurtis, who was five at the time, "Let's go." First Assembly wasn't like the Swiss convents—they praised the Lord and spoke in tongues. That fascinated her. "I guess it fit my style of who I am. And I left and I came back the next Sunday, and the next Sunday. I remembered the exact words the preacher said that pulled me to the altar. It was 'Cast your cares upon the Lord for he careth for you.' I couldn't get up to the front of the church fast enough and get on my knees. They tell me I was forty-five minutes bawling. And that was it for me, I was committed. I was *so* committed that I got into a small Bible college and learned the word, and every time the doors were open I was in church. Then my husband ran off with my brother's wife. And that put a big divot in my faith."

The divorce rate for the people who work in stunts is similar to the divorce rate for the stars they double. From the outside, the situation seems easy to explain: they live away from home for months at a time, working in out-of-the-way places, and at the end of the day, which so often happens to be the middle of the night, there they are, revved up and wired, with time on their hands, hanging out in hotel bars with like-minded souls who are almost uniformly fun, rich, good-looking, lonely, and likely to forgive. There may be other, less charitable explanations—that movie people are narcissists and adrenaline addicts who feed off a certain kind of emotional circus. But these are sociological theories. On an individual level, all you can say is that, no matter what happens in your career, one of the biggest dangers in the movie business is heartbreak.

Epper can certainly spot the symptoms in her colleagues. She was in Japan, on the set of *Fast and Furious: Tokyo Drift*, when she saw Terry Leonard, whom she's known practically since she first started in motion pictures. He was the movie's second-unit director and he was standing alone, on the set, late at night, and she knew that body language—he was going through his third divorce, from a woman he'd been with long enough that he finally started to think he was done with divorcing. She got out of the car she was supposed to be driving and they walked to each other. Leonard put his arm around her, she said. And he said, "Remember when the roofer left you?"

Of course she remembered.

"That's how I feel," Leonard said.

She talked to me about the ripple effect of her husband's betrayal, the hurt not just to her and her brother, but to her dad, her mom, the children. She sat in her living room thirty years later, making the sound of an explosion. "It was a big one," she said. "It went from everything being wonderful to almost like death. And he never came back. He never came back, he just . . . never came back. And I had to deal with the kids and my career, and he stole my money. I stayed in church, but down deep inside I thought, I'm mad at God. I kept thinking God was supposed to stop this. Well, that isn't really His job. We're not puppets. God didn't make us puppets."

But Epper is not one to linger over her problems for very long. Stunt work has trained her to take responsibility for herself: it's one of the fundamental lessons of the job. On the set, at least, she admits to being a control freak. "As a woman, you can't let other people set everything up for you. You've got to know in your head about cables and camera lenses and air bags and heights and bombs and cars. Because you're the body in that car, you're the person on the descender. Find out who's going to be on the wire, on the extinguisher, who's there to put you out when you're on fire. That's where you do all your homework."

Of course, the training works the other way, too: on a big movie, with dozens of people hired to do the stunts, you can't always be the one on fire. Sometimes it's your job to put somebody out. In fact, most stunt professionals spend a greater percentage of time on the set watching stunts than doing them. They're paid to act as backup, to help think things through, to stand off camera ready to rush in, in the unlikely event that something goes drastically wrong. And this, too, becomes an instinct with them, another form of courage. An eighteen-year-old crashed his motorcycle in front of Epper's house once, and when she saw that his friends didn't know how to handle it Epper ran out and did the only thing left: she just held him. "And all I could think of was 'I wish I knew who this boy's mother was so she could know he died in my arms and not—' " The kid was eighteen, racing without a helmet. By the

time the firemen arrived a few minutes later, there was nothing
they could do to help. They recognized the situation and left her
alone with the boy for a while, to collect her thoughts, sitting at
the side of the road in a huge puddle of blood.

A few years later, Epper heard about somebody else in danger,
her friend the actor Ken Howard, who'd die if he couldn't get a kidney transplant. So she took the tests. When she found out that she
was a suitable match, she agreed to donate one of her kidneys. "People asked me how I could, and I said, 'The same way I do a big stunt.
I decide to do it, I gather all the information about what I'm doing,
and then I get focused and I go for it.' It was July 25, 2000. It was
kind of scary, the night before, when I was in that room with all
those things in my arm. There were some mind battles in my head
the night before. But I knew what I was focused to do. I kept saying
it was like a stunt. But sometimes when you decide to do a really, really big stunt, and you've done all your homework, and you've gone
out on location, and you've practiced, and you've checked out the
spot, still the night before, when you lay on your pillow, it all starts
to go in here"—she pointed to her head—"and that's where you
have to learn to shut that off and go with what your original decision was: It's elective surgery. I *elected* to do this."

Still, even in this extremity, Epper couldn't resist tweaking the
chauvinistic impulse, since the situation proved that in the right cir-
cumstance it was possible for a woman to double a man. After all,
she said drily, "They let me give my female kidney to a male actor."

Because the stunt world is so exclusive, both hard to get into and
largely unknown to outsiders, I never got too far into a conversation on set before somebody asked, "So who else are you talking
to?" People in stunts have a right to be suspicious. Newspaper
and magazine stories usually cast them as maniacs with a death
wish, jocks so desperate to hang on in Hollywood that they'd run
headfirst into a brick wall. They consider it an insult when, say, a
photographer asks them to pose on crutches for a group photo.
So I learned to arrange my answers carefully, mentioning legends,

families, top drivers, key figures in the struggles between the big stunt groups. It was an almost Homeric ritual ("I bring word of Hector, son of Priam"), a long-form version of one they practiced on each other ("Weren't you on *Dukes*?" or "You doubled Sly, right?").

One name never failed to get a reaction: Debbie Evans. Evans is the Meryl Streep of stunts, with five Taurus World Stunt Awards, more than anybody else in the business. But when I told a stunt co-ordinator on the set of *Spider-Man 3* that I'd visited her the month before, his reaction was far too typical: he looked me in the eye and said, "Debbie Evans is one of the five best stunt*men* in the business." His admiration was legitimate, but the emphasis was meant as a slight. He needed to impugn her femininity to recognize her superiority—which she established early in her career by coming in second, at the age of twenty, in the CBS Stunt Competition, against nine of the best stunt*men* of the era. In case I missed his innuendo, he started going on about the mannishness of stuntwomen, whom he found sexually unappealing.

The stunt business is unlike business or medicine or academia, where men and women compete on more or less equal terms in an intellectual arena; at those jobs, the debate about sexual politics is a comparatively genteel matter, focused on leave and compensation and equal opportunity. But the gender dispute in stunt work happens on a more primal level, because it's one of the few jobs, along with firefighting and war and the circus, where the competition between men and women is judged on physical merit. Men will probably hold onto the lion's share of the work for the foreseeable future; the majority of action roles are written with male stars in mind, and most of the backup muscle and villainous henchmen—the guys who do a lot of falling and being set on fire—are still men. But in the years since Epper first began sending letters and speaking her mind, women have made progress. Some of this is a sign of the times: there's more work for stuntwomen because Hollywood producers think there's a market for movies like *Kill Bill* and *Charlie's Angels* that showcase kick-ass women.

But stuntmen know that's not the whole story. There are simply a lot more skilled women around now. Some, like Evans, are as good on the streets and up on the screen as any one of the men. This makes them intimidating to the competition.

Like so many people in stunts, Evans lives about an hour north of L.A. in canyon country, near a twisty mountain-pass road through the Angeles National Forest, a long cut into town favored by motorcyclists, who like to get up in the cool sierras and lean through the switchbacks beside the steep ravines. Over the years, Evans and her husband, Lane Leavitt, have turned their place into a stunt complex, with a rambling ranch house overlooking a pool, which is just a few steps away from a barn filled with every variety of rig—mats, tramps, hoists, air rams, winches, descenders, crash-test dummies. On the north end, beyond the barn, there's a bare, bumpy patch of rocks and dirt which to many householders would look like unimproved land. Evans and Leavitt see a playground for their kids, who like to take out the Quadrunners and XR100s and race around. Evans pointed to the one structure out there: "And that teeter-totter, we ride over on our bikes."

Evans is blonde with pale-blue eyes and very little to outwardly distinguish her unfussy style from that of any other beleaguered mom in jeans. She looked tired: she'd been up all night shooting *Redline*, spinning out a Ferrari Enzo on closed L.A. streets, so she poured coffee (hers into a Speed Racer cup) and we headed to her garage, past her drift car, a classic red Nissan 240 SX, to look at her motorcycles. One stood out from the row of dirt bikes: a sleek and sculpted red Ducati 996, a gift from the Wachowski brothers in gratitude for her work in *The Matrix Reloaded*. Evans doubled Carrie-Anne Moss in the freeway scene, a fourteen-minute chase shot on a two-mile stretch of private freeway built on the Alameda Naval Air Station, outside San Francisco. The filmmakers intended her feat—dodging through oncoming traffic without a helmet, in a catsuit, at around ninety-five miles an hour—to look impossible, a cool, hyper-speed accomplishment of a quasi-spiritual order, and in some way the strategy backfired: many viewers just assumed that the scene was computer generated. "Well," Evans said to a stuntman who didn't believe it was real, "there were four lanes of cars making lane changes, and one of them hit me, and that was not a CGI car."

Evans is a specialist: ninety-nine percent of what she does, she says, she does in or on a vehicle. The roadwork has shaped her. She's broad-shouldered from muscling motorcycles through the dirt and she's got a bowlegged walk that she probably shares with most of her fellow members of the Motorcycle Hall of Fame. And then there are the little things you can't see, like the slipped disk in her cervical vertebra that she'll have to take care of one of these days, a chronic injury that started on *Taking Lives*, when her car sped into a crash on an icy bridge in Quebec, and her head and crash helmet slammed around inside the car: *whack-whack-whack*, rebounding back and forth against the steel bars of the roll cage. "That really hurts," she said, in an informational tone.

Most stunt people can point to some crazy incident early in their lives that nurtured their fearlessness. Evans started riding at the age of six, in the pre-helmet era, when her father, David Evans, an enduro racer sponsored by OSSA and Montesa, took her out to a picturesque dirt pile somewhere near their home in Lakewood, California, and put her on her first motorcycle—a minibike with an eighty-horsepower Yamaha engine, which she promptly drove straight into a pile of concrete and rebar. He told her, "Get back on and ride around." In her rendition, his words sound calm, gentle, and encouraging, and it's easy to see that the advice, and the confidence behind it, has stuck with her over the years. Her free-spirited father appears briefly in *On Any Sunday*, Bruce Brown's documentary about motorcycle racing in the late sixties: he rides past the camera, over rough terrain, tracking all the way through the frame while holding his bike in a wheelie. Once when he was out in the garage working on his bikes, his wife yelled up the driveway, "Dave! Dave! Come out here please!" He ran out to find her pointing up to Debbie, twenty-five feet above them, hanging from the lamppost. He watched his daughter for a while, then called up, "You like it up there?"

"Yeah," Debbie said. She'd seen the stunt on TV and wanted to try it herself.

"Can you get down?"

"Yeah."

"Stay up there as long as you want," he said and went back to his bikes.

Evans's sister Donna is also a stuntwoman, with two Taurus awards of her own. Their dad, who figured anything boys could do girls could, too, taught them both how to ride. But off the bike, the sisters chose different styles: Donna went the head-cheerleader, homecoming-queen route, and Debbie decided to hang from lampposts and beat up boys. "I think when I was six or seven, Georgie Porgie came down and started picking on me, and I beat him up," she said. "He was *eleven*. I was kind of the defender. Donna would come in: 'Debbie, Johnny hit me!' And I'd take off after Johnny." Now they pick up each other's kids or call from the set to go over a big gag together. "Our lifestyles are very much alike now, because of the way the industry is—not knowing what's going to happen minute to minute," Evans says. "We're very understanding of each other there, where people in a regular job don't really know how it works."

Back when she was still in high school, she'd seen some motorcycle gags on TV, done by some "girl" with a thick neck and cannonball biceps, and she thought they looked like something cool to do. But before she could act on the impulse, the movies called her. She was eighteen, and a big deal in the bike world, appearing on the cover of biking magazines, winning time trials against the men, cutting out of high school on Friday afternoons to fly off to trick shows in places like the Houston Astrodome and the Pontiac Silverdome. She made her movie debut in the 1978 movie *Deathsport* ("In the year 3000 there'll be no more Olympic Games, World Series, or Super Bowl. There'll be only . . ."), a Roger Corman production, with David Carradine and Claudia Jennings. She did everything they asked—including clearing a thirty-foot ravine. For most of the shots, she drove on unwieldy bikes with sissy bars, tarted up for the movie with fifty pounds of spiked metal plates and battering rams. "Every time you'd turn the thing it would want to take a dive into the ground," she told the Motorcycle Hall of Fame. "They had us doing jumps on them and all kinds of other stunts. In retrospect, it was pretty dangerous stuff, but that's how I got into the Screen Actors Guild."

On the strength of her *Deathsport* work, she got invited to the CBS Stunt Competition. Evans's invitation could be interpreted as a token gesture of Carter-era inclusiveness or a cynical attempt by network programmers to inject a badly needed shot of teen-tomboy sex appeal into a lineup of grizzled ground-pounders. But the motive didn't matter. A lot of the stunt guys thought she didn't deserve to be there: she was too young, she hadn't done enough. Evans made her counterargument by winning the car race, taking second in the motorcycle race (after spotting the field nearly a lap—in a four-lap race—when her engine failed at the start), and placing sixth in the horse race, to tie for second overall. A lot of coordinators took notice, and the offers—for car work especially, normally a closed shop, with the top jobs jealously guarded—started rolling in.

One person impressed by her work was Jeannie Epper, who persuaded Warner Brothers to hire Evans as Wonder Woman's stunt double for the show's motorcycle scenes. Evans calls Epper her "stunt mom," and right from the start Jeannie made her feel like family. (The family ties almost became legal: for years, Evans's sister Donna dated Jeannie's oldest son, Richard. And when the two broke up, Epper was frank. "You better rethink this," she told her son. "They don't make many like her. There's not going to be a Donna Evans on every corner. I prayed her into your life.") Invariably, Evans thanks Jeannie Epper in acceptance speeches—along with God, "for protecting me for all these years"—and she nodded in recognition when I mentioned Epper's concept of set etiquette. She found the advice helpful, especially Epper's take on the politics of the job. "There's a proper chain of command," Evans said, paraphrasing her mentor. "So when you have an idea, you don't just walk up to the director and say, 'Maybe we should do it this way.' You go up to your stunt coordinator. And you don't go up in front of a bunch of guys and yell out your idea. You go off to the side and talk to him quietly. And if he wants to take credit for that idea, fine." As for the moral aspect, Evans said, "Those were my morals anyway. But it's always good to know that you don't have to change who you are in order to get a job. I guess there were others—Jeannie probably told you—who were doing two jobs for the price of one."

In 1979, Evans married Lane Leavitt, a three-time U.S. national motorcycle champ in trials competition. In the early going, Evans tried juggling job and motherhood—her first child, Steven, was born in 1981—but she found herself canceling family vacations whenever a stunt coordinator called her with a job. So when she and Leavitt decided they wanted more kids—a son, Daniel, in 1993 and a daughter, Rebecca, in 1996—Evans tried semi-retirement. "When I had the second two, I thought, 'Well, maybe I shouldn't be doing this, because of what society says.' You know, how you shouldn't go risk your life," Evans said. "But I was miserable. I backed off and didn't take many jobs and I was grouchy. Then I started working again a little bit, and I felt so much better. Because I believe God gave me these gifts—physical agility and natural balance—and I feel more fulfilled when I'm using them. And I'm a happier mom when I come home. I shouldn't have to deny what God made me because I'm a mom." She settled on a happy medium: she wouldn't take any jobs that required her to be away for months at a stretch: no Prague jobs, no Tokyo. And she sets aside a few weeks for a real family vacation, and no fakeout "location vacations," either.

The norms of society don't seem to fit Evans very well. It's not that she'd strike you as outwardly unusual. She doesn't dress like a renegade, or live like a beatnik, or exhibit behaviors that would attract the attention of airport security. She looks like a mom. But not that many forty-something moms would rent out the Dodger Stadium parking lot and call in a couple of trick riders to learn everything they can teach her in a couple of days: tank stands, stoppies, burnouts, all manner of driving styles (sitting backward with her butt on the handlebars, lying down and steering with her feet), and something called skitching, where she jumps off the back of her motorcycle and skids along behind it on her feet.

"But what are you hanging on to?"

"I rigged a strap over the seat, and what I did was I got my hands in the strap and braced myself against—"

"And how do you steer?"

"You lean it."

Champion form on a dirt bike has come to be seen as the best measure of raw talent in a stunt driver. Evans, the top-ranked woman motorcyclist in the country when she got the call from *Deathsport*, made it all look easy, and people assumed, rightly, that she could handle just about anything on wheels. "Motorcycling goes right over to the car work, because you understand things like suspension, momentum, torque, gearing," she said. "If you know how to slide a motorcycle, you're not going to be afraid of what might happen when the wheels of your car start spinning." From the beginning of her career, stunt coordinators trusted Evans to do the most outrageous car stunts. In 1986, in *Never Too Young to Die*, a race-'em-up starring Vanity and John Stamos that went straight to video, she drove a low-slung Corvette underneath an eighteen-wheeler. She repeated the gag in a souped-up Honda Civic for *The Fast and the Furious*, in a sequence that won her her first Stunt Award, in 2001. She's still amazed by some of the stuff she gets to do on the streets of L.A. while policemen close down the streets and watch. "I just got to drive a Ferrari Enzo. And I did 360s, reverse 180s, sliding around a corner," she said, obviously excited. "You'd never do that if you *owned* a Ferrari Enzo. It's too expensive. But I don't have to pay the insurance. And I don't end up in jail." When I asked how she drove on the L.A. freeways coming back from work, she said that cruise control comes in very handy; left to her own instincts, she'd wind up going too fast. "Not too fast *for me*. Too fast for the speed limit."

She has made a few exceptions to her ban on location work,

most notably for *The Matrix Reloaded*, which she and her husband decided was too good to pass up. The first movie had been a whopping hit, so the sequel would have a huge budget, and the stunt coordinator wanted her to double the female star, Carrie-Anne Moss. But she wouldn't have much margin for error. Instead of a helmet and padded racing leathers, she'd be wearing a black catsuit and sunglasses in the motorcycle scene. And as soon as she got there, they took her to the hair trailer and said, "We're going to cut your hair."

"Uh-uh," she said. "Just use a wig."

But they kept insisting, so she went up the chain of command, to the stunt coordinator, R. A. Rondell, who'd worked with her before when she was doubling Angelina Jolie in *Gone in Sixty Seconds*. One of the reasons she didn't want to cut her hair, she explained, was personal: her kids were five and seven, and she didn't want to fly home on the weekend and scare them. ("What's happened to Mom?" she imagined them saying. "She's gone away and now she looks like this?") The other was practical: In a dangerous scene where she'd be driving without a helmet, the wig gave her a small measure of protection. Her own hair under the wig would serve as more padding, and then she had the stocking cap, too—if she ever did go down to the ground, the extra layers might save her hair and flesh. She got her way, and in the end the directors, Andy and Larry Wachowski, couldn't even tell the difference: when she drove by them on set suited up in her wig and sunglasses, they called her Carrie-Anne and complimented her on her driving.

The *Matrix* trilogy remains tremendously influential in the stunt business: The original was the first big Hollywood production to rely so heavily on Hong Kong wire work in its fight scenes, and it spawned a slew of wire-fu imitators and behind-the-scenes technical innovations, such as the computerized high-speed super winches used in *Spider-Man 2* and *3*. As the first movie to provide fight choreographers with months of paid rehearsal to train the actors and stunt doubles before the shoot, it kicked off the craze for preproduction stunt boot camps, a phenomenon that has led to markedly more complex fight sequences. It pioneered the use of CGI, even elevating one such effect into a sort of leitmotif, by reserving its bravura "bullet-time" camera setup (a super-slow-motion shot taken from the bullet's point of view) for scenes that test the hero's spiritual attainment.

For stunt drivers, the *Matrix* movies stood out for their ideal working conditions. On many productions, drivers show up on the day of the shoot and hastily throw a few tricks on city streets that are locked down for a matter of hours. On *The Matrix Reloaded*, the second installment in the trilogy, they got to drive on a two-mile freeway set built especially for them—they could work all day, and never have to worry about holding up actual traffic. The production provided a nearly unlimited number of cars, donated by GM after a series of Houston car dealerships got flooded in Tropical Storm Allison, in 2001. And the directors insisted on multiple takes—at full fee every time.

I visited Evans four years after the shoot, and she still knew her sequence of maneuvers on the freeway by heart. "Coming against traffic was intense," she said. "I had four lanes of traffic, and four cars making lane changes, and my last move was to split two oncoming semi-trucks. You had to get that pattern down, and we rehearsed it over and over." She talked me through it, darting her eyes and ducking her shoulders, leaning forward in the club chair in her living room as if she were still tucked over the gas tank of the Ducati. "I cut over here and a car makes a lane change, so I cut over there, and another car makes a lane change, and then I go alongside two cars and cut back in. And this car here is supposed to clear the lane, so I take the center of his lane. And then another car clears, and I take the center of his lane, and then I duck back and split the two oncoming semi-trucks." If that sounds complicated, imagine it at ninety-five miles per hour.

What made the sequence so frightening was that one false move from nearly anyone on the freeway could force Evans to change her line, leading to a collision somewhere farther down the road—exactly what happened in one of the run-throughs. "I might have been coming a little faster" than planned, she said tactfully. "I don't know. I don't blame the guy who hit me. What we do in stunts, sure, it's all calculated. But it's not a perfect science. There's risk involved, which is why the actors don't do it." But for whatever reason, one of the cars was slow to change lanes, and she barely missed hitting him head on. But since there was another car coming behind that one, she couldn't swerve too far into traffic to avoid the collision without driving smack into the car in back of it, and as she tried to steer between the two, the car she'd just passed sideswiped her. Her reflexes took over and she hit the brakes and wrenched her front wheel around to lay her bike down, sliding to a stop down the small passage between lanes. She was uncharacteristically fuzzy about the near-death experience. "Usually I remember everything," she said. "But that was a lot of pain, so I don't remember a thing." She had another stunt person (the double for the Keymaker, whom her character was trying desperately to deliver to safety) sitting on the bike behind her, riding blind and holding onto her as tightly as he could. Both of them had to go to the hospital—her first ambulance ride in twenty years of stunt driving—but the X-rays didn't pick up any broken bones. Back at the hotel that evening, she stuck her foot in a trash bucket filled with ice and held it there until she couldn't stand it any longer. She repeated the procedure five times and then felt ready to go back to work the next day.

But to Evans, the collision that actually happened wasn't as scary as the one that didn't. Early in the chase scene, when she and the Keymaker were still riding with the flow of traffic, she was supposed to cut over to the shoulder of the road and shoot the gap between the freeway wall and an eighteen-wheeler. According to plan, the driver of the truck spots her riding beside him and swerves, hitting his brakes and slamming his trailer against the wall in an attempt to crush her. The gag required precise timing: Evans was supposed to hit her brakes at the instant the truck driver did, so she could bring her motorcycle to a stop as the trailer hit the wall just in front of her. "We did four rehearsals where I rode behind him," she said. "I told him, 'Do exactly what you're going to do so I can time it out.' And I counted to four seconds every single time." But on the fifth try, when she got in between the truck and the wall, she heard the air-release sound of the truck's brakes starting early in her count and she had to slam on her brakes as hard as she could. The trailer hit the wall just inches from her front wheel.

"That was the only time in my whole career where I just stood there and started physically shaking," Evans said. "I felt like I was going to throw up. It was just so intense."

Evans didn't have to yell at the driver of the truck. Everybody else on the set did it for her. "The rest of the stunt crew, the guys, just went after him," she said. "They were not happy at all. I, of course, wasn't happy either. The guy's done really good work other times. Communication is just really important. You have to let people know what's going to happen—you can't just change something. Especially on me—I'm on a motorcycle, with no helmet. Not that a helmet would have helped in that situation. There's no protection. I felt very fortunate to get out of that one."

She didn't mention the driver's name—no one ever mentioned the other driver in their near-death stories. And I heard a lot of them; you couldn't work at the top levels of the stunt industry without logging a few near-misses. Often, these stories hinged upon a slight miscalculation or blameless mechanical glitch. But since top stunt drivers operate with the smallest of margins—stopping inches from a mark, coming into an intersection, blind, through an opening that would be there for less than a second—these glitches and miscalculations could easily have fatal consequences.

But the stunt world is very small. I was sitting on a bus in Port Authority on the set of *The Bourne Ultimatum*, talking to a stunt driver, Kevin Scott, killing time as we waited for the cameras to roll. Scott specializes in big vehicles—he was driving the semi that Evans drove under in her Civic on *The Fast and the Furious*. He'd also worked on *The Matrix Reloaded*, and spoke of the experience in utopian terms. But when I mentioned Evans, he shook his head immediately. "I had a close call with Debbie one day," he said. "I missed her by maybe a foot, sliding the semi into the wall."

"That was you driving?"

"And I squeezed her. Yeah, that was a good one. We hugged each other after that."

I recounted the chain of events as Evans had explained it to me—how on the fifth run-through, she'd heard the air brakes starting early. But without my notes I mixed up her two calamities and thought that she'd laid down her bike to avoid the crash. Scott corrected me. "No, she stayed up. But it was literally like—" He spread his thumb and index finger a few inches apart. "Air brakes, as you know, they're unreliable. But they also have a tendency to change how they grab. And this one time it grabbed twice as hard as the other times, and the trailer just locked up and sent me right into the wall."

"So what you did that time wasn't any different from what you'd done before?"

"That's just how air works," he said.

The chase belonged on any shortlist of greatest extended stunt sequences, along with Yakima Canutt's chariot race in *Ben-Hur* and the chase scenes in *The French Connection* and *The Bourne Supremacy*. And I told her so. "When I see the things I've done," she said, "I usually look at them and think, 'Oh, that stunk.' And the second time, I might go, 'That wasn't so bad.' And then the third time, I'll go, 'That was pretty good.' Because I'm real hard on myself. But this time, when I was in the theater and I watched this thing? I was like, 'Yes! Wow! That was awesome!'"

Before I left, Evans gave me a tour of the stunt barn where she had a small gallery of film stills and snapshots: Evans working out with Arnold Schwarzenegger on the set of *Kindergarten Cop*; doing her first turnover on *CHiPs*; doing her "headstand thing" on a bike seat; doing a bike jump when she was pregnant with Rebecca ("I actually set it up so it wouldn't be a hard impact or anything, because if you set it up lower and longer, it sets you down real nice"); riding over a VW bug for *The Jerk*; in blackface, doubling Whoopi Goldberg ("They had to get special permission from the NAACP for that"); doubling Lindsay Lohan in *Herbie*; flipping upside down at fifty miles an hour, in a Porsche 911, breaking a light in the top of the Broadway tunnel in San Francisco for *What Dreams May Come*.

As she walked me to my car, past the patch of dirt where her kids played with their motorcycles and Quadrunners, it was impossible to miss her look of longing. I said, "You must come out here from time to time."

"We have fun," she said. "But Mom has more responsibilities. I've got to get stuff done around the house. I don't get to play all the time anymore."

I reminded her that playing was a big part of her job description.

"Funny you say that. When I got to a certain age, my mom and dad said, 'Okay, Debbie, you don't go out and play football with the boys anymore. You have to be more ladylike. You can't go out and do those kinds of things.' So I had to stop jumping off fences or swinging a sword."

When was that?

"Well, I remember the football thing happening when I was about thirteen. And I was just like, 'Oh man.' So anyway, I get on this show, and I'm nineteen years old, and I'm riding these motorcycles, I'm having a great time. And then they hand me a *sword*. And they say, 'We want you to run around and jump off that and swing the sword.'" She jumped up in the air swinging. It wasn't the formal jump of a stunt professional: it was the "en-garde!" jump of an eight-year-old brandishing a stick. "And I looked at them and I said, 'You're going to pay me to play?'"

Talking with Quentin Tarantino—between takes on the set of *Death Proof*, as he slugged down a "big-ass cup" of coffee—is a little like double Dutch: he can't slow down, you have to jump in. "*You're* the guy," he said, when I told him I was here to watch Zoe

Bell riding on the hood of a 1970 Dodge Challenger in the movie's big chase. And then he launched, mostly unprompted, into a lightning tour of the Tarantino Mental Archive of Badass Stunt Work. "I'm a big fan of the whole history of stunts, going back to Yakima Canutt and Dave Sharpe. And I'm also a big fan of the director William Witney, who used to work with them at Republic Pictures."

I made some noises.

"I'll tell you one of my favorite stunts of all time. *Chapter Four: Zorro's Fighting Legion*, directed by William Witney. And that gag that John Ford did in *Stagecoach*, where Yakima Canutt goes under the stagecoach and comes up again? Wild Bill Witney did it the year before and it's even better in *Zorro's Fighting Legion*."

More noises.

"Yak fucked himself up big time doing that on *The Lone Ranger*. He was positive his legs were cut off."

Tarantino likes to talk at close range, although you could hear him fine from fifty paces, and he bobs his head and works his chin and laughs unexpectedly and fast, like a tommy gun. His talk sets a stiff pace, but even if you could turn the sound off, his nervous movements would keep up the same dizzying kung-fu-fight rhythm. The experience is not unpleasant: a verbal bear hug. He's a big guy, six-one, two-fifty, with cartoonishly large features, big wide eyes, a beak nose, a jutting bad-guy jaw, and he favors slovenly hip XXL ensembles—today, in the cool mountains above Santa Barbara, he's got on jeans, Pumas, and a black-and-white-striped hoodie. He's physically impulsive and seemingly uninhibited: he can and will pick up female stars and whirl them around, out of an overflow of moviemaking joy. But through it all, behind his Nietzschean bonhomie, he mixes in little intimate movements, momentary hesitations and likable artifacts of shyness. The reaction he seems to be going for is both "Fuckin' A!" and "Awwww."

Tarantino finished the *Death Proof* script on Valentine's Day, 2006, and went straight over to Bell's apartment in Venice, California. Bell was aware that he was writing her into the movie, but she'd thought she'd be an extra, somebody who sidled up to the bar with a beer and said, "Cheers, mate!" Instead, he made her a star—the primary vehicle of his chick revenge fantasy. He never allowed her to doubt whether she could pull off the acting. "It's like you have no fucking choice," Bell told a New Zealand TV news show. "He's not telling you, 'You can't fuck it up.' He's telling me, 'You won't, because you're my decision and I'm brilliant. I don't make bad decisions.' You have Quentin Tarantino saying that to you in your living room with a script that has your name on the cover? 'I wrote this script for you.' Oh fuck—really?"

To prepare for her acting debut, Bell met with her costars and ran lines on the beach or over drinks; by the time she had to appear before the camera she had the sassy Tarantino dialogue cold. But during her action scenes, she found herself returning to her stunt-double instincts, reflexively averting her face from the camera so the editors could use the shot. Tarantino had to coach her. "Don't *look* at the cameras," he said. "But don't hide your face so much either." Her natural reaction the first time she caught a camera tracking her so closely in the middle of a stunt, she said, "was like, 'Get the fuck out the way.'"

Like Bergman or Balanchine, Tarantino fleshes out his female characters with worshipful details modeled on his latest real-life muse and artistic collaborator. With Bergman and Balanchine, these relationships were often more than platonic, and Tarantino has been dogged by similar rumors. Bell understands how the notion that she might be "shagging Quentin" got started—she pinpoints a moment on the red carpet in Cannes when the two were hugging and mugging for photographers and Tarantino slipped his hand under the fabric of her backless gown. Both have issued denials. She says, Yeah, the two of us are tight, but not that tight. He says, Zoe is like a sister. She credits him for drastically altering the course of her life on two occasions—hiring her for *Kill Bill* just when she was heading up to Canada for a utility stunts gig, and then, a few years later, turning a stuntwoman into a movie actress important enough to photograph on the red carpet. And Tarantino has enjoyed his role in the transformation, she says. "I think he takes a certain amount of pride in that: 'Yup, I was the one who got that bitch in a dress.'"

In a sense, the rumors about the director and his protégée are accurate but misplaced: *Death Proof* is a love letter not to Bell but to stunts in general. His films have always been cleverly referential postmodern celebrations of B-movie schlock, full of in-jokes, homages, and drive-in-movie cinephilia. But this time he takes a direct approach, celebrating the whole B-movie world by setting much of *Death Proof* among the industry's unsung working class; there are fewer jokes about movies and more on-set trivia and in-jokes about life in the movie industry. "I got into the business the way everybody does," the movie's designated psychopath, Stunt-man Mike, says. "Through my brother Stuntman Bob." The hero-ines of the movie's second half are crew members on location, a hairdresser, a pair of stunt doubles, and an ingenue still in her cheerleader costume from the night before. When they stop for breakfast, one of the stuntwomen, played by Tracie Thoms, men-tions working on an earlier movie—*Three Kicks to the Head, Part 3*. The license plate of her car, a vintage Mustang, says BRAND X, the name of the stunt group that Jeff Dashnaw, the movie's stunt coordinator, belongs to.

Tarantino intended *Death Proof* to be his response to the classic car-chase movies of the seventies, like *Convoy*, *Dixie Dynamite*, *Vanishing Point*, and *Dirty Mary, Crazy Larry*. Tarantino has al-ways insisted on the artistry of action scenes. (For inspiration, he hosted screenings of classic movies on location for the cast and crew.) And unlike most directors, he refuses to subcontract the ac-tion to a second-unit director. "I'm not down with the whole 'sec-ond unit directors doing all the action' thing," he told me. "If I directed a James Bond movie and somebody said, 'Hey, great movie,' it's like, 'Well, I hope you like all the exposition scenes, be-cause that's all the fuck I did.' That's what these action movies look

like. It doesn't look like the guy who's directing the movie did any
of the action, which doesn't make any sense. If I was going to
direct a *porno* film, I'm not going to let *you* do the fuck scenes." (I
believe he meant that he wouldn't let me *direct* them.) "*I* want to
do them. This is a fucking action movie, I want to do the action.
That's the whole reason I'm fucking doing it. And I want to come
up with different ways to do it. And so it's like there's no second
unit on this film. Me and the stunt guys, we come up with the gags
together."

Nearly all of the climactic chase scene was filmed on a two-lane
road that twisted through Santa Barbara ranchland up to Los
Padres National Forest—dry California horse country standing in
for the movie's purported setting of Lebanon, Tennessee. (This
egregious mismatch of landscape is in itself a winking homage to
bad movies.) The road is not entirely featureless—parts of the
chase pass Michael Jackson's Neverland Ranch and a couple of
progressive schools, including a boarding school where the kids
have farm chores mixed in with their homework. The ringing of a
bell, to call students to and from the fields, punctuated the filming.

I'd just jumped down from a work truck—it was carrying a Zoe
Bell dummy in black jeans and a tight pink T-shirt—when Bell
herself appeared in an identical getup, piling out of a car with six
others on a pee break. The women of the film looked comfortable
together, joking around offscreen with the same warmth and acer-
bity that Tarantino had written into the script. Her costar Rosario
Dawson claimed that she taught Zoe everything she knows, and
Bell smiled, picked up one of the water bottles that a production
assistant had brought over, and spun it, casually, like a hotshot
gunslinger with a six-shooter.

Early in their half of the movie, Bell the character persuades the
others to help her pull off an infamously dangerous gag called the
Ship's Mast: she wants to climb out the window of a Dodge Challenger and ride on the hood—the "bonnet" in Kiwi—hanging on by
means of two leather belts buckled to the car's doorframes. In the
movie, it looks as if the two belts are her only means of support,

and when Kurt Russell as Stuntman Mike (or Buddy Jo Hooker, as Russell's stunt-driving double) slams the girls' car from behind, Bell loses hold of first one belt, then the other, sliding around on the hood and grabbing wildly for anything she can hang onto, the bumper, the top ridge of the hood up near the windshield, the cool shark-nose engine vents cut into the Challenger's hood.

The gag (which Tarantino invented for the movie) has inspired a slew of copycat videos on YouTube, in which feisty real-life chicks in T-shirts bump along spread-eagled on a hood, hanging onto ropes or wires, arching and squirming flirtatiously for the videocam. Some dudes have tried it, too, usually (for some reason) in hoodies; their reenactments make up for the missing B-movie sexploitation element by going for a purer form of idiocy. Certain shots that never appeared in the movie have already become standard in the home-vid versions, and the additions greatly increase the feeling of mortal danger, especially the now canonical handheld shot, taken from the driver's point of view, where the camera pans from the friend flailing around on the hood, down past the steering wheel, to the speedometer, which we see inching over sixty. In one version, we hear the cameraman complaining off camera about how hard it is to keep everything in focus and still drive.

But the home-vid versions of the Ship's Mast are trying to re-create the gag as it appears on film and not as it was performed on set. When Bell came back from the bathroom, a stunt rigger came over to help her with the harness she wore underneath her black jeans. "Wicked!" Bell said. "I've got time to uncage my cooch!" She dropped her black jeans to get at the harness, a rig of straps and buckles that she referred to as her "crotchless nappy." Beneath the nappy, she wore a pair of gray form-fitting briefs, more Under Armour than underwear, whose appearance in plain sight caused somebody nearby to hoot. Bell reached down and grabbed a handful of one of her cheeks, universal sign language for "Kiss my ass." When she pulled her pants back up a few minutes later, her harness had been carefully cinched and all the buckles and wires checked over for wear. As she walked over to the Challenger to drive back to the shoot, a steel cable trailed behind her like a bridal train.

The cable connected to her harness allowed Bell to be hooked to the hood of the Challenger the way that a mountain climber is tethered to a rockface. The cable, made of flexible steel and covered with plastic sheathing to reduce friction, was threaded through a small hole in the hood, and snaked underneath the car, then back up through the floorboards to a winch bolted into the car's backseat. Before every shot, a stunt rigger adjusted the amount of play in the cable, depending on whether Bell was supposed to be clinging onto the car's front bumper or sliding around up near the windshield. The cable was incessantly checked for wear and frequently replaced. "You think you've got it safe," the coordinator, Jeff Dashnaw, said. "Then you go home at night and you don't sleep."

Casting a stuntwoman allowed Tarantino to film the chase with much more immediacy: he could show Bell's face or keep the camera close or hold a shot so that even when she turned her back to the audience you knew it was always her. This realism went with the seventies aesthetic he was looking for. But the chases of that era were often shot from the sidewalks as the cars whizzed by, and Tarantino wanted to shoot the *Death Proof* sequence so that the audience would feel as if it were inside the chase, an innovation he credited to *Mad Max* and other Australian movies from the late seventies and early eighties. To do so, he filmed it from a moving vehicle: a custom-made Cadillac Eldorado camera car equipped with a technocrane that could swoop over and around the two vehicles as they raced down the road. And he wanted to do the whole movie without ever using computer-generated imagery. "Everyone knows how much I hate that stuff, so we just tried to figure out how we could do it without using any CGI at all," he boasted to a reporter before *Death Proof* opened in England. "And we did. We pulled off some really gnarly shit. And it was all on the day, in camera."

Tarantino is fibbing. Much of the terror you feel watching Bell's stunt work in the Ship's Mast scene depends on a type of CGI. True, he never *added* any imagery using the computer, but throughout the scene he had all traces of that steel cable that kept Bell safely anchored to the hood *digitally erased*—an option that wasn't available to filmmakers back in the seventies, or, apparently, to the makers of the YouTube videos.

But even with the cable, the danger to Bell in the scene was real. Unlike the amateurs in the copycat videos, she was hooked to a car that was being continually spun out or rammed from behind or sideswiped—if her car blew a tire or slid off the road into a rollover, she was toast, a genuine risk that a normal actress (that is, one with no stunt experience) would never be allowed to take. And Tarantino could mount a camera inside the car so that audiences could see what she was feeling while this happened. "If I'm doing another action movie," Tarantino told me, "it would be almost foolhardy not to put Zoe in it, because you get so much."

I'd first met Bell the previous spring, in Venice, California, months before the shoot. It wasn't a happy time. Tarantino had promised her the part a few weeks before, but the movie was still just a script and a start date that kept getting put off. She'd been injured, badly, on *Kill Bill: Vol. 2*, and although she'd recovered and gotten a big part, doubling Sharon Stone on *Catwoman*, she'd been having trouble getting work. "People are like, 'Oh, you've won awards. You should be getting hired.' And I'm like, 'First of all, I'm not an actress. Producers are not going to give a shit if I've won awards. They're not going to be like, Latest movie starring—not even starring, *involving*—award-winning stuntwoman. No one gives a shit.' "

In the *Kill Bill* scene where she got hurt, the Bride busts into a mobile home, only to be hit by a shotgun blast to the chest. It was set up so that she'd fly back on cue, hooked to a ratchet that would whip her through the air. But in one of the rehearsals, the landing pads were rearranged and the pressure on the ratchet increased at the last minute, and Bell flew through the air, far past the end of the mat she was supposed to land on, right into her stunt coordinator. "As soon as they hit the button I knew I had too much guts," she said. "I knew I was going to clear the mat, so I kind of balled up, preparing for impact as best I could, flying at a hundred miles an

The original twenty members (minus one, who was working that day) of Stunts Unlimited, on the Hansen Dam, Lake View Terrace, California, 1970. Ronnie Rondell is seated front row left, in the silver fire suit.
(COURTESY RONNIE RONDELL)

Companion photos of Ronnie Rondell on the set of *Shenandoah*. Above, he practices the gag for the cameraman, jumping over the cannon from a minitrampoline. Below, as filmed, the jump is timed to a special-effects explosion. The effect was so convincing that an actor on set, a friend of Rondell's, ran into the frame to save him. (COURTESY RONNIE RONDELL)

Terry Leonard performs two versions of the most dangerous stunt ever filmed: above, in *The Legend of the Lone Ranger*, and below, prepping the same gag under a truck, for *Raiders of the Lost Ark*. (ABOVE: COLLECTION OF TERRY LEONARD; BELOW: COURTESY LUCASFILM)

In the seventies, championship form on the motorcycle replaced horsemanship as the prerequisite skill for the working stunt performer. Above, Debbie Evans, as a teenager, rides her Yamaha bike on Mont Blanc. Below, she doubles Jamie Lee Curtis on a commercial shoot.

Evans drives a Honda Civic under a tractor-trailer in *The Fast and the Furious.*
(COURTESY UNIVERSAL STUDIOS)

Evans doubles Carrie-Anne Moss in the freeway chase scene in *The Matrix Reloaded.*
When a stuntman told her he thought the sequence was computer generated, Evans said,
"Well, there were four lanes of cars making lane changes, and one of them hit me,
and that was not a CGI car." (COURTESY WARNER BROS)

The Louisiana stuntman and gator wrangler Jeff Galpin watches over his charges for a *Sports Illustrated* photo shoot. (COURTESY JEFF GALPIN)

Mike Kirton executes a textbook full burn. (COURTESY MIKE KIRTON)

Mike Kirton on the set of the Italian miniseries *Extralarge*.
(COURTESY MIKE KIRTON)

In low-budget pictures, Kirton honed his expertise in getting big
effects, like this limo explosion, done fast and cheap. (COURTESY MIKE KIRTON)

Jeannie Epper, seen here in a stair fall in her mid-sixties, remains a top-tier stuntwoman. (COURTESY JEANNIE EPPER)

Epper, who originally dreaded high falls, jumps two and a half stories from a plane toward an air bag on the tarmac. (COURTESY JEANNIE EPPER)

Epper, the most illustrious member of a family with twelve stunt performers, holds up Lynda Carter, whom she doubled in the *Wonder Woman* TV series. (COURTESY JEANNIE EPPER)

Tim Rigby, a former British commando, BASE jumps from the world's highest waterfall, Angel Falls, Venezuela.
(PHOTO BY JEB CORLISS)

Rigby, performing what he has described as the most frightening stunt of his life, BASE jumps from the back-seat of a Corvette convertible as it plunges off a California bridge for *xXx*. (COURTESY COLUMBIA PICTURES)

Rigby, in a typical role for a stuntman, dresses as an Atlanta policeman for *The Dukes of Hazzard*. (PHOTO BY CRAIG CAMERON OLSEN)

New Zealand import Zoe Bell rides on the "bonnet" of a 1970 Dodge Challenger for *Death Proof*, in which she plays the character Zoe Bell, stuntwoman. (COLLECTION OF ZOE BELL)

Bell relaxes with Uma Thurman during a break on *Kill Bill*. (COURTESY MIRAMAX FILMS)

Bell got her start doubling Lucy Lawless in *Xena: Warrior Princess.*
(COURTESY PACIFIC RENAISSANCE PICTURES)

Bell, Quentin Tarantino, and Jeannie Epper on the set of *Death Proof.* "If I'm doing another action movie," Tarantino says, "it would be almost foolhardy not to put Zoe in it, because you get so much."
(COLLECTION OF ZOE BELL)

Sean Graham, who frequently doubles Mark Wahlberg, at 155 pounds when the actor lost weight for *Rock Star.* (COLLECTION OF SEAN GRAHAM)

Graham and Wahlberg, both pushing two hundred pounds, on *Four Brothers.* (COLLECTION OF SEAN GRAHAM)

Darrin Prescott (far right) flies through the air on the set of *Bedazzled*. (courtesy stuntgirl.com)

Prescott, stunt coordinator and cofounder of Go Stunts, relaxes with his son Tanner before a race at the annual stuntman gathering A Day in the Dirt. The event, which boasts a slate of more than fifteen races, is widely known in the trade as A Day to Get Hurt. (collection of darrin prescott)

Dan Bradley directs Matt Damon in an action scene. "I tell anybody who'll listen that Bradley's an A–list director," Damon says. "I would do a movie with him in a second." (COURTESY UNIVERSAL STUDIOS)

An NYPD cruiser rigged on a traffic barrier for the climax of the New York City chase scene in *The Bourne Ultimatum*. (COURTESY UNIVERSAL STUDIOS)

hour about to hit the desert floor, which, you know, is like cement with rocks in it. Your brain works so quickly. I was ready: Three . . . Two . . . One . . . And they hit the thing, and all I can remember thinking is like, 'Ah shit, keep my teeth tight and chin to chest, and just ball up.' Also, 'This is going to hurt my head.' Because it doesn't matter how tight you are, when you're traveling that fast, it's really hard to not have your head whip back and hit the ground. So anyway, I hit the ground, and I'm sort of dazed and incredibly winded. I couldn't breathe. And of course everyone's worried, so they all crowd around you. And I'm like, 'Get. The. Fuck. Away. Can't. Breathe.' I know you're caring about me, but you're not helping. Then once I got my breath back, they're like, 'You all right?' And I'm like, 'Yup, but there's something very wrong with my wrist.' "

Bell has a reputation for being impervious to pain, so it confused people when she asked to go to the hospital when there was no swelling or blood, nothing visibly wrong at all. But X-rays confirmed her suspicions: she'd dislocated her wrist and completely torn the ligament. She needed surgery to have pins inserted and she had to stay in a cast for three months with her wrist immobilized. When the cast came off, she could barely move, let alone work on stunts—it took her three months to be able to grip a steering wheel. The change hit her hard: she couldn't surf, swim, do gymnastics or martial arts. She missed walking on her hands, which she'd been able to do since she was five. "It's infuriating not to be working," she said. "Not only am I bored, I suffer from a serious lack of purpose. My whole identity gets thrown into question. If I'm not Zoe the stuntwoman, who the fuck am I?"

Stuntwomen have their own associations (largely because the big male groups continue to admit only men). One reason they exist at all is to help people through a lull like that, by directing her to easier work. But Bell wasn't the joining type. "I come from a country where the fraternity-sorority culture is nonexistent," she said, as she sat sprawled on the floor of her apartment, legs akimbo in a

hurdler's stretch. There were DVDs on the floor—*Vanishing Point,
Silver Streak, Boys Don't Cry*—her film education, she called it.
"And I don't know what it is, but my whole life I feel safer when I
operate as a single unit. I don't feel safe just lumping myself in with
a bunch of women I don't know. And those women aren't necessarily going to hire me. So why? So their husbands will hire me?
Also, diplomacy is not one of my hugest strong points, so I find it's
just easier to avoid situations where I'll have to use it."

In person, it's hard to separate her openness in conversation
from her fearlessness moving around: she can throw in a leg kick
or a casual pratfall or rip off a few beats of Cabbage Patch dance,
and it comes off naturally, as much a part of her as her accent. Bell
grew up on Waiheke Island, ten miles off Auckland in the Hauraki
Gulf, and then moved to a commune on the mainland: she passed
much of childhood "pretty naked." Her parents' brand of atten-
tive permissiveness played a huge part in developing Bell's independence and her faith in herself. "When Zoe was about three and
a half," her mother told me, "we were driving in the car and she
wanted to go home, and I had somewhere to go. And she created a
big fuss. So I stopped the car and said, 'All right, Zo, you walk
home.' And she walked home. I drove the car slowly behind her,
unbeknownst to her. And she walked all the way home, several
kilometers. And every so often, I stopped and said, 'Okay, Zo, you
can get in the car now.' 'No,' she said. 'I'm doing it my way.'"

Despite growing up eighteen time zones east of Hollywood,
Bell seemed destined for stunt work, almost from the beginning.
Her parents take no credit for this, beyond buying her a trampoline early on and taking her to gymnastics meets. But by the time
she was fifteen, Bell had made it to New Zealand's national gym-
nastic squad. And at the gym where she worked out she kept
running into a forty-something stuntman named Pete Bell (no rela-
tion). While she'd be practicing flips and trying to land on her feet,
he'd be doing the same thing, trying to land on his back. They
got to know each other, partly because her trainer would call
her over to demonstrate moves. "Zoe," he'd say, "can I use you to

show him something? Could you do it right? And then do it wrong?"

When she quit gymnastics and started taking tae kwon do, the black belts kept talking about a stunt coordinator who was hiring a lot of them for two New Zealand TV shows, *Hercules* and *Xena*. It was Pete Bell again. At times it seemed as if the business was pursuing *her*; one day she ended up watching a morning TV show she hated because she was sick and felt too shitty to get up and change the channel. "Next up," the announcer said, "stunt-man Stuart Thorp!" The host asked Thorp what you need to be a stunt person, and Bell found herself paying attention to the answer. The requirements, he said, were different for men and women but the stuntwoman needed training in gymnastics ("Check," she thought) and martial arts ("Check"), and a great attitude really helps ("We can work on that").

By this point, the Bells had moved off Waiheke and back to Auckland, where her father, Dr. Andrew Bell, worked in the emergency unit of a hospital. One day a patient showed up with a big bump on his head. Her father, following standard practice, asked the fellow how he got it. A fight, he said; he was a stuntman. "Oh, really?" Andrew said. "Here's your Panadol. Tell me about this stunt thing, because my daughter's been talking about it." He came home with Pete Bell's phone number and urged Zoe to give him a call. "So it popped up in a bunch of different places in my life," Zoe said. "It was like, 'Ah shit, Give it a go, because it sounds like a dream job and if I get it, fantastic. And if I don't, I'm no worse off than I am right now anyway.'"

After she finally called Bell, she sent off a handwritten résumé and a few snapshots left over from a gymnastics tournament. And Pete Bell, who was running the stunts for *Xena: Warrior Princess*, called back to invite her to a tryout for *Amazon High*, a pilot for a show about a cheerleader who goes back in time and fights alongside the Amazons in her cheerleader outfit and pink Converse sneakers. "I think it was right before a national holiday or a school holiday," she remembered. "So basically I'd got a lift up there, and my friends were going to meet me there and we were going to leave straight from there to go camping. So I did this audition thingy and at the end Pete sat us all down and said, 'Hey, ladies, either I or my assistant will be calling you in the next couple days. I want you to know you all did an amazing job, so if you don't get the part it doesn't mean anything about *you*. There's always more opportunities.' Blah blah blah, giving us the whole speech. And right before he started talking I saw my mates pull up in the driveway and they've got a chilly bin of beers in the back of the car, and I'm like, 'Fuck, I want to go camping, the sun's out!' " When she told me this story, we were sitting at a café down the block from her apartment and Bell rocked back on her metal chair and clapped her hands. Her excitement—over the prospect of a camping trip she'd taken ten years ago—was infectious. "So afterwards, I'm like, 'Pete I'm going to be away for a week. Should I just call you when I get back? Or will you just leave a message?' And he's like, 'Yeah, just give me a call when you get back. But don't let it ruin your holiday, don't fret about it.' I'm like, 'I think I can manage that.' I'm looking at the fuckin' chilly bin full of beers, like, 'I think I'll be fine.' So anyway I get in the car. And I'm like, '*Yeah!* How's it going, guys? Yeah!' And I remember cracking a beer and there was a knock on the passenger window, and it's Pete, and I'm like"—Bell does an extended double take, looking at the beer in her hand and back out at Pete—" 'Hi, Pete!' And he said, 'Listen, I didn't want this to ruin your holiday. I didn't want it to worry you. I just wanted to let you know you got the job.' And I was like, 'Cool! Thanks, man. That's choice!' He was like, 'Cool, just give us a call when you get back.' And I'm like, 'Sweet!' I roll up the window and we pull out. And I'm like, 'Fuck! I got the job!' And they're like, 'What's the job?' And I'm like, '*I have no idea.*' "

After the pilot was made (it was never released, although sections of it were later included in a highly confusing episode of *Xena*), Zoe began to pick up work on the *Xena* series, whenever they needed an extra villager or an Amazon or a Grecian woman to get into a fight in the baths. She went to the season-ending wrap party after she'd been on the books for about six months. A rumor was circulating that Lucy Lawless's regular stunt double, Geraldine Jacobsen, who'd been there since the series began, was leaving the show, but Zoe, who was nineteen at the time, said at that point her ambitions went no further than the free wine at the party. In the middle of the festivities, Pete Bell approached her. "So, as you've heard," he said, "Geri's leaving."

"I know, mate. Fuck!" Zoe said, wine in hand. "What are you going to do?"

"Not quite the response I was after," he said. "Anyway, the lads and I have been talking and your name has come up. And we've come to the conclusion that it might be worth it to give you a shot." When this, too, stirred little response from her, he tried phrasing it as directly as possible. "How would you like to be Xena?"

That sobered her up. She took the part: at the time, Xena was almost certainly the most stunt-intensive female role on earth. Bell has jokingly called Lucy Lawless, who played Xena when the script required speech, her "acting double." Bell did everything else: falls, wire work, air rams, all manner of fights. In one episode, when Xena traveled through time to the present, Bell even took a car hit, slamming into the windshield of an oncoming Ford in her leather action skirt and black battle bustier. In many ways, Bell's hard-knock experience on *Xena* was very similar to Epper's on *Wonder Woman*: the safety standards and technical expertise in New Zealand in the nineties were comparable to those which Epper encountered in the L.A. stunt industry in the seventies. Bell got hurt on several occasions—she particularly remembers snapping her back in the middle of a wire gag, when the cable she was hooked to turned out to be shorter than expected. And she often wound up the guinea pig for the stunt crew's experimental approach. They'd look at American movies and start brainstorming: "How do you reckon they did that? Let's give it a go."

At five foot eight, Bell is two inches shorter than Lawless (and four inches shorter than Uma Thurman). But doubling an actress is in itself a form of acting, and Bell not only handled the complex action choreography with authority, but she did so while quietly adopting Xena's distinct style of movement. Lawless played her portion of the action scenes with a smirk that let audiences in on the joke, which Bell amplified in broadly comic, biff-bam-pow fight scenes. Thurman brought another style of movement to *Kill Bill*, which again Bell made her own. The scenes of high-speed hand-to-hand combat were meant to be blindingly brutal, but others played in a more lyrical register, like the final confrontation in *Vol. 1*, a fight to the death between the Bride and O-Ren Ishii (played by Lucy Liu and her stunt double, Ming Liu) in a Shinto garden as the snow (actually big gobs of soapy foam) fell quietly around them. You can ascribe the quality of Bell's movement to other sources—to Tarantino's direction or Woo-ping Yuen's fight choreography—but it was Bell who performed the bursts of spiraling swordwork with the right note of wounded desperation. It's widely supposed that the reason there's no Academy Award for stunt people is that actors are conspiring to perpetuate the illusion that they do their own stunts. What's even harder for movie stars to acknowledge is that, at crucial moments in a film, stunt people convey a potent emotional message that actors are entirely unequipped to deliver.

The separation between actors and stunt people is so strictly enforced that when Bell was cast in *Death Proof*, the underwriters who reviewed the script to ensure the production costs tried to force Tarantino to hire somebody to double her. But Bell was adamant that she not only wanted to do her own stunts, but she wanted to do all the insert work, too—when the camera needed a shot of her hand or her leg, the sort of posing that a star would often pass on to a stuntwoman or stand-in. Having a stunt double, she said, "defeats the whole purpose. Just because I'm a 'star'! It implies that I don't love being a stuntwoman and that I actually want to be an actress, and that's not really the case. One of the things that Quentin was so excited about was the stunt at the end. He described it in detail, and I was like, 'Ah! Ah! Omigod. Really?' That was the highlight. At that point I forgot that I even had dialogue. I was like, 'Sweet, dude. Car stuff! That'd be a buzz.' "

Tarantino runs a fun set. He has his quirks—cell phones infuriate him—but he backs up his anti-highbrow film aesthetic by creating a partylike, communitarian workplace. A set decorator had loaded an iPod with Tarantino-style music (Joe Tex, O.V. Wright, Magnetic Fields, and so on), which played constantly in the background. Tarantino playacted between scenes, amplifying a stray comment by quoting huge chunks of classic movie scenes verbatim or just riffing, to the guys in the camera car, while everyone drove over to the starting point of the next take. ("Shit! You assholes better push one out!" he said, mocking his own authority. Then, under his breath, "These assholes know their shit!") Stand-ins and stars joked with each other. Bell stood around catching up with a childhood friend, from back in the commune days, who'd come to visit her on the set.

But despite the good vibes and camaraderie, Tarantino still tore through a tremendous number of setups in a day's work. He started at a little after sunrise with the cars going full speed down the road, and by midmorning he had moved to a series of side-by-side racing shots, with the cars pulling nose-to-nose, then inching ahead one after the other.

"Do you know what you're doing now?" Tarantino yelled out before he called for action, trying to get in one final check on the drivers—Buddy Jo Hooker and Tracy Dashnaw, Tracie Thoms's driving double and the wife of the stunt coordinator, Jeff Dashnaw.

"We're just playing it by ear," Hooker yelled back.

"A stuntman's last words!"

They tried another shot that they had diagrammed in the dirt on the side of the road: Hooker, coming so hard in hot pursuit that he causes Dashnaw, driving the Challenger with Zoe on the hood, to spin out off the side of the road. They wanted to time the gag so that Dashnaw would slide onto a big dirt turnoff that led to a ranch. She could use the dirt there to do a nice, loose 360 and then she'd peel off back onto the road, kicking up a roostertail of dust with a screech of her tires. The dirt made the spin both more visually dramatic—it rose up in plumes when they slid around—and considerably safer. To pull off the same thing on pavement, Dashnaw would have to carry a lot more speed, increasing the risk of a rollover and making the gag much more dangerous for Zoe. "I've been on the bonnet for about three weeks now, doing all sorts of different shit," Bell told me. "But this one is definitely a moment where we're asking the cars to lose control temporarily. That requires us to be pretty serious about it. Stunts come first over acting at this point."

They tried it out, at three-quarter speed, without Hooker. Jeff Dashnaw had such confidence in his wife's ability that during one run-through he stood on the dirt waving as Tracy sped right by, missing him by a couple of feet. A few minutes later, they ran it again, with the cameras rolling and Hooker tapping them from behind to initiate the spin. Bell slid across the hood abruptly, and her arm shot out to hold onto the grille or bumper. She kept her head up, as a terrified person would (and a stunt double might not), looking for anything to grab onto. When the spin was over and the Challenger sped away, all the cast and crew who'd gathered on the ranch fences and up the nearby hill applauded.

Dashnaw drove back to the turnoff and stopped the car, and Bell unhooked herself from the hood and came over to see the playback. She seemed excited about the shot and getting the hang of playing to the cameras, and as she walked over to Tarantino she said, "Could you tell I wasn't a dummy?"

"Don't you mean, 'Could you tell I was a human being?'"

Bell reached out and gave him a titty twister.

"You do the best titty twister in the world," he said.

She was on the hood for the last gag of the day, too, in which the two cars come to a bend in the road and Russell/Hooker pushes the Challenger right into the guardrail. They continue at full speed just like that—Bell on the hood with the car sandwiched between the steel guardrail and Stuntman Mike's 1969 Dodge Charger—for about eighty feet. The camera setup was taking a long time—there was some debate about whether it was safe for a cameraman to stand on the other side of the guardrail—so Bell crossed the street to sit on the fence with those of us hoping to watch the gag from a safe distance. While Tarantino was pitching a fit (he'd film from there himself if they wouldn't let anybody else do it!), Bell smiled benignly. This was nothing, she said. She reminded everyone of the legendary screamer, a British stunt coordinator, from a family of Bond stunt doubles, and she imitated his high-volume words of guidance, accent and all. "Take the facking spank, you facking cunt!" She said that now whenever she had a big stunt to do she repeated the words: "Take the facking spank! You're getting paid shitloads of money, mate. Take the facking spank." Soon she had the whole row of us along the fence saying it with her: "Take the facking spank, you facking cunt!" She passed along a more PG version of the advice during a prerecorded intro at the Stunt Awards show, just before they announced the winner of the Best Stunt by a Stuntwoman. "If you're going to give us the same pay," she said, "then you need to beat us the same way."

A safety rigger came by again to clip her onto the hood for a few rounds along the guardrail. On the first take, Bell rattled around, just feet away from the steel rail throughout the run, sliding over the hood and screaming in terror. Just after she passed out of the shot, she spread out her arms with a flourish, like Nadia Comaneci. The sun was going down—as it so often happens, the last shot of the day was the hardest. But Bell seemed to be having a blast: she made riding on the hood at ninety miles an hour look like body boarding at Venice Beach. As she drove off to repeat the stunt for the last time, Buddy Jo Hooker called after her, "Have fun, Zo!"

She waved back lightly from her perch. "Thanks, love."

CHAPTER 7

One Wide, One Tight, Good Luck

Growing old isn't easy for anyone, but it's hell on stuntmen. The hip replacements start to add up. The eight or ten concussions don't help. And, for a guy who's used to looking at a long wooden staircase as a chance for a pretty good paycheck, it's hard to stand on the top step and wonder, Hey, can I even make it down this thing? Stuntmen do not, as a rule, look forward to the golden years of retirement. "That's why so many people have shot themselves, I think," Ronnie Rondell Jr. told me. "They just don't want to deal with shitting their pants."

We were standing on a deck at the top of a wooden staircase leading down the cliffside from Rondell's house on the Big Niangua arm of the Lake of the Ozarks, in Camdenton, Missouri. He used to come out here in the fifties when he was a kid, a California boy riding bareback over the Ozark hills, and he started returning in the nineties, after he'd established himself as one of Hollywood's top stuntmen and second-unit directors. He'd spend all summer at his place on the lake, go back to L.A. at Thanksgiving to have dinner with his dad, work through the winter, and then head straight back in spring—semi-retirement, he called it. "And it was probably 2000 that I said goodbye." He told everybody in Stunts Unlimited, the stunt group he and Hal Needham and Glenn Wilder had founded thirty years before, "This is my last meeting. I'm sixty and I'm bailing out. I'm leaving town. I'm gone. The house is sold. I'm outta here, boys. You're on your own. You gotta get it together."

Rondell was five foot ten in his heyday, but the day I met him, after forty-some years of stunt work, he was five foot six. He was a diver, a gymnast, a surfer, a desert racer, a hang glider: he was good in the air. He had a thick head of hair, Italian hair—the Rondelli family comes from Naples by way of Studio City—and a mustache that must have looked good in the seventies and still worked now, rough and vintage, almost hip. When I drove up, he was waiting for me with one leg over the grille of his ATV, in front of a garage full of cars and racing bikes that looked tuned and spit-shined and ready to go, although he dismissed the idea of getting on them himself. He kept them for his son's visits. As we walked into his airplane hangar of an office/garage, he moved, like so many older stuntmen, out of a wide stance, with a little planning.

We looked at the framed pictures on his wall, a quick tour of three generations of Rondells in Hollywood: his dad, Ronnie, as a dashing extra and occasional star in the silent era; Ronnie Jr. himself, in midair, upside down over a cannon on *Shenandoah*; his sons Reid and R. A., together, before Reid was killed in a senseless accident on the set of *Airwolf*. He had pictures of stunt friends, too: Jack Coffer, killed on the Hollywood Freeway, as a civilian, when his Porsche hydroplaned under a diesel truck; Jerry Randall, killed hang-gliding; Lennie Geer, who doubled Robert Mitchum in the fifties and got his last credit in 1986, at the age of seventy-one, three years before he died peacefully at home. "Believe me," he said, "I'm fighting like a dog just to keep walking. I'm beat up." He mentioned a few things: the artificial hips; the rebuilt rotator cuff; carpal tunnel; broken ribs, arms, wrists, vertebrae; a detached triceps; a lot of concussions; the spinal fusion. "That sorta worked out. I don't have the mobility, can't play golf anymore, but if I'm sitting or lying down I have no pain whatsoever, so I'll take it," he said and laughed. "Let me get my ass in this chair before I seize up."

The image of infirmity that he was cultivating was not entirely convincing. In 2002, two years into his retirement, he un-retired, threw his stunt gear in the trunk of his car, and drove up to San

Francisco to work for his son R. A. on the freeway scene in *The Matrix Reloaded*. R. A. put him in one of the background cars, and in the part of the scene where Agent Smith jumps from car to car, and the traffic in the background rolls and collides and turns over and over, Ronnie was right in the middle of it. As R. A. and the Wachowski brothers watched the rushes, Andy Wachowski pointed out one car that wound up riding along the center divider and nearly fell into the oncoming traffic on the other side. "Who's that guy going over the middle of the freeway?" Wachowski said. "I didn't think that could happen."

"Aw, that's my dad," R. A. said. "He's just showing off."

Still Rondell keeps at this retirement business: he has a weekly nickel-dime poker game with some friendly fellow-lake-dwellers; he goes out on his boat, *Re-runs*, and explores the Ozark lakes. One summer he and a friend entered a fishing tournament with a dawn starting time. They loaded up before first light that morning, and as soon as the official timekeeper could see the water all the boats sped out across the Big Niangua, one by one, at full throttle, sometimes as fast as seventy or eighty miles an hour, to get to a favorite secret fishing hole. Rondell, riding in his friend Gary Minnick's boat, was next to the last to leave, and it was light enough by then that he and Gary could keep the boat ahead of them in sight. So they were watching when its steering mechanism broke and the boat jerked sharply to the left: they saw the two fisherman fly out and land in the lake. But the engine on the empty boat didn't shut down, so the boat kept winding in circles, full speed, around the two fishermen bobbing in the water. Another pair of fishermen had spotted the same thing and they, too, stopped to help: everybody watched the boat circling the two guys in the water until finally it changed course enough for them to swim like hell out of the circle to safety. The guys in the other boat fished them out. That left the driverless craft—a new thirty-thousand-dollar bass boat—racing around in circles, slowly making its way toward the rocky shore. Gary's boat wasn't fast enough to stay side by side with it, but Rondell figured if they could time it right, he could get close enough to jump over and turn off the engine and reunite the fishermen with their brand-new boat. "The funny part about it," Rondell said, "when I saw the thing happen and those two guys finally got away from the boat, I started yelling at Gary, 'Gotta get over there! Get over there!' like I'm directing a movie or something! And Gary couldn't believe I was going to make the jump. But, shit. It wasn't that big a jump! And he was so good with the boat, timing it to get right there, so when I committed, I was going to be in the *boat* and not in the water, then run over by the boat. He thought I was nuts. But shit, it's a stunt. If we get it right, it shouldn't be a problem."

That's Rondell's idea of retirement. And to his way of thinking, even with the boat-transfer gag, he's still taking it easy. His old hang-gliding buddy and fellow-stuntman Freddy Waugh still flies, at seventy-two. "He came close to getting killed a month ago."

"Oh yeah?"

"The fly bar dropped off—this control bar?" He had a picture of himself up in the air, back in the seventies, when he used to test-fly experimental hang-glider designs, and he pointed out the piece that fell. "The wires come off of that. That's what holds the wings, when the air's under it. It holds them in position. And he'd worked on it and he forgot to put the bolts back in, and when he took off, the bottom fell out of the bar, and he's holding it like this"—Rondell did a convincing imitation of a man in the Iron Cross—"and he knows he's gotta crash, he's gotta crash now, because if he gets any altitude he's dead. And he held on. He said, 'Ronnie, I never fought so hard in my life for my life.' He broke his ankle on the landing, but he got it down. And he went, 'Shit, that was a cheap price to pay. When I saw that bar fall, I knew I was dead. I went, "Hello, Fred. You're dead."'" He was up in the air wrestling with it for two minutes, too far from his takeoff point to crash into the ridge, too low in the air to use his parachute, too high to survive a fall. Rondell said, "God, Freddy, what if you'd been—"

"Look, Ronnie," Waugh told him. "I'm seventy-two years

old. If it fucking kills me, it's better than dying in a goddam hospital bed."

In all likelihood, Rondell had quite a few years to consider his own exit strategy: his father died at ninety-five, in the Motion Picture Country House, just before Rondell "retired." Back then Rondell still had a house about a half mile away, in Woodland Hills, California, and the last few months he visited his father every day. The experience did not make a persuasive case for longevity. At one point, his father told him to bring a gun.

"Dad," he said. "I can't bring you a gun."

"You bring me a gun. I'm getting out of here."

"What? Are you going to shoot your way out?"

"You know what I mean."

"Dad, I can't do that. They'll put me in jail. They know where it's coming from."

His father had to immigrate to this country twice. The first time he made so much money rum-running for the East Coast carriage trade that he quit the business and returned to Italy a wealthy man. But the Bank of Naples failed and he lost everything, so he came through Ellis Island a second time and paid a visit to the entrepreneurs who'd bought him out when he wanted to go back to Italy. They said, "Ronnie, this business is in the shitter. Help us out!" Rondell described his father's rum-running as a discreet in-person delivery service, a few bottles hidden under a coat and driven to your door, not a high-volume trucks-and-machine-guns operation. It made enough money for him to bring his whole family over one by one, but the pressures of operating outside the law made his father sick—"melancholia," they called it then. Today they'd call it depression. According to his son, he just didn't give a shit about anything.

In 1923, California was still regarded as the health state, so Rondelli Sr. headed out to L.A. to convalesce. Melancholia or not, he was a dapper dresser, in the swanky Latin style of the day, and one morning when he was out walking in Hollywood, he came upon an informal casting session for extras outside the Fox

Studio and the man on the loading dock picked him out of the crowd. It was like passing through Ellis Island all over again: the studio payroll man took down his name, dropped the final vowel, and he became a citizen of the movies. Over the next twenty-five years, Ronnie Rondell Sr. played in hundreds of features and two reelers and studio shorts. He got to live all sides of the movie world's fizzy highlife, as waiter, headwaiter, party guest, nightclub patron, orchestra leader, chauffeur, croupier, ringsider, ship passenger, hotel guest, bellboy, doorman, bookie, best man, and country club extra. Central casting ran everything, and he called in all day long.

"Ronnie Rondell."

"No work."

He'd call back ten minutes later, because you never knew when a job would come in from the studios. When he was actually on the lot working, he could hustle more work, dropping by the other shows to check in with the assistant directors. But if he ever went two or three days without a job, he'd put a tuxedo in a flower box—he had his own props and wardrobe at home and wore his own clothes in half his movies—then he'd slip into his delivery-boy overalls, get on a bicycle, and pedal up to the front gate of the studio with a box of flowers for whatever big star was working that day. ("Okay, they're over on Stage Six.") Once he was on the lot, he'd head for the bathroom, change into his tuxedo, and start making the rounds.

"Ronnie! What are you doing?"

"Oh, I'm over here working. You got anything coming up?"

"Oh, yeah, Jesus! Tomorrow."

After he'd lined up a job, he'd get back in his overalls, throw the box with the tuxedo in it over the studio fence, then pedal out the front gate, waving to the guard, who came to recognize him as a regular delivery boy. As a backup plan, he had ladders hidden behind studio landscaping all over town, so he could just climb in if he had to. He kept at this life through the war—he was exempt from the draft due to his flat feet and asthma—and when the war was over, a Universal exec called him into the office and said, "Ronnie, you've been in this business since the early twenties. You know everything there is to know about it. We want you to be an assistant director. We need somebody who understands what it takes to make these things on budget."

So he switched jobs and began "steering" the directors, letting them know, diplomatically, how many people they'd need and when it was time to break or to shoot or to stop shooting. He schmoozed the stars, kept them from firing a makeup girl just because a perfume bottle wasn't in the right spot on the dressing room table. When Universal started making films in Italy, they shipped him over on the first one, *Deported*, a Robert Siodmak potboiler about a gangster sent back home. When the production was wrapped and ready to pack up, Italian officials took all the film and held it for ransom. The studio dispatched Rondell to talk with the officialdom, who may or may not have been controlled by the Mafia. He explained that the Americans came over with all this American money to spend on making a movie here, and they won't come back if they have trouble on this first one. Is there anything you can you do to help out? He was reasonable and easygoing, and he got them to bring the price down. That was his father's style, Rondell said: Don't make it a vendetta. Always give them room to negotiate.

His father brought young Ronnie to the lot on Saturdays, leaving him with the stunt guys usually, to play with their swords and guns. He'd got his first job in pictures at three months old, for ten dollars a day—his dad was A.D.'ing a movie that needed a baby in a bassinet. Then as a kid, in the early fifties, he worked extra on the Ma and Pa Kettle movies—as one of the Kettles' fifteen children—and he went through most of grade school on the lot. But when he hit high school he wanted a real life: neighborhood girls, and a car, and a job valet-parking at the Sportsmen's Lodge on Ventura Boulevard. He lettered in diving and gymnastics. For a few years he thought he'd said goodbye to pictures forever.

The morning after graduation and the senior prom, he got on

the bus with all his buddies, heading for San Diego and the Navy Reserves. They put him in mine warfare school—a handy skill for a man who would spend a good portion of his life getting blown up—and he served at a naval ammunition depot on Indian Island, just off Port Townsend, Washington. During his Navy years, he taught himself how to scuba dive, got married, had R. A. But when he returned to civilian life, his new responsibilities were hard to reconcile with a '55 Thunderbird and a surfer's impromptu approach to the job market. Because he had a family to support, he started working extra again—he had the crewcut California look that was popular in the new teen movies—but he didn't call in if the surfing looked good.

There was something about him back then that seemed to tick people off on sight. There he was, on location one afternoon, lying around in cowboy gear, with a stuntman and another extra. "So, what are you going to do in this business? Just work extra, or what?" the extra said. Rondell knew the guy didn't like him, but he didn't care.

"No, I'm going to be a stuntman," he said. "That's what I'm trying to do."

"Really?" the stuntman said. People express this ambition to stuntmen all the time. Sometimes their only experience is that they've survived a car crash.

The extra picked up on the skepticism and challenged Rondell. "Tell you what," he said. "Run along the edge of that and I'll give you a gunshot. Let's see what you can do." They'd been waiting for their call up on the lip of a ravine. It was big enough that if you weren't serious about becoming a stuntman, you could stand up, take a good look down into it, then laugh and go back to being a member of the Screen Extras Guild lying around in the sunshine. But Rondell got up, shook his shoulders the way he did before a big dive or a tumbling pass, and took off running. When the extra yelled "*BANG*," Rondell kicked into the air and turned it over, then dove down into the ravine and rolled his shoulder into the bank just enough to launch himself, end over end, straight down

to the rocky bottom. He was twenty years old. It was nothing for
him.

"Jesus Christ," the extra said from the top of the ravine. "Are
you okay?"

"Yeah. Why? Isn't that what you wanted me to do?"

"Yeah, well, Jesus. You're going to get yourself killed."

Rondell picked himself up and dusted off his chaps. When he
climbed out, the stuntman, Lennie Geer, said, "Come here." He
wrote down an address in Topanga Canyon and invited him to
come out to his place to train. His first paid work as a stuntman
came soon after, on *Deep Six*, a war movie that his father helped
sign him to, and it was very nearly his last—he came close to
drowning as the battalion of stuntmen landed their transport
boats in the surf on Catalina Island. But he considers that fall into
the ravine in front of Geer his first real stunt. It didn't happen
overnight, but that twenty-foot tumble turned out to be the tryout
that landed him in the pros.

He started driving out to Geer's place in his T-bird every weekend, to train at the ranch with a small group of Lennie's guys—
Dave Perna, Hank Calia, and Hal Needham. They practiced
fights, falls, and horse work. They'd dive out of an oak tree into a
ravine onto dingy old mattresses. They'd haul loads of sawdust in
the back of Geer's pickup truck, pour it out, then gallop through
it, taking bullet hits, falling to the left or right. They learned trick
riding and pony-express mounts. Because of his gymnastics training, Rondell could clear a horse in one jump. A trick rider who
stopped by told him he was a natural and made it look easy; Rondell told him it *was* easy. After all those flips and handstands, all
that trampoline work, he knew where he was in the air. Geer
started sending out Rondell and the other guys who trained at his
place to do charity stunt shows—jumping from a horse onto
Geer's pickup truck instead of a covered wagon, brawling with the
guys in the truck and throwing them off the back, learning how to
get it all right the first time, in front of a paying audience. They
called their little show Stunts Unlimited. When Rondell finally

traded in the T-bird for a family man's station wagon, he even painted the name on the back.

It would be a few more years before anybody thought to start a stunt association. But the structure was in place: there was a clique of older guys controlling most of the hiring. Geer started talking up his four stunt hopefuls to them. He'd say, "I got four kids out at my place who are going to be the best stuntmen in the business if somebody gives them a break." The guys listened: they were getting to the age where they didn't want to take a bullet hit and fall down two flights of wooden stairs and crash onto the ground. So when the really tough jobs came up, they'd call Rondell or Needham and say, "Hey, kid. You want to do a stair fall?" The standard response was "You bet. Just point me to it."

"In those days," Rondell said, "it was kind of phony bullshit Westerns. They were into the slick look. And the pants always fit so tight I couldn't put pads in, because then it looked like I had some kind of growth on my knees. But usually the shirts were loose enough to put an elbow pad on. I'd get up there, take a bullet, slam my head on the wall, then tip it over down the stairs, end for end for end. And the wilder it was, the more points you got from the guys hiring you. So the next time a real nasty thing came up, they'd give you a chance. They were also testing you: are you going to be a whiner or are you going to tough up and do the job? And if you hit the ground wrong and get smacked really good, are you going to get up and do it again? I have to tell you, I've seen Hal Needham work with a broken leg. I saw Jack Coffer work with a completely broken shoulder. I've separated my shoulder, never told a soul, did a take two. It was on my dad's job, and he came in back and he said, 'Did you hurt yourself?' And I said, 'Yeah, I'm hurt.' And he said, 'All right. We'll get it on this next take.' And I went back to One"—the scene's original starting position—"did it again, and he sent me home. I drove home one-handed, shifting the car like that. Oh *man*!" He crossed his left arm over his body and winced. "You never told anybody you were hurt. Because they always had another guy that could fit the clothes."

One day as he was leaving the studio with the other stuntmen, someone noticed the hand-painted sign on his station wagon. " 'Stunts Unlimited.' What's that?"

"Well, that's a group of stunt guys," he said. "We do charity stuff, you know, on weekends—Stunts Unlimited." When they started to make fun of it all—fighting for charity, the whole half-ass hotshot idea of a few inexperienced stuntmen calling themselves Stunts Unlimited—Rondell said, "Well, think of something we can't do and maybe we'll change the name." He laughed at the memory. "I guess I was a bit of a smartass."

He was also a new kind of stuntman. The old guys were tough—former rodeo riders, boxers, football players—but they couldn't do what he did. Rondell was no horseman, but he could fall off a horse in any direction: over the head, off the back, to either side. He had a diver's timing and precision: he could come so close to hitting his head on the way down that people would gasp. The old guys who saw him land just out of reach of a horse's hooves told him he'd be dead before he turned thirty, but the truth was they couldn't do half of what he did in the air. He'd grown up jumping on trampolines—his good friend's dad ran a trampoline supply business and he'd go to the showroom and bounce for hours—so he could come down and hit a target almost without looking. When he first began, he said, he still looked like he was performing for the judges, but after a while he learned to do what he became famous for: roughing up the perfect form, leaving a leg out awkwardly or twisting his arm around so he looked out of control. He still had the gymnast's spring and the height in his jumps and he could still nail the landing, on his feet or his shoulder or his back, but in between the takeoff and the landing, for the camera, he looked desperate. In other circumstances, you'd call it acting. Rondell just says, "I sold the stunt."

Just the way actors can be sorted into bit players and leading men, stuntmen fall into two categories: utility men and big-gag performers. Rondell had been working for five years before he got the chance to do his first premier stunt in *Kings of the Sun*, a wigwam saga about tribal warfare in the Mayan era, sort of an early-sixties *Apocalypto*, starring Yul Brynner. The shooting script called for a forty-foot fall from the top of a burning pole. But the fall wasn't designed as a straightforward drop onto a pile of pads and empty liquor boxes below. It was more of a long topple, over the melee of an ongoing battle between the Mayan forces, their local allies, and an invading tribe, with the stuntman doubling one of the Mayan chieftains holding onto his perch up in the primitive guard tower as the pole caught fire and tumbled like a felled tree. Then, at the last possible instant, just before the pole slammed into a village hut, the stunt double would leap from the pole straight through a dry thatched roof, which would then burst into flames. Rondell said three guys wanted the gag, Billy Shannon, Hal Needham, and himself.

"Hal wanted it, and he could do it," Rondell said. "He was a tree trimmer. He swung on ropes and climbed—one of the best stuntmen ever. Anyway, I got the shot. And up on the top of the pole there was a platform, two-and-a-half by two-and-a-half." In the office, he had a lobby-card-size film still that showed him half naked with the pole on fire, and another one taken near the end of the fall, just after he'd pushed off from the pole. He was spread out in the air, right over an X marked on the thatched roof. Just standing on top of the pole was something of a feat, he said— "Forty feet up on that skinny-ass pole, things moved around"—so he had them build him a footrest on the platform, and a handhold at the top, so he could hang on in the wind. Rondell used to go up on his lunch break to eat there and imagine the pole falling. "So the day comes to do it. And I climb up there. I'm on the pole, ready to go. They get all ready, and the clouds come in—there's extras and hundreds of Mexicans and all the stunt guys mixed in with them, fighting and doing. It's a huge shot. In the movie, it's gigantic because the star is up there, putting arrows in the enemy. Then you cut to a stunt guy getting an arrow. And they were live arrows shot by another stuntman. No screwing around. It was the real deal."

Film sets are something of a law unto themselves; they aren't covered by OSHA regulations, and even the local police can find it difficult to get on a set. Although some union rules were put in place in the seventies and after to protect the crew, safety standards, especially for stuntmen, are largely a matter of convention. (And part of the point of working in Mexico, back in the sixties, was to avoid what few regulations there were.) In many cases, the level of caution exercised in a given maneuver is determined by trial and error, with safety adjustments made only after someone dies trying to do it; stuntmen who talk with their counterparts from previous generations are often shocked by the seemingly senseless risks they took. But no matter what the era, shooting live arrows at other human beings, in the middle of a crowd—moving targets in a mass of extras—sounded impossibly dangerous and foolhardy.

"No," Rondell assured me. "It was the real deal. A seventy-pound bow with a broadhead arrow: just *jhzwump!* We wore a steel plate with that much balsa wood"—he spread his thumb and forefinger about four inches apart—"to catch the arrow."

"How did you know that he wouldn't hit you in the face?"

"Because I was an archer, too. I thought it would be a good skill to know." Rondell assured me that a lot of the stunt guys had signed up for the privilege of being shot at, because every arrow they took was worth a hundred dollars—about seven hundred dollars in today's terms. Rondell was so eager to make that kind of money that he put his name on the fitted steel-and-balsa breastplate that he'd wear for the gag, and hung it up in a safe place so he could find it in a hurry whenever they needed a body to get shot. The guy doing the shooting was Richard Farnsworth—the stablehand turned stuntman turned actor, the same one who got two Academy Award nominations later in his career. Apparently Farnsworth was a crack shot, and once he knew which stuntmen he'd be shooting at, he invited them all out to a nearby beach for a demonstration. He set a tin cup about forty feet away—and missed it every time. "He never hit that cup the whole time we were there," Rondell said. "But he did that on purpose. He was just jerking us all off. And I'm going, 'How can he shoot so good when the pressure's on, and he can't hit the broadside of a barn?' Anyway, the day comes for his first shot at me, and I run in and somebody'd taken my breastplate. I'm going, 'Goddamit,' because they were all made to fit you. 'Fuck! I'm not losing this hundred bucks.' So I just grabbed one off the wall." He put on the burlap covering that the Mayan warriors wore, and they doused that in rubber cement so Farnsworth could hit him with a flaming arrow and he'd go up in flames—the addition of fire made the gag worth an extra fifty bucks. "So Dick's all ready. They roll cameras. I kill this guy like that, I turn and go to kill another guy and I give him the shot"—he stood still for a second so Farnsworth could aim—"and he shoots and I scream and I fall over into the sand and I'm thrashing around and the fire's coming up. And fucking people are panicking and running around and I'm going, 'What the hell is going on?' I'd felt the arrow. You feel it—it's coming . . . you know, a seventy-pound bow, *BOOM*, that thing goes in there. And I looked down and the arrow is sticking out of my groin!"

Farnsworth had missed his mark in the worst possible way. But Rondell was lucky. "The breastplate, the wrong one that I put on, was too long for me. When Dick shot—it was *not* Dick's fault—when he shot, one of the feathers came off and the arrow corkscrewed, and that's what happens." Rondell imitated the path of the arrow dropping like a sinkerball. "Dick nearly died. And I screamed: I sold the stunt. So now he *knows* he's just shot my balls off. And everybody on the set sees it. They're going, 'Oh GOD, it's stuck in his pelvis somewhere.' And I'm going, 'What?'" They yelled "Cut," and put out the flames, and eventually Rondell stood up and everybody saw that he was fine. But after that incident, Farnsworth didn't want to shoot another arrow. "Now everybody's pissed off at *me*, because if Dick doesn't shoot the arrows, we don't make the hundred bucks. I went over to tell him, 'It's cool, Dick. It's cool. Shoot me again. Get an arrow.' He finally got back on line, but that scared him. He started moving up. Before he was making long shots, now he's getting closer. And *he* got a hundred bucks every time he shot one. You do that several times a day you make a lot of money back then."

While I was still laughing, Rondell went right back to the story of his burning-pole gag. His storytelling style was more comic picaresque than cowboy machismo, and sometimes in the middle of a story he'd forget a name and say, "That was my eighth concussion." But modesty aside, his recall for stunt work seemed remarkably precise. He could walk me through a split-second decision from a gag he did forty-four years ago. The first time I heard a stuntman shaving the thought process into fractions of a second like that, I thought it was just exaggeration or good storytelling. But so many of them describe the experience that way, I came to see it as one of the few traits that the best in the business have in common, this ability to slow time in a crisis, to sort through the possible outcomes till they hit upon the most survivable option. And they seem to do so at will, on an adrenaline surge, whenever the director calls "Action."

"Anyway," he said, picking up where he left off, "the clouds come in and they stopped. The next day, I get up there again. It's an afternoon shot, because they want the sky a certain way and the light and all this bullshit. They light the pole on fire, so now the heat is coming up around that little box I'm standing on. I'm going, '*AaaaaaAH!*' I'm acting! I'm doing all this acting shit. And, fuck man, it's hot! And I hear somebody yell, '*Cut! Cut! Cut!*' Man, the fucking pole's on fire! *Cut*? What am *I* supposed to do? Climb down?" They'd stopped the scene because one of the safeties, a Mexican hire charged with manning a hose in case the fire got out of hand, started watching the action instead and didn't notice that he had aimed the spray from his hose right at the generator, which killed the water pump. It took another hour for them to fix that and redo everything: reset the hundreds of extras, cover the pole with fresh burlap to set on fire.

"What happened to you and the fire?"

"Finally, somebody turned the gas off. The burlap kept burning, but that's not as bad." After the delay, he got back on the pole, for the third time, and they started the scene again. Once they lit the fire, he needed to draw his bow a few times—in the final version, they would intercut closeups of the Mayan chieftain taking the shot. "Then I hear them yell, 'Trip it!' So I know the thing is going to go. I'm ready. Man, I get my foot up on the deal for my takeoff, and the pole goes *whish-whoo*"—it started swaying back and forth, as if deciding which way to fall. "I'm looking: Behind me there's a picket wall to the fort, with pointed pikes, and it's forty feet to the ground. And I don't know which way it's going to go. There was a moment when I went, 'This is it.' And I'm thinking, 'Shit, should I bail here to land on people?' You know, anything to break my fall. But then it starts to go, and the rest was easy. But there is a trick to it." Since it's impossible to jump clear of a falling object in midair—there's nothing solid to push off from— Rondell had to wait until the pole had fallen halfway to the ground. Only then could he get enough thrust, by pushing at the platform the way a swimmer pushes off from a pool wall. If he mistimed it, he'd go nowhere and land on top of an adobe wall. But if he timed it right, he could clear the pole and the wall and land on his mark in the middle of the thatched roof. "So I pushed against the pole, and I got off just enough to clear everything. Now I go through, I hit the mark. See me throw the arm?" He pointed to the second glossy, where he hung in the air about a foot above the big X on the roof. "I'm getting ready. It looks like I went through on that arm, but I did that so I could finish my turn and land on my back on the pads and tortilla boxes."

In Mexico, the only boxes the stuntmen could find in any quantity were tortilla boxes, which were only about a cubic foot. Rondell said it took a million of them to make a catcher.

"Now the effects guy had gone around and sprayed gasoline in the eaves, so that when the burning pole came through it would start a fire on the roof, because the whole village is going to shit. Well . . ." he chuckled, "the fumes had seeped up into all these palm fronds, so when I came through—I went right through, I

land in the boxes, I go YES!, I can see the hole I made in the roof—
and it goes *BWOOOM!* It turns into a ball of fire, burning palm
fronds are falling everywhere. My safety guys run in, it's an inferno, and the next thing I feel is Big Roy Jensen"—an ex-CFL all-
star who went on to a solid career in the movies as a big galoot.
"He comes in and gets me by the pec muscle, because I didn't
hardly have any clothes on. His hands are this big and the first
handle he gets is my pec muscle and my neck and he throws me out
the door to get me out of the falling burning shit. But unfortunately, his aim sucked, so my head hit the doorframe, so I end
up going *puhnff*"—he made the expiring noise of a knockout
victim—"and they go, 'He's hurt!' " He gave a sarcastic chuckle in
agreement. "Shit, I'm hurt. He tried to kill me! I was fine till he
got me."

The pole fall in the middle of the movie's climactic battle moved
Rondell to the top ranks of the business, on any shortlist for a big-
dollar gag. It was an unusual gag and it highlighted Rondell's
blend of fearlessness and precision. The same gag today would almost certainly be done with a stuntman laced into a harness, with
his fall (and the fall of the pole, as well) controlled by wires,
winches, and computer. Or it would be broken up into safer bits
and filmed in sections (Shot One: the platform teeters. Shot Two:
the pole topples. Shot Three: closeup on actor in wind tunnel. Shot
Four: a stuntman falls about fifteen feet through a roof). Certainly
nobody would suggest doing the gag in a single long shot, without
any wires at all, to show off the fact that an actual human being
had bravely, and successfully, dared the fall. Partly, this is an aesthetic choice—today's audience would know instantly that the guy
falling was a stuntman, and directors (and second-unit directors
and stunt coordinators) live in fear of setting off such alarms. You
often hear decision makers on the set saying that they don't want
their stunts to look "too stunty." The action director needs to stay
just this side of the audience's threshold of disbelief.

In 1965, on *Shenandoah*, Rondell did a flying front flip with a
half twist, in Confederate uniform, over a cannon that blew up an

instant before he leapt into the air. Rondell invented the move—
not the aerial maneuver, but the use of a cleverly concealed
minitramp to add extra height and air time, with the blast and the
jump timed precisely so that it appears that he has been thrown
into the air by the force of the nearby explosion. The gag, now a
staple of war movies from *The Patriot* to *Saving Private Ryan*, has
been updated—stuntmen are now launched violently into the air
by means of an air ram, a pressurized steel platform that catapults
a body much farther than a minitramp could. It's exactly the sort
of gag that directors and stunt coordinators now tend to shy away
from. But in 1965, when Rondell first tried it, the move was so in-
novative that the actor George Kennedy, who'd wandered by during the filming of the stunt, was convinced that the whole thing
was real and he ran into the shot, heroically, to see if Rondell was
okay.

Rondell has two photographs of the sequence that he and Hal
Needham, who was running the stunts on *Shenandoah*, trotted
out for directors. One shows a test run without explosives, with
Rondell upside down over the cannon, the form on his front flip
slightly scrambled in rag-doll fashion. A nearby Confederate soldier stands motionless, almost unnaturally still, like a figure in da-
guerreotype. The second photo includes the explosion; the nearby
soldier has come to life and recoils from the blast, which is blow-
ing the cannon apart and throwing smoke and dust and wood into
the air. In this photograph, which appears to be shot at the same
instant of flight, with Rondell at the apex of the aerial, his limbs
appear in the identical rag-doll arrangement. Taken one at a time,
the pictures are amusing. But looked at side by side, they're an impressive display of what a good stuntman can do, able to safely reproduce the appearance of life-threatening danger on take after
take.

In 1961, Rondell was asked to join the Stuntmen's Association,
as a charter member of the first "fraternal organization" dedi-
cated to stuntmen. The group began out of necessity, following
the collapse of the studio system. From the silent era on, the studios

always kept their own gang of reliable gag men and barnstormers and ramrodders and specialty extras—whatever name they used for the stuntmen of the era. But once the moguls left and the studios came under corporate control, the money men figured it didn't take much skill to get hit for a living, and started hiring extras to do the job in an effort to cut costs. Predictably, this resulted in chaos, which came to a head on the set of *Everything's Ducky*, an interspecies comedy (in the style of *Francis the Talking Mule*), in which Mickey Rooney and Buddy Hackett play a couple of Navy men who come into possession of a talking duck. The script called for an extended bar fight between a dozen Marines and a dozen Navy guys. When the cut-rate hires still couldn't get it right after ten days, Rooney approached Loren Janes, a former pentathlete who'd doubled Steve McQueen in *The Magnificent Seven*. "What's wrong here?" Rooney asked him. "This couldn't be going worse."

"Well," Janes told him, "you've got one stuntman on the Navy side and another stuntman on the Marine side and the rest are extras and they don't know what they're doing."

Rooney walked off the set and refused to return until the production hired professionals to complete the scene; when the producers gave in and met Rooney's demand, the pros got the fight done in one take. This embarrassing brouhaha prompted Janes and another veteran stuntman to put together a group of recognized, reliable guys who'd been working steadily, so producers could make one call and know they were hiring capable and experienced stuntmen. The two got SAG approval, and the Stuntmen's Association of Motion Pictures was inaugurated, with an initial membership of fifty.

Many such groups exist today and several key ones rival the original in their innovation and importance to the trade, but the Stuntmen's Association—or simply the Association, as it is known among stunties—continues to be the largest and best established. Several groups consciously pattern themselves after them (the Black Stuntmen's Association, the Stuntwomen's Association, the

Stuntmen's Association of Serbia, and so on), and all have built themselves on the template that the Association quickly and profitably established.

For the first nine years, though, the Association was the only game in town. And, according to Rondell, during their years as a monopoly, they became complacent. In the early years the founders had recognized the need to bring in young guys and new talents—that's why Needham and Rondell and the rest of Lennie Geer's guys were invited to join. But by 1970, the younger generation had begun running shows and hiring people, and they started to feel that the Association wasn't keeping up with the times. Needham was doubling Burt Reynolds on the TV show *Dan August*, and he was stunt coordinator for both *Chisum* and *Little Big Man*. Rondell was running the stunts for *The Mod Squad*, and doubling Michael Cole, the designated white guy in the flower-power detective trio. As stunt coordinators, they needed both raw recruits who could hit the ground hard and more skilled performers who could pull off the new brand of stunt work that directors were calling for, the car jumps and pipe ramps and cannon rolls. On the set, stunt coordinators hire and manage the stunt crew and choreograph the action; they also go to meetings to negotiate with producers and set the standard fees for every gag in the shooting script. The two strongly believed it was time to raise the standard prices, which hadn't changed much since the Association began. But their attempts to raise rates were doomed to fail if other stunt coordinators didn't follow suit, and they couldn't get the issue onto the agenda at Association meetings. They got the feeling that the older generation had a greater allegiance to the producers who gave them their jobs than to the stuntmen they had to bargain for.

Rondell's first idea was to start an agency—if the coordinators in the Association couldn't get together to set the prices, he thought he could represent enough stuntmen to set a better standard. But once he and Needham started making discreet individual inquiries—to see how many stuntmen would be willing to give ten percent of their salaries to negotiate higher weekly fees and better rates for standard stunt work—a few Association members got wind of their plans and brought the matter before the Screen Actors Guild. In short order, their idea was officially quashed.

That power play got them angry. Rondell and Needham and another friend, Glenn Wilder, were all running shows. Between the three of them, they had enough jobs to support a good number of stuntmen on their own. So they decided to break away from the Association and start their own group.

"What are we going to call it?" Needham wondered.

"Shit, Stunts Unlimited," Rondell said.

"Perfect."

He drew up a full-burn logo—a circle filled with flames, with three tiny birds, representing Needham, Wilder, and himself, escaping the blaze—and he placed it on the center of his scriptbook and started leaving it out in places around the set where other stunt guys were sure to see it.

"What's that?"

"It's Stunts Unlimited," he'd say. "We're going to start a group."

"You're *what*?"

That was all it took to get the word out. Less than a week after Rondell started provoking gossip in the small world of working stuntmen, he and Wilder and Needham showed up at the regular Association meeting. Rondell had a speech prepared, but when he tried to get the floor, they told him that he hadn't followed parliamentary procedure and he wasn't on the agenda.

"So, we can't talk? That's it for us?"

"No, we don't want to hear you."

But there were sixty people at the meeting, a greater showing than the sleepy affairs usually attracted, and the animosity was palpable. Finally the mixture of anger and curiosity overwhelmed the objections of the parliamentarians, and Rondell was allowed to speak. "Look, you guys are doing nothing," he said. "You hold these meetings. But you're not hiring out of the group. There are guys working all over the place that aren't part of our group. The business is changing. The day of the big studio is dead: now you can go anywhere and shoot. You've gotta move. You've gotta modernize. But it's not happening here, so I'm giving you my resignation tonight." Rondell and Needham and Wilder, and about ten other guys that the three had persuaded to join them, stood up and walked out, over the shouts and jeers of the Association.

Hollywood was a simpler place then. Stunts Unlimited got an office with a secretary—something the Association, which at the time had no corporate staff or headquarters, had never thought to do. They took out a full-page ad in the trades: all twenty original members (except Needham, who was working that day) on the Hansen Dam, with an amazing array of seventies coifs and sideburns, long hair and Afros, big curly manes, a dirt bike helmet and scuba goggles set down on the rocks. Guys wore fire suits or parachutes. One stands by his skis. Three guys are shirtless, one wears chaps, still another holds onto a surfboard with a boxing glove. Standing seductively in the middle of this testosterone show, there's a single high-cheekboned fashion model in a slinky maxidress. The ad said, "Do you know Stunts Unlimited? A one-stop shop for stunts."

According to Rondell, the Association members started a whisper campaign against them with the studio heads. They said Stunts Unlimited was going to drive up the price of stunts, that they were bringing in a new group of stuntmen with so little experience that they'd make the sets unsafe for everyone. The story of this original apostasy has become legend in the small world of stunts, and I'd heard exaggerated versions of it from other guys, including one where a Green Beret turned stuntman threatened to take out the Unlimited founders. Rondell's recollection of events was milder and more realistic: he did remember making up some stickers that said "Stunts Unlimited will get you if you don't watch out" and pasting them in studios all over town, on mirrors and in bathrooms. But as for the cloak-and-dagger element, he laughed it off. "There were guys that got drunk, called the house, threatened to kill us. They'd tell our wives, 'We're going to kill 'em.' But you know what? Nothing every happened. Fact is, one of the guys that did that became a member of Stunts Unlimited a few years later." For all the drama of the breakup, he said, in the long run it worked out fine for all sides. The business was growing, so there was enough work for everybody, and after a couple of years, he said, "we hired them and they hired us and it all more or less loosened up and we were all friends again."

From 1970 on, Rondell ran the stunts on TV action shows like *The Mod Squad*, *S.W.A.T.*, *Baretta*, *Charlie's Angels*, *Hart to Hart*, and *Baywatch*, along with a few of the more tempestuous soaps, like *Dynasty* and *Falcon Crest*. Compared with feature films, the TV budgets were small, the schedule was tight, the action was raw and unrehearsed, and there wasn't a lot of room for mistakes. On most of his shows, they had one car and you had to hit your mark on the first take. "Shit, television," he said. "They gave you two cameras and that was it. One wide, one tight, good luck."

The advantage of TV was that he did almost all of his work in L.A. and had weekends at home. Rondell raced motorcycles with his sons, R. A. and Reid—he'd run his Triumph out in the desert, bring it into the shop on Monday, get it out the next Friday, and do the same thing. "Me and the kids, we'd all go racing. Barstow to Vegas: out through the desert under the road, then on into Vegas, one hundred sixty miles, through rough hill climbs and big sand washes." His evocation of desert stillness, expressed in movie shorthand, was filled with motorhead awe. "1965. Twelve hundred motorcycles on the starting line: not an engine running. Truck about three hundred yards out and you can hear a pin drop. The desert: not a sound. And the banner goes"—he dropped his arm, the way a starter would—"like that and twelve hundred motorcycles go *BWWAAAAAAA!* And leave. Just funneling onto the desert."

R. A. and Reid both became stuntmen. Rondell's second wife, Mary, used to show visitors a set of three pictures on the wall of their Woodland Hills home. "This is my family," she'd say, and point out the trio, all of them enveloped in flame. Full burns make good family photos; Rondell keeps a few of them on his wall, including one with R. A. safetying his brother, Reid, who has just been lit on fire. The job—full as it is of danger, professional calm, and brotherly solicitude—provides plenty of opportunities for such family portraits. And while any stunt family can probably point to some dark, mysterious, and unique genetic element that draws them en masse to the profession, the most logical explanation for the surprisingly wholesome family atmosphere in the stunt business is much simpler than that: the kids love it. At just the age when kids look upon their parents as heroes, kids in stunt families have parents who actually perform heroic acts. These parents come home, and instead of squelching a child's natural recklessness, they're much more likely to give the kids how-tos in the high fall, or build them a zip line from the upstairs porch to the backyard tree house.

Reid Rondell was twenty-two, with seven years' experience doubling Jan-Michael Vincent, in 1985, the year he was killed. He'd started working as Tom Cruise's stunt double in 1981, appearing in *Taps*, *The Outsiders*, *Risky Business*, and *All the Right Moves*. "Reid was the first stunt guy who was my age," Cruise said (they were born eight days apart, in July 1962). "He was generous and encouraging. He'd say, 'Aw, you can do this.' He was the first guy to really teach me about stunts." A long-term double does more for an actor than simply appear for him in action scenes: he goes over the day's shot list and walks through the set or location until he's certain that the actor will be safe every time he gets out of his trailer. The double argues for changes if he feels something's too dangerous, and after he's made sure that a sequence is acceptable for the franchise actor to do himself, he'll break down the risk, step by step, so the actor knows exactly what he's getting into. "Reid was the first guy to do that for me," Cruise said. "He'd say, 'Look over here. Always walk through the scene before you do it.' On *Taps*, before the scene where I got shot, Reid and the head stunt guy and I, we went through and looked at every squib"—the small explosive charge that simulates gunfire. "They took me through every shot that was going to be fired, pointed out all the stunt guys, who was going to be firing and where they'd be. They showed me the 'loaded' weapons—to make sure that a weapon wasn't really loaded when it was loaded. I got my primary education there." Cruise would have picked Reid to be the stunt coordinator on all his pictures, he said, if he'd lived.

The accident occurred in January, during a shoot for the CBS action series *Airwolf*. The show was named for a helicopter, a supposedly billion-dollar supersonic prototype, played by a Bell 222 painted in a black-and-white killer-shark configuration; Jan-Michael Vincent played the moody renegade who recovers the chopper from Libya, then acts as its pilot on top-secret CIA missions. Of course, the teleplays called for a lot of helicopter work. On the morning Reid died, he wasn't doubling Vincent—he wasn't a qualified pilot, so his doubling duties extended only to those scenes where the actor was on solid ground. But he'd showed up for work on time, and the body double who was supposed to sit beside the pilot hadn't. So Reid volunteered to ride along. This wasn't an unusual chain of events: with L.A. traffic, being late for work sometimes is almost inevitable, and riding in a helicopter was fun.

The scene called for a chase through Pico Canyon, in the Santa Monica Mountains north of L.A. After the first take, the three choppers involved in the scene—a lead helicopter, a pursuit helicopter, and a camera helicopter—paused for a moment in the air, then turned to go back to One, for a second take. But as they were heading back, the pilot of the Huey that Reid was flying in, Scott Meher, started showing off, and he dropped out of the line to skim over the top of a knoll. But instead of just grazing the crest, or missing it entirely, Meher caught a skid, and the helicopter snapped into the ground. The turbine engine, which was mounted behind the passenger compartment, crashed through the Huey and crushed Reid. Fuel spilled everywhere and the chopper burst into flames, and the crew members on the ground ran in to save the pilot. But they couldn't do anything for Reid, who was either killed instantly by the engine or trapped by it, unreachable but still alive as the helicopter burned. The autopsy was inconclusive, but the second-unit director, an ex-military man who'd been working with helicopters in Hollywood for years and had even flown in scenes with Ronnie, assured the Rondells that Reid was dead by the time he reached the wreck.

Steve Davison, one of the younger stuntmen on the set, who'd worked with Reid before on several shows, made the call to the family, and Ronnie, who was home that morning, picked up. He remembers the conversation word for word. "Hi," he said.

"Ronnie?"

"Who's this?"

"Steve."

"Hey, what's happening, man?"

"There's been a really bad accident."

"Wait. What show are you on?"

"We're on *Airwolf*."

"Fuck, it's Reid." In the stunt business, a call from the set saying that someone's been hurt isn't entirely unexpected. He wondered if Reid had broken a leg or had a concussion or been knocked unconscious. "How bad is it?"

"It's as bad as it gets."

"Oh, bullshit. What happened?"

"The helicopter hit a hill and crashed and burned."

"Did you guys look around to see if he was thrown out?"

"Ronnie. He's dead."

He managed to say "Okay, Steve" and hung up. Then the phone started ringing and more and more people came over. He said he told Mary, and the news almost killed her. He called his first wife to say, "You just lost your youngest son."

Rondell found it all hard to believe. It wasn't so much that a stuntman had died. "I could have been killed a million times, you know?" he admitted. "I just wasn't." He understood that the chance of dying was an element of the job, a mathematical possibility that could never be entirely eliminated from calculations. He just couldn't believe it had happened to Reid. Reid had always been the one who could survive anything. "This whole freaking building could fall on him," Rondell said. "And he'd be in a corner somewhere, tucked in, you know? When we finally dug the entire building out, we'd find him down on the bottom."

The senselessness of his son's death infuriated him. As Rondell saw it, Meher's behavior had violated a cardinal rule of professional conduct. "You drive your cars as fast and hard as you can going to do the gag, and on the way back you go slowly and carefully," Rondell said. "You rest your horses. You don't gallop them back to One. You drive your car slow. You get in formation, you wait to go, and you fly your helicopter back. And this guy was fucking off and he killed— You know, he got my son killed because he's stupid and— Not that he was a bad pilot. He was a hotdog, and that cost my son his life. I'll never forgive him for that. I went after him with everything and I got his license pulled. Doesn't mean he can't go to another state or whatever, but I got him out of the picture business anyway. So he wasn't going to kill another stuntman."

For years after that, Rondell served on the Screen Actors Guild committee for stunt safety, and whenever there was a serious accident, he'd be part of the official investigation. In 1994, when Sonja Davis, Angela Bassett's stunt double on *Vampire in Brooklyn*, pushed off for a forty-foot fall down an air shaft and rebounded off the air bag into the adjoining brick wall, Rondell showed up to look over the edge of the roof. Despite all that he'd been through, he argued that stunt work was safe, comparing it favorably with logging or commercial fishing in Alaska. He seemed to know many more stuntmen who'd died in accidents off the set—like Jack Coffer and Jerry Randall—than those who'd died, as he put it, "in the business." It was a tricky calculus: his son had died on the set, but, technically, he wasn't performing a stunt.

The same thing happened to his old friend Dar Robinson—Mel Gibson's double in the *Lethal Weapon* series, and the son of the family that owned the trampoline business where he'd spent so many hours as a young man. Robinson had done some pretty theatrical gags in his day, on film and in exhibitions, like jumping from one airplane, falling a mile, then climbing into a second plane without ever pulling a chute. But on the day he died, he'd already finished his big gag, crashing his motorcycle into a guardrail and falling down a hill on the other side. After that wrapped, they'd sent the ambulance away from the remote location in northern Arizona—a fatal mistake, as it turned out, because when Robinson, after performing a routine drive-by past the camera, turned his motorcycle to head back for another pass, he dumped the bike unexpectedly, slid off the soft shoulder of the road, and fell down a hill that was littered with boulders and sharp brush. He waited two hours, in Page, Arizona, more than a hundred and forty miles from the nearest hospital in Flagstaff, for an ambulance that never came, and died of wounds that he would most likely have survived with timely medical attention.

I'm not suggesting that Rondell dismissed his son's death on a technicality. His voice never wavered when he told me about Reid—perhaps working on the SAG safety committee had helped him turn some elements of the personal tragedy into professional perspective. But his eyes were full as he spoke, not with tears, but with the effort of confronting a permanent emotional loss that went to the heart of his family and his life's work. On several occasions during our conversations, Rondell referred to Reid casually in the present tense ("There's Reid," he said, laughing and pointing to a picture of him as a young boy. "There's the little shit right there. His nose was always peeling from the sun"). But there didn't seem to be any denial in it. It felt more like a quiet determination that no accident or twist of fate could deprive him of the pleasure he took in his son.

Thirty-some years after Rondell left the Stuntmen's Association, another gang of stuntmen decided it was time to strike out on their own. The circumstances will sound familiar: the well-established professional fraternity showed signs of age, failing to keep up with trends or to sign enough young guys to pull off the latest gags. Once more, a Rondell spoke up. This time, however, the aging group was Stunts Unlimited, and it was R. A. forming a new band of stunt expatriates. Ronnie, of course, understood. "I'd no sooner left the group," heading off to his Ozark retirement, he said, "than I started getting phone calls, and guys were going, 'Man, we're unhappy. I know you started the group, but we've gotta move on.' And I said, 'Then you've gotta move on.' I said, 'You guys are the young, hot, go-for-it dudes, and the old guys, well, they're making the same fuckup that the Association made. It's time to go.'"

R. A. had been a member of Stunts Unlimited for twenty-five years. "I grew up with these guys," he said. "I love them dearly, but the group evolved. They all do. It evolved into a kind of politics that I didn't want to be part of anymore." He was coordinating big shows, and he felt responsible for hiring the best people available, "no matter what colors they fly." But with the aging of the Unlimited ranks, he found that the group's hiring quota was holding him back. "So I told my dad, and he goes, 'I totally understand. I respect you for staying as long as you have. That's the reason I left the Stuntmen's Association.'" R. A. and a few other former Unlimited guys called their new group Brand X, which was partly a nod to the X Games and the type of renegade adventure athletes they hoped to recruit. But it was also an inside joke: back in 1970, when the guys in the Stuntmen's Association tried to convince producers that their rivals were dangerous and cut-rate, they'd refer to Stunts Unlimited only by the derogatory nickname Brand X.

A few weeks after my trip to Missouri, I visited R. A. Rondell on the set of *Next*. They were filming an extended daylight shootout sequence on the piers at Long Beach—a high fall, a rollover, an explosion, some long-range sniping, a cat-and-mouse exchange of gunfire in a warehouse full of catwalks and storage containers. The day I came, they'd scheduled a few big-action paychecks for the crew of stuntmen, but there were also a lot of transition shots and mop-up work on the slate, stunt doubles running down corridors or walking through doorways, so R. A., who was coordinating the stunts and running the second unit, had some free time between takes to talk about his dad. Like Reid, R. A. worked in the business from an early age, and he used to safety for his father a lot. He remembered a stunt competition twenty years ago, part of a halftime show, in which his father worked with a special-effects man named Dutch Van Derbyl to create a car that would disintegrate on cue for the live audience. They planted a series of strategically placed explosive charges, so Rondell could drive into the stadium and slide the car, press a button, and the thing would completely blow up: the doors, the windows, the trunk and hood, everything would blast apart and disappear in a huge fireball. "And *the guy*"—by which R. A. meant his father, since the point of his story was the almost extraterrestrial nature of his dad's bravado—"had a little pod that he would sit in for all of this. So I'm a safety guy. He comes in, slides the car"—R. A. imitated the screeching sound of wheels locking under the emergency brake—"the blast comes, there's fire everywhere, the whole works. I run right to where I'm supposed to go, to his side to get him out, and as soon as I get there I look at him. And he locks the door and just looks at me. And I'm standing at the door, but he's just sitting there, and I know what he's doing. Needham runs in, thinking that I'm not taking care of business. He pulls me off to the side, and tries to grab the door; he's running around grabbing fire extinguishers, thinking his best friend's dying in the car. And the audience is quiet. And everybody's freaking out." For several long beats, while the car went up in flames, Ronnie sat in the pod and watched his son and partner flail around. "Finally," R. A. said, "he steps out and takes a little bow and gets a nice round of applause. You know? Here are all the rest of us panicking and getting . . ." He stopped there. It was quite obvious, even twenty-some years later, what effect his father's theatricality had had on him that day. "Yeah, it's good stuff."

After all I'd heard from Ronnie, I couldn't bear to ask R. A. a direct question about his brother, Reid. But I did want to check on one story that his father had told about a near-miss back in the mid-seventies. I wanted to hear R. A.'s version of events. Ronnie was working on *Baretta*, running the stunts and doubling Robert Blake, and the script called for a car to drive off a pier into the ocean. Ronnie assigned the gag to himself. Both R. A. and Reid were certified scuba divers, and even though R. A. wasn't much older than twenty, Ronnie made him the chief safety for the gag. His son would get his first experience overseeing the dive team and recovery process and coordinating the heavy machinery—like the big crane they kept on hand to haul the wreck out of the water in case anything happened.

It was a twenty-seven-foot dive from the pier to the water, and the water at the intended entry point was about the same depth. The day before the shoot, Ronnie dove it to scout the bottom; R. A. did the same thing the next morning. Both of them found it to be soft and silty, and R. A. poked around with a pole to see if he could scratch a hard bottom underneath the muck. The car had been prepped to hit the water and sink. The windshield was smashed out, and Ronnie had had a little metal splash plate welded onto the hood: when he hit the ocean surface the splash plate would deflect the incoming water over the open windshield and his head, so it wouldn't hit him full in the face and knock him out, jarring loose the mouthpiece to his air supply. Ronnie also put a thousand pounds of lead in the trunk, to keep the car from flipping over after he went airborne, and he had holes cut in the bottom of the car, so it would fill up with water and sink quickly to the bottom. Just before they started filming, the director leaned in to ask him to keep the mouthpiece connected to his air supply out of his mouth until he went underwater. Ronnie agreed—then put it in anyway as soon as he drove away.

He flew off the pier, caught a glimpse of the sky and the camera boat, and then nothing but water as the car dove straight down ("Like Greg Louganis, *BOOM!*"). It bobbed back up just enough to show the taillights, then started sinking. Ronnie, now underwater, knew that the take was over and he could start planning his escape. But as he was putting on the mask he'd taped to his arm, he felt a huge jolt. The car had hit bottom, hard. He cleared the water from his mask, but he still couldn't see anything: it was pitch black. He reached through the space where the windshield once was: mud, so hard he could barely scrape it with his fingernails. He was upside down and stuck inside the cabin. He started to calculate how much time it would take for them to extract him: they had to find the car, bring in the crane, send down a cable, hook it to the rings they'd welded to the four corners of the car's chassis, and then haul him up. How long would that take? A half hour? And what if they hit a snag? What did he need if it went as badly as it could possibly go? He had a long regulator hose so he could move around, and he was hooked to a bailout bottle that was small enough for him to maneuver out of a window and make it up to the surface if he could find an escape route. The bailout bottle had eight minutes' worth of air. He had another thirty-five or forty minutes in the big tank in the backseat. He decided to switch to the big tank. He remembers thinking, "Now I've got an hour, maybe more, because I can skip breathe, go into Zen, just hang here."

The roof of the car had caved in, so he didn't have much room to move around. But before he curled up to wait it out, he pushed at the back windows and found one that collapsed so he could reach through it. He worried about moving away from the car and getting stuck, or getting lost in some cave that the safeties couldn't locate. But when he reached out with his hand he couldn't feel anything at all so he decided to risk sticking his head out of the car to look around. As soon as he did he saw green—a murky dark green, because the impact of the car had stirred up all the silt. But he'd seen enough light that he thought he could make it. He got back in the car, switched to the bailout bottle, and squeezed out of the window. As he headed to the surface, he looked down one last time: he spotted the white heavy-duty shock absorbers they'd installed to hold up all the lead, so he knew the car was upside down. "And I saw my kid, down by the driver's window, trying to dig his way in there," Ronnie said. "But I didn't have a weight belt on, so once I got out of the car, I couldn't turn around and swim down to him." The only thing he could do was float up to the surface and wait.

When his father drove off the pier, R. A. had been in the water already, hanging onto the pilings, waiting to dive down and help in the recovery. As soon as he saw the car hit the water and begin to sink, he went underwater to follow its progress. At first the water was clear enough for him to see bubbles and trace the path of the sinking car. But as soon as the car hit bottom, it kicked up the silt and created a blackout. At first, he could still follow the trail of bubbles escaping from the car's trunk and passenger compartment. But soon that stopped, too. There was no more air left in the car, and R. A. swam down to the bottom and found nothing. The car had disappeared. So he got down on his hands and knees in the mud and started digging. Finally, he hit the exhaust pipes and differential housing, and he realized that the car was upside down; the windows (and therefore all the escape routes) were stuck beneath the mud, and there was no air escaping anywhere. He knew his father was a resourceful stuntman and a great diver, but at that point, as he reviewed the possible scenarios he couldn't stop thinking of the worst one: that he'd tried to escape and gotten pinned underneath the car.

He raced to the surface and signaled for the crane to get into position, then swam back down to keep digging around. The first thing he did was clear the bottom of the car and locate the rings welded to the four corners of the car. Then he started to tunnel through the silt to find doors or windows, any way to get in. Again he swam up to the top, to direct the crane arm and the hook into position, and then swam back down, to dig for the windows, which were all stuck in the mud. Finally, he broke through one of them: he found the steering wheel and the empty seat belt where his father had been. He was gone.

"So I spring back to the surface to reposition the crane arms," R. A. told me. "But as I pop to the surface again, he pops up next to me, about that far from me, and he goes, 'How was it?' And I just looked at him and I just started crying.

"I said, 'Don't—' I said, 'You can't do that.' " R. A. remembered the conversation the way his father remembered the call from the *Airwolf* set. He told his father, "You can't do that to me."

"What?" Ronnie said. "How was it?"

"You're fuckin—"

"It's okay. It's okay. It's okay."

"Oh my god. Dude, you can't . . . You can't do that to me."

"I didn't do anything."

Ronnie remembered the scene only slightly differently. In his version, he was bobbing on the water when R. A. popped up. But R. A. had surfaced with his back to his father and immediately started shouting to the crane operator: "Get the crane over here, right fucking now!" Ronnie grabbed him from behind and said, "R. A! R. A.!" And the instant R. A. turned to see him, there were tears in his eyes. "And he just started swimming away," Ronnie said. "And I went, 'Hey, it's okay. It's okay. You did the job.' "

Ronnie grew more emotional telling that story than he'd allowed himself to be as he remembered Reid. "It really freaked him out," he said, as he pictured R. A. swimming away. "That was a big part of him realizing, Shit can go wrong." The story seemed to take both of them by surprise. No matter who did the telling, by the end of it, each of them had clearly remembered another day where they couldn't get there to tap a kid on the shoulder or help him scratch his way out of the wreck.

"He was so calm, looking at me," R. A. said, and he imitated his father's cheery, unruffled greeting one more time. " 'What? How was it?' First I wanted to kiss him. But then I wanted to choke him. But then I wanted to kiss him again, you know? I had to swim off by myself for a little while. Just, 'Oh my God. What was all that?' "

As the Rondells can tell you, it's not unusual to have a couple of people from the same family in a stunt crew. It's not even that unusual to have one family member setting up a risky gag for another and running the safety crew for him or her. Whenever that happens, everybody pays attention. R. A. did his first cannon roll on one of his father's shows. And Ronnie watched the whole thing from a helicopter. "He practically jumped out of the helicopter before it landed because it looked so violent in the air to him that he was a mess," R. A. said. "He didn't let that show when he got to me, but the people with him told me that. By the time he got to me, he said, 'You all right? Good. Here we go.' And he was on to something else." That sort of incident sets the standard of care for the whole industry: once you've seen a Rondell (or a Picerni or Orsatti or Epper or Gill or Gilbert) jump out of a helicopter and race over to check on his own family, you always know how fast a body is expected to run.

CHAPTER 8

Skid and Burn

At the start of my stunt-driving lesson, I was riding in a black Hummer with Adrien Brody. We were lost. Brody was at the wheel in a wife-beater, camo pants, combat boots, and Yves Saint Laurent sunglasses, and who cares what I was wearing—something beat up, for sure, because it's not a good idea to wear your best new clothes to hang out with a stuntman. We were driving around an industrial park in the Santa Susana Mountains one hour north of L.A. It was June, hot, six o'clock; we had a couple of hours of sunlight at least, and nobody around, maybe four cars parked in the entire canyon of half-built big-box warehouses. I got on the cell to Sean Graham, who'd chosen this place, and was somewhere nearby driving the car I'd rented that morning—a silver sport-series Mini Cooper, the same kind of car he'd driven up the walls of an L.A. water main, doubling Mark Wahlberg in *The Italian Job*.

Graham had taught me the lesson about new clothes when I'd dropped by his house in Venice a few weeks before. He was sitting on his porch, double T-shirt, puka shells, his hair sea-bleached a subtle shade of orange. He's a prodigious talent, with two stunt awards and a big rep that he doesn't hesitate to let you know about. Even among stuntmen, he's a standout, known for his eccentric combination of Hollywood hustle and barefoot brother-man surfer vibe. On the one hand, he is, as he puts it, "a sponsor whore," with a shifting constellation of endorsement deals from the likes of GM, Quiksilver, Yamaha, Steve Walden surfboards, Simpson racing gear, and Polaris Quadrunners. On the other, as we were headed to his garage he saw his next-door neighbor, an old lady not much taller than the wooden fence between us, and, with less than a one-step prep, cleared the fence to help her take her trash out to the curb.

His good deed done, Graham got out a pair of battery-powered scooters from his stunt garage—a mess of ATVs, hang gliders, rackets, surfboards, roller blades, motorcycles, stunt pads, climbing gear, and so on—and we headed off to a bar by the beach. He carved a big wide path down the empty streets, slaloming and popping wheelies; I bisected his wake, beelining behind him on a scooter with considerably less horsepower than his. When he disappeared down a footpath between Venice backyards, I ducked in after him. "Okay," he called back at me, as we headed into a corridor where the shrubbery had been manicured to form an archway just over our heads. "Don't let up on the throttle the whole way here." He disappeared at full speed and when I tried to do the same I got whipped in the face by rosebush branches and ran over something screechy. Graham waited for me at the other end, smiling like a man who knew how to duck, and as soon as he saw me emerge, he headed off again, back onto the road toward the beach. I followed his route precisely but failed to notice that he'd popped a wheelie to make it safely over the curb, so I hit the concrete lip with the front wheel at full speed and spilled over the scooter's handlebars, hitting the pavement and rolling a few times. I ripped the *Big Fish* film-crew jacket that Graham had given me to wear and tore up a pair of khakis I'd bought just that morning. Graham laughed and then pretended to care for a few seconds before I waved him away and got back on the scooter so we could go have that drink.

I didn't mention that story to Brody. Mostly we were talking about cars and motorcycles. I grew up in Detroit, where everyone speaks Car, and Brody's a car freak, too: in the past few weeks the Queens native had been busy driving in the Gumball 3000, an annual semi-legal road rally which that year followed a route from Paris to Madrid to Marbella to Casablanca to Barcelona to Cannes. The Hummer (he called it his "truck") was a gift to himself after he won the Oscar for *The Pianist*: black on black, privacy glass, Alpine stereo, custom bass enclosure, TVs in the headrests, PlayStation in the back. On the ride over, he kept turning the air-conditioning on and off to save gas. He'd cool off for a minute, turn it off. Talk. Start sweating, turn it back on. "Look, I've had this car for about a year," he said. "And there's three thousand miles on it. I drive my motorcycle most of the time. I don't like to be wasteful."

We finally spotted Graham and the Mini Cooper. It wasn't hard, since we hadn't seen another motorist the whole time we were circling, but any doubts we might have had about his identity disappeared as we watched the Mini Cooper speeding directly toward us, with the preposterous intention of playing chicken with a Hummer. But just before the seemingly inevitable collision, we heard a screeching of brakes, and the Mini pirouetted around, doing a 180 that landed the rental car neatly behind us, drafting on our rear bumper, heading the same way we were. "That's awesome," Brody gushed. "I want to drive like that everywhere I go. I just want to drive like that."

Graham pulled out ahead and led us to an intersection at the far end of the industrial park, where the deserted roads dead-ended in a dry arroyo. I'd offered to rent a parking lot somewhere for our lesson, but Graham had heard a buddy talking about this place and its new, empty, and absurdly wide streets. The guerrilla approach seemed more his style. Jumping out of his car, he picked up a couple of traffic cones left behind by some construction crew and positioned them in the middle of the street. He pointed to a fire hydrant. "I wish we could turn that on, dump some water there," he yelled. "I should have brought my tools. Would that be awesome or what? The cops would have been here in no time."

With Graham at the wheel of the Mini Cooper, we piled in, stuntman and star in front, journalist in the rear. "We're going to practice how to 'ride the slide,'" Graham said, and immediately introduced the essential element of stunt driving. "Before you do any tricks, you gotta make sure you set the e-brake." The timely application of the emergency brake, he explained, makes a car slip over the road and provides the essential screech. He pointed to the e-brake, which on the Mini Cooper is just inches away from the gear shaft, right between the two front seats. "Like when I slid next to your truck: if I turn the steering wheel first, there's a chance I could roll the car. But once the tires are locking up, then I can control the turn."

Brody pointed to the nipple-like button on the top of the e-brake. "So do you keep that thing pressed in?"

"Always. This time, all you're going to do is you're going to come in, ride the slide for a while, and stop it for me." Graham demonstrated, starting his run with the Mini backed against a cyclone fence where the road ended, and accelerating through first and second gear to about thirty miles an hour, at which point he pulled hard on the e-brake. On the first run, he simply steered straight ahead, enjoying the squeal of the tires and letting us appreciate, in isolation, what the e-brake contributes to any trick, the feel of the rear tires locking up, the smell of burning rubber as the car skims forward over the pavement. Then he released the e-brake and brought the car to a stop with the foot brake.

Because the car had shuddered a little bit, he reached out to the dashboard and switched off the traction control. Such safety features pose a real problem for stunt drivers—newer cars, especially the more expensive models, have so many built-in safety gadgets that it can be hard to pull off stock chase-scene maneuvers. Stunt teams often have to beg car-company engineers to show the movie's chief mechanics (or "action-vehicle supervisors") how to turn off all the factory-installed features: the anti-lock brakes, the traction control, the electronic stability systems. Stunt driving used to be something everybody could learn: all you needed was a production car and a healthy disrespect for motor-vehicle regulations. Try it on most cars now and the brakes won't lock or the engine will stall. All the "out-of-control" driving you're used to seeing in chase scenes is becoming archaic, a relic of a dirt-road rear-wheel-drive America, a film convention that's increasingly difficult to reproduce in real life. The ideal stunt car is a muscle car built before the oil crisis, but you can't find those models at your local car rental, so we were making do. Graham had driven Mini Coopers for six months on *The Italian Job*, and while he didn't lust after them, he'd come to regard them with grudging respect. "I hate to say it, but this is a great stunt car," he said. "Cheap as these things are, it's like a little go-kart."

Graham backed up to the fence, to demonstrate again. "Ride the slide as long as you can, and when you want to stop, just release your e-brake and step on the brakes. You come in, you're hammering the e-brake. You're riding the slide, ride it, ride it, ride it—"

"Do you let it go and then press your brakes?" Brody asked.

"You can hold it the whole time and just push the brakes to stop it. But the right way to do it, you feather it. You release the e-brake while you're stepping on the brake." He started a second run, and got up a little more speed. "You can keep the car straight. Or you can slide it around like this." He hammered the e-brake and began fishtailing back and forth over the road. On my tape, the screech lasts for six full seconds. It's followed by silence and appreciative chuckles.

"You want to try that?" Graham asked.

"Let's try that."

"I'll just show you one step past that one." Graham turned back toward the intersection, parked the car, and placed his left hand firmly at the top of the steering wheel. "This time we're going to do exactly the same thing: we're going to come in, we're going to set the e-brake, and once you feel good lockup, all we're going to add is a quarter turn. We're just going to turn the wheel this far." He moved his left hand, crisply, from 12 o'clock to 3.

The students nodded.

"And that's it: we'll throw a 90." Again he started driving, stomping on the gas until he hit thirty miles an hour. "No cars coming. Come in . . . and . . . ride the slide." He set the e-brake, and in four seconds of screeching, he turned with a quick cut on the wheel, more of a jab or a jerk than a turn, and the car slid around the corner (Witherspoon Parkway and Avenue Penn, in case you're ever in driving distance of Valencia, California) in a neat sharp line. Graham explained that, to avoid going into a spin, you begin the recovery in the turn, countersteering just the way you would on an icy road.

"The e-brake is what gets all of this stuff going." He was on a roll and decided to show us another trick. He drove back to the starting point, by the fence on Witherspoon, in line with the traffic cones. "So all a 180 is, you just hold it for a hair longer."

"It's a quarter turn, huh."

"Always a quarter turn. You don't ever need more than that. You see people doing big things with the steering wheels." He laughed, and there was a tactful instant where he did not say a word about any particular actor behind the wheel, in a hero car set on a raised platform behind a truck, with cameras all around, filming, while said actor pretends to be careening down the road, hauling around a disconnected steering wheel like he's steering the *Lusitania*. Instead, Graham showed us the crisp move again, in both directions: 12 o'clock to 3. 12 o'clock to 9. "It's just that. That's all it is. Okay. I'll just show you a 180 here. This is cool."

But before Graham could begin, a security guard in a Buick drove past slowly and we waited for him to decide what to do. In the end, he just crawled past at a passive-aggressive five-mile-an-hour pace, then turned a corner and disappeared forever. Graham laughed and resumed the tutorial. "This trick is not that loud, so I don't think we'll be making much of a ruckus. Now remember, you're coming in, set the e-brake and, just like any other sport—motorcycle riding, skiing, anything else—it's all your eyes: target fixation. If you look over here, you're going over here. So you want to look at your target. If I'm trying to slide into the box—" He drove past the cones and stared at them, demonstrating target fixation, keeping his head fixed on a single point as he drove by. "I'm looking at the box, even when I'm sliding into it, I'm still looking at my box: Boom. Stop on my mark."

"Slide into a box" is stunt language for "throw a 90 or 180 into a parallel parking space." Graham has won stunt competitions with the move and even set a world record, sliding into a parking space with only about thirteen inches of extra space. He drove back to the starting point. "This one we'll throw. I'm going to go just past the cone. I'm going to set the e-brake, I'm going to throw the steering wheel, and I'm going to slide all the way past, to 180, and stop. You're doing the same thing as a 90. It's not any more difficult—it's just holding the slide for just a hair longer." Graham accelerated, pulled at the e-brake, tugged the wheel, and the car rocked around the traffic cone. When he hit the brakes, we came to a complete stop, nestled between cones, facing the direction we'd just come from.

Graham switched to the passenger seat so Brody and I could both try the move. He was right: the 180 was easy. Practically all you have to do is hit the e-brake, turn the wheel, and enjoy the ride. The 90 took more work, since you have to throw the trick, then somehow manage to keep yourself from spinning the car as you're trying to drive away. The last thing you want to do is throw a 115 and then stall out, as I did.

Brody caught on quickly and got hooked, and Graham coached him through a series of reps and variations: left- and right-hand turns, uphill and downhill. He urged him to increase the speed and stay on the gas throughout the turn for a "race-car drift." ("Mmmm," Brody said, appreciatively. "That's dangerous. You're teaching me bad things. Let's do it the other direction.") But the trick that was the most fun and impressive actually wasn't all that hard: the reverse 180, that is, a 180 that starts while you're driving in reverse. "It's one of the easiest tricks," Graham said. "The drift-reverse 180. It's a fun one to throw at a party. My buddy rolled his truck doing that, in front of a bunch of chicks. He's a real good stuntman, too. But his truck wasn't set up for it."

Graham's right. A reverse 180 is easy. The reason I know is that I just got up from my desk and took my '94 Honda Civic out to a dirt parking lot deep in a nearby state park. A few months after the stunt tutorial, my wife, Amy, and I moved to the country with our kids, a lifestyle change that required one car per adult. I wound up with a scooty beater with manual transmission, built before Hondas got traction control, and it has performed well on the series of irresponsible maneuvers detailed here. The 180s are addictive, the 90s throw up a lot of dirt, and while I've never managed to drive smoothly out of the reverse 180—so far every time I make it all the way around, the car has come to a full stop—I'm sure I will soon. I'm determined to pass something of value on to the kids.

To tell the truth, I've been out more than a few times. Procrastination is a serious hazard of my job, and it's invigorating to procrastinate by doing something that's actually hazardous. Here's one of the first things I discovered: the e-brake is a surprisingly versatile little driving enhancement. There's about three miles of dirt road before I actually get to the parking lot, and it's wide enough that I can set the e-brake and fishtail around ess-curves through the woods. It seems to be more efficient than foot-braking or downshifting, since you can pretty much keep your foot on the gas. I do worry about the trees on the side of the road, but I checked with my accountant. Repairs would be tax deductible. New tires, too.

Don't let me misrepresent my skills. I'm trying this stuff in the middle of a hardwood forest. Half the time I screw up and stall or stop too soon or wind up far away from any place I thought I'd be going. I've gotten a crick in my neck from attempting a reverse 180 and I make myself carsick a lot, so I don't feel like eating much afterward (the stuntman diet!). I've heard stunties talking about being able to do a gag but not being ready to perform it on the set, where you have to hit your mark on camera every take, and you have to have enough confidence to guarantee the safety of the crew and the surrounding equipment. I'm trying to work up the courage to show my eight-year-old.

In the tutorial, however, Brody was doing fine and enjoying himself. Driving the Mini, Brody was likable and unguarded. Brody in the Hummer was a bit of a prig. But in front of the stunt-man, he dropped all pretension and caginess and had fun stalling, starting over, peeling around corners, and subjecting the passengers to horizontal g-forces that seat belts are not designed to withstand. "One more reverse, then I'll let you guys take over," he said. "Heh, heh."

"We've got to finish with a clean 180," Graham said.

Brody threw the reverse 180 into a spot on the street that Graham had sprayed with some Black Magic Tire Wet, a product that's marketed as a way to make your tires look shiny and clean but is widely used as an aid to automotive hijinks like smoking out your tires for YouTube. "Oooh," Brody said, pleased with the trick and his dawning sense of mastery. "That'll scare people. You pull up like that to a party? I have arrived!" He made the screech noise and drove back into position to try it again. From my spot in the backseat, I had the best camera angle to catch the indie star adding a bit of humanity to his action shot: this time, as he pinned down the gas and hammered the e-brake, he bit his lip a little and still pulled off the trick.

Graham, who doubles Tobey Maguire as well as Mark Wahlberg and knows how to handle the talent, cheerleads. "Now that was the fuckin' trick. Yeah!"

"I'm going to give it one more shot."

"We've created a monster."

"I know. It's bad."

Graham reached into the backseat for more product. "You want me to wet it down one more time and show you what a 360 is?"

End of tutorial. Also, end of demystification. You, brave reader, may now go forth and drive like the Driver in *The Driver*. Just commit the foregoing to memory—or tear out the chapter and tuck it up under the visor for ease of reference—and away you go.

Of course, there are legal issues involved with the content here, so let me preface this by saying don't be an idiot. But, if you have reason to believe you might be chased by rogue agents or rival moonshiners or Illinois state troopers, or if you just want to make a good impression the next time you show up at church, by all means, hit the gas and hang it out there. You now have all the necessary intellectual grounding.

On the other hand, this next trick, the full burn, I do not recommend trying without a full crew of stunt professionals. It's not like stunt driving, where if you make a mistake all you do is stall or blow a tire or land upside down on the hood of your new truck in front of your future wife. If you flub a full burn, that's it. You're toast, literally: you're a brittle piece of charred carbon residue ready for the knife.

I know this because I've done it. I had to, really. What would be the point of watching all these elaborate stunts if I never tried one myself? And thanks to the vigilance of five legitimate dues-paying SAG stuntmen, I survived. Three weeks later, I finally told my wife what I'd really been doing in L.A. over the Labor Day weekend, and the news spread, in spite of my attempts to control the story. The next morning, I was out in the backyard with my three-year-old son, Jack. We were talking. I had a coffee in one hand and from time to time a Wiffle ball in the other. He had a bat.

"Anyone can be on fire," he told me.

The day before, I'd printed out a picture for his older brother and sister. In the process of booting them out of my office, I showed off some digital snapshots of me on fire. If you clicked from one to the other fast enough, it was almost like a movie: Dad. Dad and man with fire suit and fireproof balaclava. Dad and two men with fireproof balaclavas who are ducking around him with blowtorches. Fire rising up Dad's outfit. Dad gesturing with arms on fire and flames threatening the familiar bald head. Dad falling facedown to the ground. Guys in balaclavas emptying a fire extinguisher on Dad, putting out the fire completely except for a runaway bit of flame that continues to burn around his sock, unnoticed by everyone, except Dad. Finally Dad, who has been instructed not to breathe while being doused in a fog of chemicals, managing to twitch his foot enough that somebody with a fire extinguisher notices the rogue blaze and squirts that one out, too.

As a parent I understand the value of hypocrisy: I warned Jack that he should never think of setting himself on fire, never play with fire, never even blow on the Sabbath candles, ever. This is not the vibe I picked up from stuntmen. The very first one I spoke to, in person, in a production office in Santa Monica, treated a full burn like a youthful prank. "In our youth we used to do that shit all the time," Freddie Hice said. "Go to a Halloween party, a costume party, and they'd have a judge in the backyard, you're putting your fire suit on. And they call your name: Here's So-and-So, dressed as . . . And you light yourself on fire and walk into the room. You're fully on fire and everybody just freaks the fuck out, you know?" Hice laughed. He made it sound innocent, just a fad the kids were into, like streaking or cramming into VW Beetles. "Usually directly after that the police arrive. But that's been done a number of times, at a few parties. It's kind of old hat now, you know. I don't think anybody's done that in years."

Then I visited the set of *The Punisher* and saw what a stuntman goes through to get ready for a fire gag. The day I was there, Mike Owen, doubling the Punisher, was getting blown off a pier, supposedly by the sudden explosion of several barrels of oil. Owen was focusing all his attention on the ratchet that would toss him into the air; the other part of the gag—the part where he'd be blasted in the face by a wall of fire—seemed almost incidental. The fire blast was important. It was a turning point in the story. It made the gag more lucrative. And the preparation for it—putting on a few layers of Nomex underwear soaked in a fire-retardant liquid, getting the exposed portions of his skin slathered in protective gel—was meticulous. But the business part of the gag required very little from him: determination to go through with it, confidence in his team and their attention to detail, enough discipline not to betray overt signs of anticipation, willful indifference at the moment of contact. For something that looked so violent and life-threatening, it was all pretty passive on his part.

I keep a running tally when I visit stunt teams and second units, a completely hypothetical "Could I ever do that?" list. (High fall: No. Stair fall: One take, maybe. Basic smacking around: Sure. Horse fall, horse-to-train transfer, horse anything: Ha. Hang gliding, BASE jumping, parachuting into a moving sports car: Ha-ha. Parkour-style jump from a rooftop in the Casbah through a window across the street: No way. Firearms, scuba diving, mountain climbing, free-swimming with sharks: No, no, no, no. And so on.) Most stunt professionals have a similar list, except for them it's a printout of specialties that goes with their head shot. Their lists tend to grow longer as they stick around the business, since most start as specialists and then systematically add to their skills. That's why they're so much more likely to be hurt off the set than on it: they're building the résumé.

So when it came time for me to try one big stunt myself, I had the perfect choice: the full burn. The gag was both legitimately terrifying and, according to my research, the only one that I could reliably survive. It seemed ideally suited to my situation: it required a high degree of professionalism but none of it on my part. For a full burn, it was okay that I had about as much talent as a candle. The only thing I needed, really, was to find somebody who could put me out.

When I called Dan Bradley to see if he knew somebody who could help me, he said he'd set it up himself. I'd met him a few times, most recently when he was shooting the climactic chase scene in *The Bourne Ultimatum*. Luckily, when I reached him he was between jobs: he'd just got back from Hawaii, where he'd been directing the action on *Indiana Jones and the Kingdom of the Crystal Skull*, and he'd given himself about a week in L.A. before he had to start work on the next Bond film in Italy. I called him first not because of his style on film, which is raw and unsettling, but because he has a reputation for being extremely safe. A sergeant in the NYPD Film and TV division assigned to the *Bourne* shoot said he'd never seen a safer set.

So I flew into L.A. on Labor Day weekend, the day before Bradley said he could do it. He e-mailed me: "I've got a couple of guys lined up for fire safety and I have the fire extinguishers!" Just like that, with friendly exclamation points, like he was inviting me to a cookout. (Great! I'll bring the Merlot!) Then he gave me an address in the desert foothills north of L.A., up where they made all the blood-and-thunder serials back in the silent era.

I pulled up around noon with a couple of friends and witnesses. He already had a big black backdrop set up in his driveway. There were two coolers by the garage door, a few sawhorses, some drywall, a furniture pad thrown down on the cobblestones, a big black Rubbermaid bucket filled with water, a C-stand sitting on a tarp, a few industrial fans. As we walked up the drive, a guy in an International Stunt Association T-shirt was getting off his bike. I also recognized Pat Dailey, a key grip turned "wire automation operator" I'd met at a *Spider-Man* stunt rehearsal (Dailey made up the title, and he helped make up the job: he ran the software controlling the high-speed winches that flew stuntmen through the air). Bradley rents a condo when he's in town, but this is his desert getaway, the one he never gets to. It looked and felt more like a movie set than a weekend house. The next-door neighbor stuck his head over the fence and apologized for all the noise he was making: he had his dogs out and his music playing, he said, while he was fixing some stuff in his yard. "No worries," Dailey said. "We're just going to light this guy on fire."

I'd brought a shopping bag full of old clothes to burn. And that was all I'd done to prepare. Bradley'd taken care of everything on the safety checklist, and as I was wandering around with my friends (Sara and Josh, watching through a video cam, and Craig the photographer), he came out to greet us with a couple of bags of ice that he handed to Frank Lloyd, the guy in the ISA T-shirt, who started loading them into the coolers.

"What's all the ice for?" Sara asked.

"Beer later," Lloyd said. "Right before we light him on fire we all drink two or three beers. It's just one of the old habits that stunt guys started out doing years ago."

"How long before we do this?" Dailey asked Bradley. The workaday quality of the question actually relaxed me, the same way you'd be glad to hear that your surgeon had done four thousand vasectomies.

"Well, Paul's not here and he's got most of the Nomex."

"I've got two layers," Dailey said.

"Well, Paul's got the Kevlar suit. If we use that we can go with just one layer of Nomex and he can go dry."

Nomex looks just like long underwear. It provides a good deal of protection on its own—a lot of firefighters wear it on the job and it's often sold as "stationwear." But being near a burning building—or even in one—is not the same as being doused in gas and lamp oil and then ignited. (The gas in the mixture gives volume to the flame and the lamp oil burns a rich orange that reads better on film.) At some point in the nineties, stunt designers discovered that if you soaked the Nomex in flame-retardant gel and kept it on ice, you could do away with almost all other protection. You can easily spot this shift in technique on film: before the discovery, stuntmen wore heavy suits that made them look like astronauts, and the full-burn sequence was usually filmed in long shot to disguise this bulk. But once stuntmen started wearing wet Nomex and covering it up with the character's normal clothes, the sequence could be shot much closer. And dressed in the slimmer Nomex, stuntmen could move more naturally, even nimbly. Still, I didn't have to move—all I wanted was an author photo—so Bradley thought I should "go dry," or wear a Kevlar fire suit, which would be slimmer than the hazmat-style suits that stuntmen used to wear but still a little bulkier than the wet Nomex look. Imagine the sort of overalls the NASCAR drivers wear.

"Maybe wet's better," I said, hoping to look as slim as possible.

"You'll be wet enough."

"So I can wear my glasses?"

"I think that'll be okay. We're going to want to keep the flames off your head anyway," Bradley said. That's why he had the fans, to point at my face and blow the wall of flame away.

Dailey asked why I wanted to do a full burn, and I mentioned the book and how it didn't feel right to go through the whole project without trying something myself. I thought a full burn seemed like the best choice, about as low risk as I could get.

"Low risk?" he said.

Bradley said, "It's only low risk if you've got two guys ready to put you out." And everybody chuckled, remembering the dicey setups they'd been through. "Like if you're doing a low-budget movie, and they haven't tested the fire extinguishers because they're afraid of spending the money."

When Paul Short showed up with his big gear bag, things started to move quickly. Bradley explained the advantage of the Kevlar suit—you can do multiple takes, which you can't do if you're wearing layers of wet Nomex, because the gel soaks through your clothes and inhibits the flame. The constraints of the author photo—I'd be still, as for a portrait—posed additional problems. In most full burns, the stuntman is moving. This is both logical, since nobody stands still when he's on fire, and safer, since a stuntman on the move gets himself out of the superheated air. Bradley warned me to hold my breath, to avoid burning my lungs. "We're not going to go very long. You can easily hold your breath, because it'll be like ten seconds," he said. "The minute you feel anything, you just go down. We'll put a pad, a wet furniture blanket, in front of you. Your going down is the cue to put you out. We have the two CO_2 extinguishers. We have the wet furni pad that'll be on the ground. And there'll be somebody holding another one. The CO_2 displaces the oxygen instantly. The furni pads take longer because it's all about oxygen starvation—you're trying to smother the fire. So we'll primarily be using the CO_2, but if it's taking too long . . ."

"You'll just roll me up?"

"Yeah," he said. " 'Where's Kevin?' 'He's a taco.' "

Bradley led me inside to a bathroom so I could change. Short gave me a Kevlar suit and some baby powder to keep me dry. The suit was legal-pad yellow, stiff, and bulky—once I put it on, I looked much stockier and couldn't easily bend down to tie my shoes. I reached in my bag for Burnable Outfit Number One and put it on over the suit: a gray cotton shirt, a pair of khakis, and some old-school plain-white sneakers. As I came out of the bathroom, the radio in Bradley's living room was playing "Stayin' Alive."

"So, how do you feel?" Bradley asked. "Ready?"

I nodded.

"Worst-case scenario," Dailey said, pointing out the wet furni pad, just steps from the black backdrop. "You walk away and go down here."

"Just go down on your knees," Lloyd said. "Then down to your stomach. And I'll say, 'Hold your breath.'" He held an imaginary fire extinguisher, ready to put me out.

"But you don't want to put your arms underneath you," Bradley added, "because they'll be on fire." He and Lloyd began double-teaming me with advice. "You want to get out."

"Spread-eagled."

"So it's a pretty quick move from your knees forward. Because if you do this"—Bradley mimed going down slowly and in stages—"the flame'll come right back at you."

"Go down like a prisoner."

"The fact is, they'll start shooting you with the CO_2 before you get down all the way."

Bradley handed me a pair of what looked like falconry gloves with a big cuff that went halfway up my forearm. He soaked a rag with gas and lit it for me so I could get the feel of waving the flame around. The gloves and the suit worked: even though I was whipping the flame around, letting the rag fall against my arm to get a feel for the fire, I hardly noticed it through my layers of protection. After fifteen seconds or so, the heat started working its way through the thick glove and I walked, as casually as possible, over to the Rubbermaid bucket and dropped the flaming rag in the water.

Meanwhile both Short and Lloyd had changed into fire suits of their own. Short had the blowtorch out and Bradley picked up one of the buckets of fire-retardant gel from a cooler, opened it, and held it up to my face. "You know what this smells like? Tell me. What does that smell like?"

Lloyd started dipping his hands in it and slathering it on my face.

"It smells like solvent?"

"No. It smells like money."

The gel was thick as rubber cement and Lloyd couldn't keep the grin off his face as he slopped handfuls of the stuff over my forehead and then smushed it around my head. I appreciated his thoroughness. After he'd covered me with one layer, he started another, enjoying the mess of it all. "It's like playing with mud pies," he said. I closed my eyes so he could get the slime to cover my eyelids. Meanwhile, Short took care of my hands, taking a pair of gel-soaked Nomex gloves out of the cooler and helping me put them on.

"He's covered good."

"Keep that gel on his face, Frankie," Short said. "Especially the front. Do it one more time before he goes."

"Here," Bradley said, guiding me over by the garage and out of the desert sun. "Step over into the shade."

"I'm not hot," I said.

"No, if you stay in the shade, it helps protect the gel."

As Lloyd finished up on my face, Dailey smeared a little gel on the earpieces of my glasses, so they wouldn't melt to my face, and then positioned them perfectly on the bridge of my nose like an optometrist. He mentioned that he'd been working on the 1984 Pepsi commercial when a fireworks display ignited Michael Jackson's Jheri curls. Dailey said he had been the one to put Jackson out. This was somehow reassuring.

"You ready, dude?" Bradley said. "We'll stand him in place and fuel him up right. We ought to do it closer to where we're shooting. Fuel him up here and he'll just take one step." He guided me to the spot where my photographer friend Craig thought I should stand. I moved stiffly, partly because of the suit and also because I didn't want to shake off any of the gel. Out of the corner of my eye, I could see Short dousing my arms and legs and back with his plastic pitcher of gasoline.

"So you're stepping from this position. Here we go . . ."

Short turned on his blowtorch.

"Keep your finger on the trigger," Bradley said to Craig, making sure he was ready to shoot. "He's going to get lit. Right now. Here we go."

Short pointed the flame at my arms and my back first, then ducked under and got my pant legs one at a time.

"You're burning," Bradley said, though, of course, I knew that. I followed his instructions and held my arms out wide in an all-embracing public-speaker gesture ("I still believe in a place called Hope"). Almost immediately I could see the flames rising on either side and dancing up my arms. The bigger wingspan did two things: it made the fire look more impressive and it cut down on the heat going straight to my head. The gel gave me a couple of seconds of invincibility: I could feel the touch of the flames on my face and head without feeling any of the heat. I could hear it, too, the fire rolling over my arms, flickering and snapping overhead, the fuel burning fast and spreading out. But after about five seconds of this sensory experiment, the invincibility came to an end. The heat slammed me from behind and I bowed my head, went to my knees, fell forward on the furni pad, and Bradley and Lloyd shot a few snowy blasts of CO_2,—*brsssshhhhht!*—and put me out. I'd been on fire for seven seconds.

"You hot anywhere?" Short asked. "A little hot anywhere?"

"A little hot back here, just on my occipital bone," I said. Short slathered the gel on it. The area affected wasn't that large—just a patch of skin blistering on a little ridge of bone—but it had been enough to bring me to my knees. (It scabbed over during the week that followed, and because it was on the back of my head in a spot I could only feel, I asked my wife to describe it. She took one look at it and insisted on calling a skin doctor. "A weird lesion appearing on a person's head all of a sudden?" she said. "You should have it looked at. I'm serious." I still hadn't admitted that I'd flown across the country to set myself on fire.)

"Anywhere else? Any other hot spots?"

"Maybe here," I said, pointing to the outer edge of my ear.

"You didn't wait to see how long you could stand it, right?" Bradley said. "You're just going down as soon as you feel it?"

"I was not challenging the boundary."

"You can't."

"Once you do that, it's too late," Short said. "If you have any kind of inkling, get out of there."

There was still a good deal left of my shirt and pants, so I didn't have to change before the second burn. But Lloyd needed to re-fresh the gel, which is effective for no more than five minutes. Lloyd just slathered more on top of what was already there, and the combined layers of gel began to pool and drip until it looked as if I'd been pelted with egg whites (I know because Craig took a lot of pictures of this stage). The stuff was now so thick that I had trouble opening my eyes and when I parted my lips I felt the goo stretching across my mouth in that howl-of-a-rabid-animal way. I certainly didn't mind if it meant I could keep my face. Also, Lloyd was having so much fun.

"I'm starting to feel like I'm huffing glue," I told him.

"You're so glossy. You're like an egg."

"Like I just got born. I'm Mr. Placenta!"

The second go was much more casual. Bradley told me to step to my mark, then told Short to set me on fire. ("Light him. He's lit.") Maybe there was something in the gel, but somehow this time around the absurdity of the whole proceeding hit me and as the fire roared around me I began to smile like a lunatic, like a Christian martyr. I was enjoying it. This wasn't a metaphor: I was on fire!

The second burn lasted ten seconds—or fourteen, from the per-spective of my foot. After that, I took off the Kevlar suit and they slathered gel on my shoulders and triceps, which were beginning to feel a little sunburnt. Short brought out a freezing wet Nomex shirt for me to wear under the fire suit. By the third take, in my second outfit, they wanted me to wave my arms and move a little—I could hear Craig and Bradley directing me—and with just that small change, simply by moving out of my author pose and into cooler air, I was able to stretch the burn out to more than fifteen seconds.

"I hope you guys got enough," Bradley said after that. "Because I think we've found enough tender spots." In 1995, he'd gone about as long as you can go on a full burn, running through the streets of West Hollywood on Spike Jonze's video of the song "California" for the band Wax—and I was more than happy to take him at his word and stop playing with fire. Bradley handed me a towel and I went inside to clean off the goop.

It took about four hard full-body scrubs with some grapefruit exfoliant that I found in Bradley's shower to get the gel off, retroactive proof of the stuff's effectiveness. If I'd been doing the gag for the movies, I would have earned $750—times three—for my three takes, another large deposit of hypothetical assets into the wealth-of-experience fund. Sara's husband, Josh, was taking video of the event, so I've seen it all again since, but I'd have remembered everything without it: some days in life just stand out from the rest (waking up to the Mexico City earthquake; meeting Amy at that potluck picnic in Riverside Park). But let's not kid ourselves. I was not going to be setting myself on fire with any regularity, or, with any luck, ever again. Still, watching the others and trying to act as relaxed as they were, I could see how a full burn could become . . . not routine, but well practiced, every instant of it calculated and precise. When I got back out, Dailey handed me the remains of my first outfit, ghostly and burnt, the cuffs and collar barely hanging on to a few scraps of shirtfront. You could see straight through it.

CHAPTER 9

I Never Saw This in *Hooper*

Six months before he set me on fire, Dan Bradley stood on the roof of the Port Authority parking garage telling Matt Damon what to do. It was uncomfortably cold with a bitter wind coming off the Hudson, and, on paper at least, Bradley's suggestions didn't make a lot of sense: he wanted Damon to drive, in reverse, as fast as he could, and then, with the car heading straight for the roof's edge, duck below the dashboard and close his eyes. Damon nodded, as if he were being given the best advice in the world. People tend to do what Bradley says, not because he is six foot five and somewhere north of two hundred and sixty pounds, although this factor cannot be entirely ignored.

The two men were filming the climactic car chase in *The Bourne Ultimatum*, on location in New York City, under Bradley's direction. For this *Bourne* installment, Bradley wrote, designed, and filmed the movie's action, often making use of setups and equipment invented by Go Stunts, a company he cofounded along with his frequent collaborators and principal stunt coordinators, Scott Rogers and Darrin Prescott. The credits list him as the second-unit director, but the title, originally a grandiose favor for studio-era underlings who filmed background scenery, is practically an insult when applied to Bradley and everything he handles in a film today—like calling Scorsese the "dialogue coach."

Damon leaned out of his Audi A6 and followed the instructions with the same combination of feral intensity and choirboy raptness that he brings to the role of Jason Bourne. Clearly, he trusts Bradley not just with his career but with his life. In the Moscow car chase at the end of *The Bourne Supremacy*, Bradley put Damon inside several high-speed, high-tech contraptions that Go Stunts had invented for the film. Damon's Audi was hooked up to one now, the Go Mobile. The nearly unbreakable 500-horsepower camera car has a low-slung chassis and adjustable platform that can accommodate almost any vehicle: the entire hero car can fit right onto the Go Mobile. Though the Go Mobile does the driving, the wheels of the hero car still touch the road, the actor can still hang onto the steering wheel, and Bradley can film both star and car, from nearly any angle, in action, up close, in the middle of a chase—while a stuntman sitting in a tiny driver's pod out of sight of the camera handles all the high-performance maneuvering. Techno-cranes mounted elsewhere on the Go Mobile give the cameras almost complete freedom to sweep in and around the hero car. The nearly 360-degree panoramas of the action convince the audience of the reality of the scene. It seems obvious that the actor is doing all the driving. Apparently, it feels that way, too. Damon refers to the Go Mobile experience as "N.A.R.": no acting required.

In this scene, Bradley wanted his star to duck on the call of "Ready and" and close his eyes on "fire!" The ducking was scripted—Bourne's instinctive reflex in the middle of an improvised escape. He hot-wires a car, and, with two "CRI" agents shooting at him from a Crown Vic, he floors it through two parked cars, up a guardrail, and off the Port Authority roof. It was Bradley's idea of how the movie's climactic car chase through Manhattan should *begin*.

"But I don't want you opening your eyes after the explosion," Bradley warned.

"Gotcha," Damon said.

"Don't look back this way at all till we stop driving. Keep your eyes closed."

"After the explosion."

"Keep down. But do the action as if you're still driving."

"You got it."

Closing the eyes was a safety measure: the audience would never see it. Special effects had rigged seven squibs, or small explosive charges—the explosion that Bradley was warning Damon about—which would blow what appeared to be bullet holes in the Audi's (candy-glass) windshield at the same instant the rear (breakaway-glass) window would shatter completely. With all that glass flying around the moving vehicle, Bradley wanted Damon to close his eyes so he didn't wind up blind.

"Fire in the hole!" the assistant director yelled. "Roll cameras! Pulling out!" The Go Mobile accelerated toward the Port Authority guardrail. Damon ducked and shots rang out and a half second later the stunt driver in the driving pod came to a stop just short of the guardrail. "Cut," the A.D. yelled. Damon's assistant threw him some earmuffs.

"That was cool," Bradley said. "Get him out of the car."

Bradley works fast, with an impatience for error and a knack for getting it right in one take that he honed over years in low-budget films like *Hell Riders* and *Hollywood Vice Squad*. Speed is his signature, onscreen and off. He grew up in the San Fernando Valley, street racing around Van Nuys Boulevard in the seventies, and he made his name in the eighties with some terrifying-looking car tricks—like the one in which he raced off the corner of a plateau, flying through the air smack into a VW van parked eighty feet away in the middle of a field. (The impact looked horrific—all sorts of refuse and wreckage flew out of the VW—but in fact, Bradley had stuffed the van full of rags and newspapers, as a way to cushion the landing.) In his early days, he even worked on thrill shows, doing live car jumps at state fairs and in domed stadiums where the only way to make money was to cut corners on his car's safety features. You learn a lot about the way steel crumples when both your life and your livelihood depend on it.

Now that he's moved to the other side of the camera, he's made it his mission to show what such an experience really feels like. He and the Go Stunts crew have invented a few high-tech gizmos that bring the audience, and the actors, closer to the action than ever—including the Go Mobile; the RDV, or "remote-drive vehicle," with its driver's pod stationed on the roof of the hero car; and a system of high-speed super-motion-control winches that allows them to fly actors, stuntmen, and cameras through the air in any direction with nearly absolute control and safety, as they did in *Spider-Man 2* and *3*.

But you don't sense any of this technology onscreen. Bradley's action scenes feel unpredictable and almost dangerously unrehearsed, like the Moscow chase in *The Bourne Supremacy*, or the brutal car crash in *Adaptation* that prompted the Volkswagen people to call Bradley out of the blue and say, "Did you ever see *Adaptation*? Can you make us some commercials with crashes like that?" He likes to slip into movie theaters and watch how such thrill work affects the audience, and the reaction he's looking for is not, he says, " 'Oh, that was a cool stunt.' It's 'Omigod, that was a real person suffering something real.' I don't care about wowing people with a super stunt. I want to tell an emotional story. And my palette is the world of action."

This method approach to stunts has been known to confuse stuntmen. "A lot of guys just want to know how fast to go, like, 'Tell me, you want forty miles an hour?' 'No, I want you to go as fast as you can, and get in that intersection, and I want it to feel like you saw your opening late, so you're throwing the turn just a little late.' And it frustrates guys, because they just want to know, 'You want me to do a 90?' "—meaning a classic screeching ninety-degree turn around a corner—" 'No! I don't want you to "do a 90"! The story isn't about "doing a 90." It's about this guy who's desperate to get away and at the last second he sees an avenue that offers some hope.' I can't say that in miles per hour."

Critics rarely credit action sequences with creating mood or deepening a sense of character, but in *The Bourne Supremacy* it was Bradley's chase scenes, filmed in a handheld style somewhere between New Wave and war reporting, that nailed the film's anxious emotional state. "I read it, and I could see it," Matt Damon said of Bradley's fifteen-page shot-by-shot breakdown of the movie's Moscow car chase. "I turned to my wife and I said, 'God, if I don't do this, this is going to be in some other movie and I'm going to watch it and wish that I had done it. This is just the greatest car chase in modern movie history.'" As he spoke, someone from makeup came over to touch up his speckles of "blood"; somebody else rubbed his hair and shoulders with "broken glass" from the Audi—actually bouncy, shredded bits of clear rubber. "I tell anybody who'll listen that Dan Bradley's an A-list director. I would do a movie with him in a second. Look, I've been really lucky. I've worked with people widely considered to be the best directors around, and I put Bradley right on that list with those guys. He's that good."

The director Spike Jonze, who worked with Bradley on *Adaptation* and *Being John Malkovich*, says, "Bradley knows stunts: how to film them, where to put the camera, how to make it look exciting. But more important than that, he's a filmmaker. He's looking to tell the story of the characters. He's trying to make things more natural."

To do this, Bradley often pushes stunts to the periphery. Matt Damon brings up *Saving Private Ryan*: he remembers Spielberg insisting that big stunts and explosions that would be featured in other movies get only background treatment in his. "And Dan's the same way. If you look at that tunnel sequence again"—the final segment of the Moscow chase—"there are amazing spinouts, all these things happening to cars in the background, but it all appears in the corner of the frame. Somebody else wouldn't be able to resist putting a camera there. But Dan leaves you with the action, following one character, one story."

Over at MGM, Bradley's raw approach inspired a case of franchise envy, and the producers of James Bond repackaged their product in Bourne's image—a strategy they confessed in a courtesy call before the premiere of *Casino Royale*. (Then, after Bradley finished shooting *The Bourne Ultimatum*, the Bond team hired him to direct the action for the next film in the franchise.)

The new bare-knuckle Bond revitalized the box office, but Bradley, who studies other movies to see what *not* to do, pointed out the flaws in two big action sequences—Bond's Aston Martin flips over on a country road remarkable for its emptiness, and in the scene where Bond stops a tanker truck from driving into a prototype plane at the Miami airport, the only other vehicles to appear in the scene promptly and obligingly crash. Bradley tries to avoid shooting in such sterile environments, the empty Sunday-morning streets you see in movies like *Bullitt*. "I loved *Bullitt* when I first saw it as a kid," he said. "But if I were to deliver that chase, shot for shot today, they'd fire me. It does not hold up." He preferred the shifting lanes and "organic mess" of New York traffic. "I like it cluttered, so it feels more dangerous," he said.

Bradley grew up as one of six kids, five of them boys sharing a ten-by-ten room. He wound up in the garage a lot, in part because his siblings were always practicing on brass and wind instruments in the house: he may be the one man in America who started monkeying around with muscle cars for the peace and quiet. This soft-spoken side of Bradley was one of his primary attractions, according to his girlfriend, Jen Eddy. "He loves what he does," she says, "but he's not reading *Dirtbike* magazine in his spare time."

Still, a movie set full of stuntmen has a lot in common with a house full of brothers, and Bradley, boss or not, has to stay aware. Each time I stopped by the shoot, there were more than thirty stuntmen listed on the call sheet, and the guys he'd hired spoke in hushed tones about his gifts. But no matter how awestruck they were about his ability to run "the biggest, baddest, and best shows around," they still judged him instinctively on core stuntman values: for his amazing strength, his surprising speed, his ability to beat anyone on the set at slapsies. Several people brought up an incident where Scott Rogers, his Go Stunts partner and a former track star and football jock, ran at Bradley and launched himself through the air, ready, he believed, to deliver a perfect blindside tackle on the unsuspecting boss. Instead, at just the right instant, Bradley ducked and Rogers sailed over him and landed facedown in front of him.

Remembering the missed tackle, Bradley laughed. "He forgot I grew up with four brothers. A lot of people tried to ambush me and they never managed to do it. I just heard running footsteps, coming closer. And the second the footsteps ended, I ducked, because the cessation of footsteps meant that he was in the air. He expected to completely obliterate me. But when I ducked, I got to see him go right over the top of me and crash into the concrete. That was pretty damn entertaining."

Most stuntmen think of their profession as a sensible one. After all, it's safer than whatever they were doing before: dirt biking, underwater bomb disposal, tree trimming, wakeboarding, racing the Baja 1000, doing product testing for an experimental hang-glider design outfit. And they're getting paid more in the movies. Add it all up—the improvements in safety and the rosier long-term financial prospects—and you understand why parents of stuntmen tend to greet the news of their child's new career with a sigh of relief.

Set visits strengthen the impression: stuntmen at work resemble nothing so much as a group of incredibly fit structural engineers, calculating stress and recoil and impact velocity. They take risk seriously and do everything in their power to eliminate it. Still, their idea of eliminating risk is not yours. They grew up nailing maneuvers most people wouldn't try on their best days, so they have no problem seriously considering propositions that sound ridiculous to a person with standard-issue reflexes or a normal sense of self-preservation—say, "slide this motorcycle underneath the eighteen-wheeler that'll be coming through that intersection soon," or "drive this rig into that parked police car at about seventy miles an hour." The best ones shrug and hit their mark and make everybody from the makeup girls to the producers feel that the spectacular is all in a day's work.

There's one way they do differ from engineers: in their calculations, reducing risk does not necessarily mean eliminating pain. "There's things that there's no trick to," says Darrin Prescott, who helped run the gags for Bradley on *Spider-Man 2* and the *Bourne* series, among other movies. "If you're going to jump in the air and land on your back, flat on the floor, it is what it is. Flat backs: There's nothing good about them. They're going to hurt. You're going to be *okay*. You're not going to go to the *hospital*. But it's going to hurt." On Bradley's films, Prescott is often in charge of hiring, and he has a huge database of talent, from X Gamers to ex–Navy SEALS. "But I think one of the best talents that a person can have is the ability to turn off their own self-preservation. Repeatedly. Almost anyone can talk themselves into doing a stair fall—once. But then you've tweaked your knee, your legs are all black and blue, and your elbow hurts. And you want the second take to look as good as the first. To be able to turn it off at that moment and just chuck yourself? It's a neat talent."

But in the past few years stuntmen have been facing a risk they can't prepare for: the likelihood that their entire line of work will soon be rendered obsolete. The problem isn't about losing a few jobs, although stuntmen, like most of the film industry, have suffered as productions turn to cheap local hires in Prague, Vancouver, Australia, Louisiana. The problem is that computer-generated imagery, or CGI, threatens to make them obsolete, turning stuntmen into a movie version of typewriter repairmen. It's not unusual for stunt coordinators to show up at preproduction meetings to find that a film's most spectacular sequences (and the lion's share of the stunt budget) have been farmed out to CG outfits like Industrial Light and Magic. More and more, stuntmen are finding their workload on a picture reduced to a few days of hopping around in a motion-capture suit as animation programs translate their athleticism into data streams.

Bradley is a realist in both his film style and his approach to his job. Ever since he started out in the eighties, working "fast, cheap, and exciting" in low-budget films like *Hell Riders* and *Joyride to Nowhere* (a prophetic title, he said), he's had the reputation for inventing gags that looked better than the movie deserved. He could see that stuntmen were facing extinction, but he also knew what directors liked about CGI: it gave characters a capacity for

superhuman movement, a crucial advantage in comic-book and fantasy franchises. So Bradley got together with his cohorts Prescott
and Rogers and they started experimenting, to see if they could pull
off the same maneuvers the directors were looking for, on camera,
in broad daylight, at full speed, with a crew of stuntmen.

They didn't get the effect they wanted all at once. But they
figured out the first piece in the 2001 feature *Swordfish*. The
movie lives on mostly in Google searches ("halle berry top-
less"), but in the stunt world it's famous for the balletic explosion that opens the film. As the camera careens through walls
around the epicenter of a terrorist explosion, you catch incredi-
ble footage of real bodies snapping through the air in ways they
never had before—the first application of what Bradley called
the "twisty ratchet."

Up to that point, there weren't many choices if you wanted to
film a guy flying through the air. He could jump. You could shoot
him out of a pneumatic device or bounce him off a trampoline.
You could hook him to a high-powered ratchet and jerk him up,
up, and away. If you wanted something elaborate—as in the Hong
Kong wire-fu movies—you put him in a body harness attached to
wire-and-pulley setups. Then a bunch of guys off camera would
heave-ho on cue so the hero could soar like a wushu warrior.

For this reason, every stuntman keeps a flying harness in his gear
bag. The standard version, before the Go Stunts team started playing with it, can be hooked to wires at eight built-in anchor points,
or pick points, on the hips and down the centerline, front and back.
This limited arrangement allows for very few styles of flight: basically straight up and straight back, with minor variations depending
on where you place the ratchet. For *Swordfish*, Bradley tinkered
with the harness, adding dozens of new off-center pick points, so in
the explosion you saw bodies cartwheeling crookedly through the
air and tumbling haphazardly back and up. He tried using multiple
wire attachments, too, so a body would start spinning one way and
then get wrenched off the opposite way—a change in direction that
looked like the result of sudden impact, even though the body

had, in fact, hit nothing but air. When the film came out, the scene looked so violent that even stuntmen, who usually know better, thought that the guys in the explosion were actually getting hurt. A little while later, Prescott ran into Todd Renschler, who specialized in the creation of form-fitting climbing harnesses built out of titanium and Spectra—basically, bulletproof fabric. These ballistic-grade harnesses, tailored like a second skin, made their debut on *Spider-Man 2*: the new harnesses eliminated almost all the buckles and bulk of the traditional setup and made it possible to show flying bodies in greater detail. The first time Rogers flew through the air in a state-of-the-art harness, Bradley shook his head and said, "This is the next level. This is going to revolutionize the stunt industry."

Bradley came up with the next element in the battle against CGI on the hip-hop chop-socky heist film *Cradle 2 the Grave*. He'd designed a chase scene where a character on a Quadrunner races full speed down a hallway and out a tenth-story window, over an alley, to land on the next building and drive away over the nearby roofs. Bradley hoped to pull the gag off by hanging both the stunt double and the Quadrunner on cables, then pulling them through the shot with a high-speed winch. The special-effects coordinator, thinking the setup was dangerous and unworkable, ignored his requests and kept designing roller-coaster-style rigs with metal tracks that couldn't be hidden in postproduction. Luckily the guy was fired for an unrelated screwup, so at the last minute Bradley got the chance to set it up himself with the equipment he had originally requested. He strung the cables, rented the winches, and got the shot. It didn't turn out quite as spectacularly as he'd planned—winch companies seemed afraid to provide him with equipment fast enough for his tastes—but the limited success convinced him that he was on the right track.

At this point, the Go Stunts crew has sunk well over a million dollars of their own money into their advanced equipment: the Go Mobile, the ultra-high-speed motion-control super winches, the remote-drive vehicle, and so on. In its first three years, the company has proved less of a moneymaking venture than a bargaining tool: you can't get Bradley and his crew without their state-of-the-art equipment, and you can't rent the breakthrough technology without hiring the crew. The team and the toys are a package deal, and right now the studios can't afford to say no.

But Scott Rogers wanted no part of it at first. The financial risk didn't spook him, he said; it was the emotional liability. "When you're winging people around, it takes a toll on you. Look at an NBA game, Michael Jordan taking the shot to win the finals—it takes a certain level of *huevos*. But we're doing a shot where a guy's flying around hooked to a wire, and there's an explosion, and the timing's got to be just right, or, one, you don't get the shot and you piss away hundreds of thousands of dollars, or, two, you're late and the guy gets hurt. Look at it that way, and taking a shot in a basketball game seems like nothing."

While Rogers was working on *Spider-Man 3*, I stopped by the set. Out on the parking lot at the Steiner Studios in the Brooklyn Navy Yard, the whole Go Stunts flight setup—the cranes and Tomcat truss boxes, the wooden crates and rental trucks, the weight bags hanging from a cat's cradle of tension wires, all of it arranged around the ultra-high-speed motion-control super winches—looked like a high-tech circus stripped of its tent. Which, in a sense, it was. Go Stunts commissioned the winches from Fisher Technical Services, of Las Vegas, and the setup they designed together was a modified version of the one that Scott Fisher first built for Cirque du Soleil.

The difference between the two versions is speed: the top speed for acrobats in Cirque shows like *O* and *Mystère* is about ten miles per hour; right now, Go Stunts can whip you through the air at well over thirty-five. (And the camera can be wired to move at the same speed, safely, and within inches of the actors.) But the trademark of both systems, and the reason Rogers can sleep at night, is precision: the movement and timing of the winches is computer controlled with a margin of error measured in hundredths of an inch and fractions of a second. And now the programs that run the motors and monitor the stuntmen integrate easily with animation software. For *Spider-Man 3*, for instance, Scott Fisher was able to map out the stunt choreography with Bradley and then send the director, Sam Raimi, fully animated renderings of Spider-Man and the Green Goblin in action, the way it would look through the lens. "And once he said, 'Yeah, I like that,' " Fisher recalled, "we'd generate the flight profiles—at frame whatever, we want to be in XYZ position—for the actors and any tracking cameras."

That makes it sound as if there were nothing left for the stuntman to do except strap in and fly. But each body moves through the air differently, and even those individual characteristics change depending on the speed. So flight profiles have to be individually tailored, or dialed in, on site. The day I visited, Rogers was working on a gag where Spidey would stop a pickpocket in the middle of a crowd, whip him through the air, smash him into a paddy wagon, and web him there for the police to find. A New York–based stuntman, Manny Siverio, had been cast as the pickpocket—and he looked like what his Web site said he was, an expert in knife fighting, martial arts, and mambo dancing. It was his first time on the Go Stunts rig, and he was apprehensive.

Perhaps his apprehension could be traced to the unusual pick point Rogers had chosen for the gag: in addition to the conventionally placed attachments on either hip, Siverio had a wire hooked to the bottom of his harness, between his legs. The hip lines served to launch him into the air, and the third wire, engaged just after he got airborne, would send him ass over teakettle out of the shot. On the first couple of tries, Siverio grabbed for the wire, a protective reflex that, counterintuitively, only increased the pain at the attachment point.

"That made it worse," he said, taking a breather. "I've been tossed sideways, but never . . ."

After one run-through that left Siverio wincing, Chris Daniels, who'd doubled Spider-Man on all three pictures (and still, from time to time, finds himself watching TV in Spidey poses), said, "I never saw this in *Hooper*."

"The full grundle," Rogers said.

Siverio looked confused.

"We call it the grundle pick, because the grundle's that little piece of skin between your nuts and your ass." Rogers's toughness is legendary in the business. His dead-body gag in *Adaptation* is famous: on multiple takes, he flew through the air onto packed earth and landed as a dead body lands, facedown, with no movement to soften the blow. Just now he was having a hard time hiding his scorn. "My six-year-old did a full grundle and didn't say boo. He did like fifteen takes. Let's go!"

It all came together after lunch. Siverio stopped anticipating, so it really looked as if he'd been snatched off his feet by the web-slinger, and he tumbled through the air with increasingly convincing awkwardness. As Siverio grew more confident in flight, Rogers increased the speed, over and over ("My favorite note: faster"), until they were going at 125 percent of their target speed, which explained the Go Stunts motto: One hundred percent is not necessarily full speed.

At this point, the Go Stunts high-speed winches have helped stuntmen (and the Go Stunts team in particular) take the upper hand in the battle with CGI, winning back screen time for stuntmen and grabbing the attention as the latest and most sought-after film effect. But the sophistication of the equipment may be outstripping current applications. "Directors ask, 'Well, what does it do?'" Rogers said. His stock answer—"Anything you want"—isn't exactly what they like to hear: innovation isn't every director's strong suit. In the long run, the best advertisement for the technology's range will most likely be the work of the man who first envisioned it: Bradley himself.

A few weeks after *Spider-Man 3* wrapped, Prescott began work on Spike Jonze's adaptation of *Where the Wild Things Are*. Jonze has worked with the Go Stunts crew on several movies, and largely because of those experiences he chose to shoot his new film with as much live action as possible. When I dropped into the Paramount lot to see a stunt rehearsal, you could tell how far Go Stunts had come in their rivalry with CGI from the way Prescott talked about the Wild Things: he sounded exactly like an animator or a Disney imagineer. "When we started the show, I was looking for reference creatures to see how they move—grizzly bears, and T-rex dinosaurs, bipeds that are that big. You can see this monster's huge, but the legs are this long." He pointed to a short-legged costume across the soundstage. "So how far can you stride? You can't cover seventeen feet—it starts to look like *Crouching Tiger*," he said, referring to the Ang Lee film in which mystically gifted warriors fly over the landscape.

The movement style he came up with—more playful than *Spider-Man*, according to Prescott, "more like kids on the playground, just smacking each other and tossing each other around"—presents a greater technical challenge. In *Spider-Man*, everything moved at top speed, but the stuntmen wore tight costumes and weighed about a hundred and seventy pounds each, so fine-tuning the movement was easy. The Wild Things are nine feet tall with ninety-inch waists and ninety-pound costumes. Since it takes a big stuntman to carry all that, most Wild Things weigh in at over three hundred pounds. Imagine negotiating the aerodynamic properties of Jackie Gleason after months of flying a crew of Fred Astaires.

Studios often balk at paying for the rehearsal time that flying requires. But fine-tuning on the soundstage translates to savings on the shoot, where expenses are highest: once the flyboys get it right, their flight software allows them to repeat it exactly for the camera, with the press of a button. For even the most elaborate gags, the director rarely needs more than one take.

So it makes economic sense that seven stuntmen are busy on the Paramount soundstage, rehearsing a gag where a big Wild Thing picks up a small Wild Thing, slams him into three trees, then takes off with him at high speed down a forest path, whacking him into every tree trunk that they pass. Dave Kilde, the big one, weighs 205 pounds, and wears a neoprene rehearsal costume that makes him sweat. At five foot six and a hundred and fifty pounds, Craig Silva, whom everyone calls Frosty, is the small Wild Thing; since the production didn't want to pay for two rehearsal costumes, he's wearing a generically fuzzy getup leftover from *The Country Bears*, which smells, as Frosty noted on a run-through where he wrapped his legs around Kilde's shoulders, like "wet ass."

The day I was there, Prescott raced behind Frosty, while he was still suspended on a wire, and zapped him with a toy—Lightning Reaction Extreme—booby-trapped to administer continuous electric shocks.

"Dude," Prescott said, innocently, "I couldn't shut it off." Prescott helped Jonze on *Jackass*—a few of the gags on that movie were ones that he and the guys had invented while goofing off. And Jonze sees the slapstick horseplay of the Wild Things characters as a more child-friendly version of the *Jackass* impulse.

"He's doing the salmon," Kilde said, watching Frosty flail around. "It would've been awesome if the bear suit caught on fire."

Frosty said, "It would've been awesome if you had two bear claws slashed across your face."

And then one of the riggers interrupted their shenanigans to point out a plywood impact barrier that shifted around dangerously whenever Frosty banged into it. "We should lag bolt this to the ground," he suggested. Prescott switched instantaneously from torturing Frosty to providing for his well-being. "We could put that scissor lift behind it," he said.

"Copy that," the rigger said.

I've spent a lot of time fucking around on the job, and there's usually an instant of transition before settling down to work—shutting off e-mail, refilling a coffee cup, closing a door. With stuntmen you can't tell the difference. One sort of gag serves as a warmup for the other, easing tension, sharpening reflexes, even testing the limits of pain and reaffirming trust. Prescott, who invented a series of practical jokes he called "Fun with Frosty," thought that it all served a purpose. "It's just such a weird personality, to be in charge of people's lives, you know? But never to have really grown up."

Prescott admits to having a hockey body now—he's six feet tall and weighs about two hundred pounds—but his size is deceptive.

In his early teens, before he outgrew the sport, he anchored an East Coast squad of freestyle bikers, and he retains much of the litheness of a gymnast: he can still do a standing backflip. Like many stuntmen, he can't see a new sport without wanting to master it, and his garage is stocked with the equipment he's picked up along the way: surfboards, street luge, racing leathers, kites for kitesurfing, triathlon gear ("They have a Clydesdale class," he joked). Prescott prefers the company of stuntmen among whom this sort of promiscuous sporting interest is second nature. "I can't speak for everybody," he says, "but I don't hang out with anybody but stunt guys. If I go to family functions, or anything outside of my community, I'm lost. It's very hard for me to sit and talk. A couple of my in-laws are doctors. It's cordial, just kind of hard. It's such a cool thing to just be able to"—he gestured out at the sound-stage where a few of the stuntmen were experimenting with a new kind of skateboard he'd brought in—"to be able to work with these guys all day and then be like, 'What are you doing after work? Let's go surf!' And have like twenty or thirty guys to play with all the time. It's like first grade never left. Because everyone's pretty much of the same cloth.

"When I first came out here, I talked to an old stunt guy and he said, 'Let me tell you right now. I don't recommend this business at all. It's not like what you think. It's not like all these guys hanging out and buddy-buddy.' And to this day I don't know what he was talking about. 'Cause it's awesome. The funny thing, I could go to another country, meet a stunt guy, it'd be the same. Go to Hong Kong, meet a stunt guy, they're pulling pranks on each other. They're always looking for the next fun thing to do. Go to Australia or Germany and they'll have this new little gadget and all of a sudden everyone's on it. You can just go there, and it's like, 'Hey, man, we're going to go motorcycle riding this weekend. Wanna come?' It's the same."

The mind-set isn't easy for everyone to understand, Prescott admits. "My brother-in-law's a policeman. And they were doing canine training. And they let the dog go, and it jumped on him and he tore his ACL, he got a concussion—he got all these things from a dog jumping on him. My mother-in-law was telling me this and I started laughing. And she said, 'How can you think that's funny?' And I said, 'It just amazes me with what I see every day that a dog could jump on this guy and he could sustain that amount of injury.' I mean, I watch guys get tossed out of cars, rip themselves through walls, fall down stairs, and they get up and walk away. And they'll do it again. They'll do it five times in a row and be fine. How does this happen? How does a guy get this mangled from a dog jumping on him? Part of it, you're laughing because of that, and part of it you're laughing because you're just happy it wasn't you. A lot of times, these guys will auger themselves"—stuntmen are big on action verbs, and auger is one of their many synonyms for "get badly injured"—"and everyone else is laughing 'cause they're just glad it wasn't them!"

Not surprisingly, the cruel joke is something of an art form among stuntmen. And with so many cameras around, some of these downtime gags achieve their own brand of immortality. On the *Bourne* set in New York, everyone was talking about another "Fun with Frosty" incident, from the *Wild Things* shoot in Australia. Frosty happily showed the clip to anyone who asked. He'd doubled the smallest Wild Thing, and the clip begins with him napping between takes in his chicken suit as his friend and fellow stuntman Chris O'Hara sneaks up behind him with a skink—that's Australian for lizard—which he tosses inside Frosty's beak. The chicken beak was hard and permanently frozen in the open position, and, as an added advantage (from the practical joker's perspective, not Frosty's), it rode high enough that Frosty could not reach inside it with his hands. So when the skink landed inside the costume and stuck to his face, the only thing Frosty could do to rid himself of it was to jump up and begin punching himself about the head—a wild chicken violently whacking himself with his feathery wings. Then, when the punching got no results, Frosty started to slam the beak into the ground repeatedly, at which point the camera pulls back to reveal the crew and the rest of the Wild Things, doubled over in laughter.

The only-in-New-York qualities that make the city so attractive to the movies—grit, volume, traffic, attitude, bipolar intensity— make it a horrible place to film a high-speed chase. There's a reason you can remember only one New York City chase scene in cinema history (*The French Connection*, shot in the seventies, in far-outer-borough Brooklyn, with just one rogue cop chasing a *train*). At the end of the *Bourne* shoot, on the day they'd set aside for a mammoth crash under the Brooklyn Bridge, Bradley was exhausted from dealing with the New York bureaucracy, Prescott was worn out from dealing with Bradley, all the stuntmen were stir-crazy from sitting around in cars waiting for somebody on a walkie-talkie to call "Action," and the beleaguered production assistants, who were getting squat for pay, had to face another day locking down public thoroughfares full of New Yorkers caffeinated to the point of rage or just drunk and belligerent, since today was St. Paddy's Day. On top of that, the night before, a nor'easter had dumped five inches of slush on the streets.

Still, this was the day they were shooting the "K-rail gag," a violent piece of movie magic that Bradley had been dreaming of for years, the sort of thing that even stars and producers who could skip it showed up to watch. The gag occurs near the end of the movie, with Bourne driving his third car of the chase, a stolen NYPD vehicle—Bradley's solution to the how-can-you-go-fast-enough-through-Manhattan-for-a-chase conundrum. Bourne's got one bad guy still on his tail, who crashes into him, so his cop car spins sideways onto a stretch of concrete traffic dividers—called a K-rail on the West Coast, and a Jersey barrier back east—and Bourne's momentum carries him up along the rail for sixty or seventy yards, tilting dangerously, sliding on the car's undercarriage. "Basically, he's going to do a grind," Bradley says, but not in a Disneyfied, *Herbie the Love Bug* style—more scary and out of control. "I want people to watch it three times before they really understand, 'Omigod, that's a skateboard trick.'"

The sun came out, melting the snow and turning the runoff from the Brooklyn Bridge and the FDR Drive into a localized storm condition. At one point, two snowplows clearing an exit ramp overhead scraped a mess of slush down onto the camera car, breaking lenses and dousing operators. Somebody yelled, "New York City avalanche!" But the street at least was clear, and the wet-down helped, if your job that day called for sliding down the street and crashing into a car at sixty miles an hour.

For much of the morning, stunt drivers ran takes of background traffic, a stream of oncoming cars whose speed in the opposite direction would add to the impression of speed and danger in the final print. After lunch, Bourne's cop car was carefully set in place, suspended on a heavy-duty version of the hardware you'd buy to install a sliding closet door, and cabled to a ratchet, or air ram, on a flatbed truck far down the street. As crew members parked old cars along the road—for cushioning between the upcoming crash and the nearby buildings and bridge supports—two mechanics inside the cop car welded support struts where the engine had once been, strengthening a single wheel hidden under the car to help it roll along the street at a dangerous angle as soon as the ratchet started wrenching it along the rail at sixty miles an hour.

For this gag, Scott Rogers was driving the bad guy's car, a new VW Touareg. Bourne's cop car had a dummy behind the wheel, with a bad wig and the same speckles of blood that Damon had, so Rogers would be the only stuntman in the collision. It was the third Touareg he was totaling in two days—he'd done two takes of a head-on collision the day before. This one had spent some time in the shop: it now had a roll cage, and the steering wheel, brake, and accelerator had been modified so that Rogers could drive from the backseat.

He had to drive from there, because halfway down the rail the rear end of Bourne's cop car was going to slam into a Con Ed truck parked on the other side of the divider, and that collision would throw Bourne's car off the rail, right onto the Touareg's windshield. To pull this off, Rogers had to match the speed of the cop car sliding along the rail, staying as close as possible to ensure, if that's the right word, that when it fell, it would slam down on his windshield. According to Bradley's plan, the resulting crash would send the Touareg sideways, at which point Rogers would hit a button to send his car flipping down the road. He'd have about three seconds to do it all.

He didn't look any more worried than a guy giving his regular Wednesday sales presentation. "Yeah, if I'm any more nervous than I am right now," he said, "I shouldn't be doing this." He had a black fire suit on, and inside the car he had a five-point harness, a helmet, and a big neck brace all ready to go. "I'm in there. I'm built to hit something. The only thing that could go wrong is a dead stop. Those are bad. You want this thing to hit and bounce and kick off and spin. You don't want to go"—he made a noise like vibrating tuning fork.

Prescott joined the safety discussion. "I have absolutely no concerns," he said. "I'm more worried about property."

"You know my feeling about property," Rogers said. "People ask, 'What made you want to be a stuntman?' Well, I had to take a real honest look at what I was good at. And I was good at breaking things."

Bradley minimized the danger, pointing to the parked cars that Rogers would soon be bouncing past. "The cars should act like baby bumpers at a bowling alley."

Ten cameras were aimed at the scene: two remotes mounted on the rail, one facing each way, and another balanced on a box beside a catcher car; a few Steadicams in a vacant lot under the bridge, and one fitted with a long lens on a corner nearby; one on the flatbed; an overhead camera mounted under a highway off-ramp; another mounted on top of a rally car that would race alongside, following the action from a parking lot by the piers. Bradley stood by a set of monitors in the vacant lot, watching the cameramen nervously practice their tracking moves. A few of them held a cordless reciprocating saw near enough to the camera to impart a nervous jiggle to the image. They swept over the street again and again. The three seconds of the gag cost somewhere near a quarter million dollars. Bradley hoped the two cars would stay within the frame, but if there was a choice to be made, he told them, stick with the cop car. It was literally a one-shot deal.

"Nick," Bradley called impatiently to an assistant director, "what are we doing?"

"Waiting for the air ram to charge." It took about twenty minutes for the air ram to achieve the necessary pressure of two thousand pounds per square inch.

Prescott came up to report on his final preparations. "So my plan is, I'll probably move a couple of these guys up." He pointed to the background traffic across the street. "Everything goes on 'Go.' Scotty goes on Go, the traffic goes on Go. And they just get after it. So hopefully they're close when the wreck happens."

Over by the Touareg, Rogers was joking with the safeties about losing his arm in the wreck ("My right elbow used to hurt"). Beyond the wreck site, Chris O'Hara sat in a yellow cab, ready to hit the Touareg and bring it to a stop, if it threatened to roll out of control beyond the set. Frosty stood behind the cars, with a fire extinguisher, the designated first man in.

Matt Damon and Pat Crowley, one of the producers, came over to the video monitors, just in time to watch. "They about to go?" Damon asked.

"They're just charging up," Bradley answered. "Probably the guy with the best job right now is Scott."

"Why? What's he driving?"

"The Touareg."

"Oh, God, so he takes the hit?"

"He's got a lot of wheel and a button. And as that car slaps him, he's gonna hit the button. Then it's going to be: sky-ground-skygroundskyground. And maybe a little concrete rail."

"Where's he land—about there?"

"No. I think he's going to eat that van right there. It'll be a very busy hundred feet."

Damon was impressed. "Excellent."

Nick's voice came over the walkie-talkies: "Effects is going hot. All right, guys, here we go! Let's roll camera. Three . . . two . . . one . . . GO!"

Rogers floored it, and when he hit his mark, a guy from effects pushed the button on the air ram and the cab sprang into action, accelerating from zero to sixty almost instantaneously. Rogers stayed close enough for the cop car to collapse his roof and shatter his windshield—so close, in fact, that when he hit the button that was supposed to send him into a roll, there wasn't enough room to do it. Instead, the Touareg rose off the ground, and landed on its nose, sliding on its front bumper for about thirty yards, lifting the cop car dramatically toward the overhead camera. The cop car tumbled away, the Touareg bounced off the van, and everything came to a stop.

"Cut," Bradley yelled.

While the safeties ran in to check on Rogers, Bradley and Damon and Crowley stood over the monitor, reviewing each camera angle on the crash. The Touareg's unexpected liftoff looked, if anything, more violent than what they'd planned, and the three men moaned or chuckled in appreciation, their voices rising each time to the crescendo of the wreck, until they saw one shot where it looked as if the Touareg had shouldered the cop car and shrugged it off straight toward the camera, and they shouted like guys at a prizefight. "That's your trailer right there," Bradley said to the producer. "People are going to want to see this."

Everybody walked over to the two cars to check on Rogers and examine the wreckage, somehow a more somber record of the violent collision. The Touareg had crumpled, and Bourne's cop car had landed on its roof. Damon looked in, checking on the dummy in the Bourne costume, still buckled in but upside down, head resting on the ground, wearing the same placid dummy expression. Its arms had fallen away from the wheel. A few feet away, a single hand lay on the pavement.

"Hey," Damon said, to no one in particular, "the dummy lost a hand."

Epilogue

You see a lot of impressive limps at the Taurus World Stunt Awards: wincingly fresh ones, subtle stiff-legged chronic ones, bad-habit limps from old injuries, swaggering limps disguised by ball gowns and cowboy boots, and proud lifetime-achievement limps that seem to incorporate a full halt in every step—a sign of double hip replacements.

The event is often referred to as the Academy Awards of the stunt world, but unlike the Oscars, they have no set date or location; every year—or so—the Red Bull people put together the money, the awards committee decides on the winners, and the few hundred people at the center of the insular stunt world come together to celebrate their best work. The first time I went, back in May, 2004, a throng of Hollywood photographers stood by the red carpet as a procession of stunt doubles piled out of limos and were ceremoniously ushered onto the Paramount lot. (Perhaps the studio honchos didn't like the idea of stunt people freewheeling in their own vehicles up to an awards ceremony.) Everyone was incredibly fit and good-looking, but the photographers seemed flummoxed: nobody knew who was famous enough to photograph. Among the mystery guests was Zoe Bell, getting her first nomination for *Kill Bill* and spouting Kiwi to the press ("Oh fuck, oh *fudge*, oh jeepers!"). Terry Leonard showed up in big lapels and a bolo tie held together with a turquoise cinch, and Debbie Evans, who later won for her *Matrix Reloaded* work, walked arm in arm with her husband, Lane Leavitt, he in black tie, she in pearl-drop earrings and a full-length red dress decorated with primroses.

The show itself was full of live and prerecorded celebrity stunts (the cohosts, Dennis Hopper and Carmen Electra, wingsuiting onto the Paramount lot; Michelle Rodriguez crashing through the stage floor in a red rally car, then climbing out of the hole wearing Christian Dior). Keanu Reeves took the stage and, to much applause, confessed that he had never done a stunt in his life. Halfway through the show, Hopper introduced Arnold Schwarzenegger ("I like to think of him as my Republican twin," Hopper said), and the governor, who has appeared at all six Taurus award programs, strode out to make a few jokes and to confess his debt to stuntmen.

You can dress up a stuntman and walk him down a red carpet. You can give him a big award (it takes a stuntman to heft the thing: the Taurus statuette, of a winged man with the head of a bull, is nearly three feet tall and weighs twenty-six pounds). But you still can't make a stuntman behave like a star. One honoree started his acceptance speech by saying, "Tell you the truth, I can't really remember much about that job"—a classic stuntman shrug, tweaking the whole idea of awards shows. The younger generation may feel a little more comfortable than the old guard about taking credit for the extraordinary things they do, but nobody got into the business because he secretly dreamed of accepting an award on TV.

I'd been seated next to Ronnie Rondell, there to receive a lifetime-achievement award. After Hopper and Electra announced his name, a highlight reel appeared on the big screen, billed as a montage of his best stunts. Rondell, who was dressed in cowboy boots, black leather pants, and a matching sport jacket, started grinding his bootheels into the floor and cursing: his lifetime-achievement clip was full of stunts that didn't belong to him. "They got some kind of foreign shit from different countries," he told me later. "You see a shot with a guy on a horse and the guy knocks the horse down with a punch—and I didn't even work on the movie! And yet I'll hold my stunts up against anybody in the business."

A more suitably rambunctious celebration of stunthood occurs every year, on the last three days of Thanksgiving weekend, at an event officially called A Day in the Dirt but widely known in the trade as A Day to Get Hurt. In it, hundreds of stuntmen and stuntwomen in racing leathers (and their little stunt children in Evel Knievel suits) gather in campers, RVs, fun runners, and toy haulers to spend the long weekend launching over jumps and muscling through tire ruts in a two-mile track at the edge of a dirt quarry north of L.A., out in the heart of canyon country.

The race weekend is a link to the old guard of stuntmen and their penchant for high-speed good times. It has its roots in a series of seventies-era races started by a film-industry motorcycle club called the Viewfinders; Steve McQueen, regarded in the stunt community as a sort of patron saint, was a charter member, as were Ronnie Rondell and many other top stuntmen of the era. Their combined pull made it possible for them to stage an annual Grand Prix motocross event on a movie lot. That race was the grandfather of this one, and many fathers and mothers at Day in the Dirt were children of that first generation of stuntmen.

When I visited, the racecourse had the look of an Old West movie lot. Stage-set red barns and decorative stretches of picket fence mingled with functional hay-bale impact walls. The indiscriminate mix of bikes and riders and foot traffic on the campground passageways gave the whole place the rhythm of a cattle town. You could stand in the coffee line at the Pines Café Express behind tanned and windblown women, dirt-streaked men in worn leathers, and feel the puff of exhaust from a vintage two-stroke engine nuzzling your hand like a horse. By the end of the event, after more than fifteen hours of racing, you could spot plenty of the long stares and wide-straddle walks of the old frontier.

A quick visit to the tents and trailers left the impression of

motocross-based social clubs—campfire conversation and cook-
outs by the RVs took precedence over racing, up until the roar of
engines at the starting line made socializing impossible. When the
races began, though, they were hotly contested, with hundreds of
stuntmen competing on a varied slate. There were family races,
with dads and kids putt-putting together. There were serious con-
tests, with moonlighting pros from the dirt circuit competing
with older riders who had given up professional biking to pursue
a career in stunts. Race leaders were easy to spot: they threw
themselves into the jumps, gyroscoping skillfully in the air and
slingshotting around heavier competitors on the high mud curves.
The biggest dangers involved good riders getting inspired: one veteran camera-bike rider pitched an endo (an end-over-end roll over
his handlebars) when a novice racer drifted into him as he tried an
aggressive pass. Tim Rigby was circumspect, though, driving carefully in a few races on Saturday before heading out to a shoot the
next day. "We were scheduled to shoot my 'Triple X' stunt right
after Day in the Dirt a couple years ago," he said. "And the whole
weekend Lance Gilbert, the stunt coordinator, kept begging me,
'Tim, whatever you do, don't get hurt.' "

But even this celebration may be too high-gloss for some. Darrin
Prescott has twenty acres up in Idaho, near the Canadian border,
that he plans to turn into his own private motocross track, and he
dreams about taking the event back to its roots: loading up a couple of box vans of minibikes and inviting a small number of stuntmen and stuntwomen. "We used to walk around Day in the Dirt
and see everybody we knew. You couldn't go ten feet without
somebody saying, 'Hey, man, what's new?' Now if you don't stay
in the Stunts Unlimited and Brand X area, you don't know anybody, because it's gotten huge. And there's pros out there, and
they yell at us because we're not as fast as them."

But for now, at least, the big event, pragmatically timed to coin-
cide with an industry-wide break in the shooting schedule, still
draws the crowds up to Palmdale, about an hour or so north of L.A.
There are plenty of classic dirt-bike scenes—"Dirty Girl" and "Shift

Happens" T-shirts, the lone rider pirouetting his bike on an empty patch of dirt in the parking lot—but the event derived much of its charm from the sincere mixture of calculated risk and quality time with the family. There's a sandbox near the grandstands, so onlookers can take pictures of the race or the kids. And in a small enclosure at a curve in the track, dads rode after little ones on minibikes like cowboys trailing the herd. One puzzled young girl watching the race asked, "Mommy, why don't you ride motorcycles?"

"Because somebody has to drive to the hospital," the mother said.

Acknowledgments

The stars here—the stuntmen and women who routinely risked their lives on these pages—deserve more credit than they get in the movies and more personal acknowledgment than I could put in this book. Nobody gets into stunts for the acclaim, and they had nothing to gain from helping put all this together. Their generosity, on and off the set, made this whole extravaganza possible. All the central figures here spent hours explaining their livelihood, but none more so than Darrin Prescott, Scott Rogers, and Dan Bradley; Tim Rigby, Sean Graham, and Ronnie Rondell; Jeannie Epper, Debbie Evans, and Zoe Bell; Jeff Galpin, and, inimitably, Mike Kirton.

Getting to these stunt professionals was not easy. Movie studios, accustomed to setting strict limits on set access, viewed my frequent requests to watch entire stunt sequences performed on location with extreme suspicion. I couldn't have written this book if a few magazine editors hadn't sent me out under their banner; not only did their excitement and enthusiasm for the stories help shape mine, their assignments turned the studios into cheerful collaborators, a change of heart that was essential to the reporting process. (The press secretaries would say, "God, *GQ*! I thought you said you were writing a *book*. Hah! Well, let's see when we can get you on the set.") Several chapters appeared in different form in their publications, and I owe a great debt to the following tough-minded pros: Seth Fletcher at *Men's Journal*; Lucy Kaylin at *Marie Claire*; Henry Finder and Daniel Zalewski at the *New Yorker*; Andrew Essex at

Details; Paul Reyes at *Oxford American*; and, above all, Mark Kirby, Michael Hainey, Mark Healy, and Jim Nelson at *GQ*, who not only sent me racing after a car chase through Manhattan, but then allowed me to disappear from my regular post at the magazine to finish this book.

In fact, two independent film publicists, Deb Wuliger and Will Casey, broke from the pack to provide invaluable assistance. They were tremendously creative in finding ways to get me right in on the action. I owe them big time for that.

The book's D-day, the full burn of *The Full Burn*, would have vanished like a Mojave mirage without the efforts of Craig Cameron Olsen, who photographed everything, and Sara Mercurio and Josh Nichols, who got it all on video.

For all the camaraderie of the set, the actual writing was a solitary pursuit that left me in a position much like that of Laika, the space dog, on *Sputnik 2*. Diane Belfrey saved me from Laika's fate by reading the stuff here, as it came out; her encouragement was vital to my surviving the ordeal.

At my house, a book doesn't get done without closing a door. I am grateful to my kids, Max, Sarah, Jack, and Gloria, for leaving me alone until they just couldn't stand it anymore. I am equally grateful for their busting in on me. Whether the door was open or shut, Amy, my wife, has kept me going all the way; my gratitude to her is all the more absolute and unconditional.

Above all, my thanks to the green light gang at Bloomsbury: to Karen Rinaldi, the publisher, who listened to a few daydreams and bankrolled this action adventure; and to Nick Trautwein, who turned my rough cuts into a full-length feature and finally said what every editor dreams of telling his author: any chance you could set yourself on fire?

A Note on the Author

Kevin Conley is the author of the national bestseller *Stud: Adventures in Breeding*. A correspondent for *GQ*, he has written for the *New Yorker*, *Sports Illustrated*, and the *New York Times Magazine*, among others. He lives in Connecticut with his wife, Amy, and their children, Max, Sarah, Jack, and Gloria.